THE POETRY

AND THE

RELIGION OF THE PSALMS

The Croall Lectures, 1893-94

THE POETRY

AND THE

RELIGION OF THE PSALMS

BY

JAMES ROBERTSON, D.D.

PROFESSOR OF ORIENTAL LANGUAGES IN THE
UNIVERSITY OF GLASGOW

AUTHOR OF
'THE EARLY RELIGION OF ISRAEL'
ETC.

WIPF & STOCK · Eugene, Oregon

Wipf and Stock Publishers
199 W 8th Ave, Suite 3
Eugene, OR 97401

The Poetry and the Religion of the Psalms
The Croall Lectures, 1893-94
By Robertson, James
Softcover ISBN-13: 978-1-6667-6175-7
Hardcover ISBN-13: 978-1-6667-6176-4
eBook ISBN-13: 978-1-6667-6177-1
Publication date 10/11/2022
Previously published by Dodd, Mead, and Co., 1898

This edition is a scanned facsimile of the original edition published in 1898.

PREFACE.

THE following pages are devoted to a consideration of the Place of the Psalms in the History and the Religion of the Old Testament, and under that title they were delivered as the Croall Lectures for 1893-94.

I have to thank the Trustees for extending to me the time allowed for the publication of the Lectures. The delay has enabled me to return once and again, as I was desirous of doing, in something of the attitude of a critic of my own positions. When one's conclusions do not agree with the current views of those who are regarded as authorities, it becomes him at least not to be rash in the publication of them.

Besides rearranging the material in the more convenient form of chapters, I have not hesitated to refer to such works as may have been published or may have come under my notice since the Lectures were delivered. After the book was all in print, there appeared in the 'Theologische Literaturzeitung' (No. 7 for 1898) a review of Wildeboer's 'Commentary on the Proverbs,' by Graf von Baudissin, with some very seasonable and suggestive words on the subject of personal religion in Pre-Exilian times, to which scholars would do well to take heed. I have lately also discovered that, in regard to some points, I have been anticipated almost in identical terms by so competent a judge as Mr Schechter, in his 'Studies in Judaism,' as, *e.g.*, on pages 229 and 295 of that work.

The Psalms are hallowed by so many personal associations that one regrets writing anything of a controversial character on the subject. At the same time, the ordinary reader who takes an intelligent interest in the progress of Old Testament criticism cannot fail to be aware of a change of attitude towards these compositions, and will be prepared to consider the bearings of the questions involved. With the verdict of such readers I am content to abide; as a friend says to me, *The Psalms will take care of themselves.*

In sending the book to the press, I have to express my indebtedness for valuable suggestions made to me by my esteemed friend and recent colleague, Dr Dickson, Emeritus Professor of Divinity in the University of Glasgow. I have also to express my thanks to two former students, Rev. William Moffat, B.D., minister of Elgin, and Rev. George Gordon Duncan, B.D., minister of Glendevon, for much help in the reading of proofs; and to my assistant in the University, Rev. Thomas H. Weir, B.D., for taking the trouble to verify the references. For the convenience of the reader, these references, where it is not otherwise stated, are made to the English Version.

CONTENTS.

CHAPTER I.

INTRODUCTORY.

Three aspects of "religion."—The religion of the Psalms specially interesting (1) because touching human nature so closely; (2) to the theologian as bearing on the connection between the Old and New Testaments; (3) for the history of religion generally, and the question of the order of development. *Prima facie* case for the existence of heart-religion from the beginning. The problem of the Psalms is part of the broader problem of the Old Testament. Not to be settled by assumptions but by method of historical inquiry . . . . Pp. 1-18

CHAPTER II.

HISTORICAL SKETCH OF PSALM CRITICISM.

Survey of the history of criticism of the Psalms: 1. Earliest Jewish opinions. 2. The Church fathers—Theodore of Mopsuestia. 3. Foundation laid for *historical* criticism by Calvin. 4. Inauguration of modern critical treatment by De Wette, whose view was carried out (*a*) negatively by Hupfeld, and (*b*) positively by Ewald and Hitzig. 5. Olshausen perceived a background of *national* history, and referred the Psalms to the Jewish *Church* of the Maccabaean period; similar position of Reuss. 6. More recent writers carry out one or other of the lines already laid down, thus:—(*a*) Delitzsch goes on the lines of Ewald and Hitzig—There is a back-eddy in Hengstenberg and Hävernick. (*b*) Smend develops Olshausen's idea of the personified Church. (*c*) Stade, Wellhausen, Kuenen, Duhm, proceed on Reuss's conception of the history. (*d*) Giesebrecht works an argument from the language of the Psalms. (*e*) Cheyne, basing largely on conclusions of Olshausen and Kuenen, elaborates an argument from groups. (*f*) Nowack, Baethgen, Sellin, Beer . . . . Pp. 19-46

CHAPTER III.

THE PROBLEMS OF THE PSALMS.

Conclusions from preceding historical survey : (*a*) The inscriptions cannot *per se* be taken to determine date and authorship of the Psalms ; (*b*) nor can we start from a limited number of admitted "Davidic" psalms ; (*c*) nor is the argument from "groups" workable. But the whole discussion raises one broad question : Are the Psalms, or a representative portion of them, the expression of pre-exilian religion ? The arguments for post-exilian origin may be reduced to five : (1) Examination of first argument, that *the Psalter was the book of praise of the Second Temple*. (2) Consideration of the *linguistic argument*. There remain three arguments, which resolve themselves into the question, What were the pre-exilian history and religion of Israel ? They are these : (3) The *historical allusions and situations* do not fit pre-exilian, but do fit post-exilian time. (4) The stage of *religious consciousness* is too advanced for pre-exilian time. (5) The *Speaker* in the Psalms is the personified post-exilian Church. Instead of taking up these several points controversially, it is proposed to institute a historical inquiry on the following lines : (*a*) to look at evidence, outside of the Psalter itself, of the existence of a Psalter, or of the practice of psalmody, in the period before the exile ; (β) to consider whether the Psalter itself gives evidence of a pre-exilian origin. If these two lines of proof show certainly, or with the greatest probability, that the Psalter originated in pre-exilian times, it will then be proper to examine the literary, historical, and religious features of the Psalms, in the light of pre-exilian history
Pp. 47-66

CHAPTER IV.

EXTERNAL EVIDENCE.

What is implied in the term "Canon," and what is known as to its formation and completion. For our present purpose we have to look for evidences of the Psalter being actually in the Canon at certain dates, and draw legitimate inferences from that fact. Evidence of extra-canonical books: (1) The existence of the Psalter in the LXX. Version, and the inferences involved. (2) The testimony of the books of the Maccabees. (3) The testimony of the book of Ecclesiasticus . . . Pp. 67-88

CHAPTER V.

EXTERNAL EVIDENCE—*continued*.

Evidence from the canonical books as to Psalter, psalms, or psalmody: (1) Ezra, Nehemiah: "singers" returning from the captivity. (2) The books of Chronicles, with references to (*a*) singing, &c., and (*b*) actual psalms now in the collection. (3) The book of Jonah. Pre-exilian books — Kings, Samuel, Amos. Summary of the external evidence, with the strong confirmation of Psalm cxxxvii. . . . . . . Pp. 89-124

CHAPTER VI.

TESTIMONY OF THE PSALTER ITSELF.

(1) Not the work of one time or of one man. (2) Five books. (3) Smaller collections. (4) Not in chronological order; yet a hint of such an order at Ps. lxxii. General conclusion; earlier psalms towards the beginning. Two *termini*—the age of David, and the age of the Maccabees. Both possible. At all events it is legitimate to go back to pre-exilian times for commencement
Pp. 125-145

CHAPTER VII.

POETRY IN PRE-EXILIAN TIMES.

The foregoing evidence not only invites but compels us to go back to pre-exilian time for the origin of psalmody. Three lines of inquiry before us: (1) Whether, in pre-exilian times, the poetic faculty was so well cultivated that lyrics of this kind were possible. (2) Whether there were occasions sufficiently varied and sufficiently outstanding to explain national and religious references. (3) Whether the religious consciousness had attained a development sufficient to produce lyrics like the Psalms. In the present chapter we confine ourselves to the *first* of these.—The stimulus to poetry furnished by the scenery of Palestine—the wealth of imagery so produced—the metaphoric element in the Hebrew language. Proofs of poetic effort from the earliest times—indications of technical and professional attainment—variety in the kinds of poetry. Now in the Psalms we find the same features of parallelism, metaphor, &c., as are exhibited, *e.g.*, in poetical fragments in prose books and in hymnic pieces in historical and prophetical works. Conclusion that pre-exilian antiquity was capable of producing poetry of the high literary standard of the Psalms. Question arises: What led a people so musical to assign to David the highest place in music and song? Argue that he must have given a new stimulus and a new direction to music. (Parallels in our own literature.) With him begins a distinctive kind of sacred poetry, the sacred lyric or psalm . . . . . Pp. 146-173

CHAPTER VIII.

THE NATIONAL ELEMENT IN THE PSALMS.

Inadequacy of the attempts to classify the Psalms according to their matter; and the reason for this. Yet certain dominant features recur. Present chapter confined to the *national* element, which assumes various phases: (1) The contemplation of the past history. The movements, conflicts, &c., of pre-exilian times were exactly of a nature to call forth such patriotic songs; and in the historical books we find outbursts of song just at the crises in history when we should expect the poetic spirit to be stirred. Here we can see the justification of the tradition that ascribes psalms to David. (2) Psalms which concern the king; these by their mention of David and David's house justify the same tradition. (3) Jerusalem psalms: but it was David that made it the capital. The enigmatical reference to Melchizedek. In connection with the Temple psalms may be taken the "guest" psalms, which also might appropriately begin with David . . . Pp. 174-204

CHAPTER IX.

SUBJECTIVE ELEMENT IN THE PSALTER.

Pause here to answer an objection that arises. If, as we claim, the Psalms, or some of them, may be referred to historical occasions in pre-exilian times, how should there be any uncertainty in determining the definite occasions? Answer:—(*a*) The records we possess of pre-exilian history are scanty. (*b*) When closely examined, the identifications claimed by critics with post-exilian situations are equally shadowy. Then (*c*) metaphor is not a photographic picture of an incident; it is the coinage of a phraseology to express inner feeling. (*d*) The Psalms are chiefly and essentially subjective, not objective. Therefore the Psalms may belong to times of which we *do* have records though they do not picture the events but express the feelings. The idealising tendency seen most strikingly in the kingly psalms, and proved by the failure of critical attempts to refer those especially to Gentile monarchs. Views of Hitzig and Cheyne here . . . . Pp. 205-234

CHAPTER X.

RELIGIOUS ELEMENT IN THE PSALTER.

This is an element in all the Old Testament books; even the history is sacred history. But in the Psalms we have religion by itself. Two great themes: (1) What the writers say or imply as to God Himself, His character, and His attitude towards creation; and (2) what they set forth as the attitude of nature and the world as related to God, especially man's relation to Him (and by implication the attitude of men to one another). (1) God's existence taken for granted. So-called Anthropomorphism. Ethical character — not metaphysical — God's near contact with His works, especially His control of and observance of Man. Here consider theophanies, which all have a gracious object. (2) Men are broadly divided into two classes, variously designated. These various designations on both sides,—the reciprocal attitude they imply, and the active conduct which is the result. The moral world here presented. Difficulty of forming a concrete connected picture of it, because it is described in metaphorical language, and largely idealised. As to the date at which such a conception was possible, there is no doubt implied an education in the handling of language to express spiritual experiences. Yet the experiences described are possible in very simple states of society. They are the situations largely dwelt on by early prophets. Compare the social condition of the East at the present day
Pp. 235-257

CHAPTER XI.

THE SPEAKER IN THE PSALMS.

The religious element in the Psalms, constituting them the highest embodiment of personal piety in the Old Testament, gives particular interest to the inquiry, Who the Speaker is, and under what circumstances he wrote them. This inquiry emphasised by the position of modern critics that the Psalms are spoken by the Jewish Church collectively. Personification a common figure in the Old Testament, and clearly to be seen in certain psalms. The modern theory of personification stated, and illustrated. Support sought for the theory in the position that the Psalter was the praise-book of the Temple. Examples of psalms held to be spoken by or in name of the assembled congregation. Examples to the contrary; and objections to the theory of personification :—(1) that nothing is gained by it, and greater difficulties remain ; (2) that it is inconsistent with the lyrical character of the songs ; and (3) that it exhibits a retrograde view of the religion. An examination of the literary process leads to the conclusion that individual conception, observation, and experience must underlie personification ; therefore personal individual religion must precede collective representation of religious experience, and this is the vital point in question. Arguments here drawn from the experiences by which prophets were taught the truths they proclaimed, from the feelings with which psalms of a personal tone would naturally be recited by a body of worshippers, and from the religious consciousness in all ages . . Pp. 258-290

CHAPTER XII.

PERSONAL RELIGION IN PRE-EXILIAN TIMES.

Every step in the preceding discussion shows that there is an underlying question as to the quality of the pre-exilian religion, which must now be considered. As explained by the critics, the post-exilian spiritual religion turns out to be a "corporate" religion, not personal piety. To which there are two objections :—that this is no essential advance on earlier religion, and that it is not adequate to account for the spiritual tone of the Psalms. The question in dispute comes to be : whether, early or late, the individual did not count for more than these critics allow.—Although the religion had always a national sphere and boundary, yet, within this corporate religion, there was room for the free exercise of personal piety. From the records of pre-exilian time, it is argued that :—(1) Law implies recognition of individual responsibility. (2) The books, and the very function of the prophets, imply a distinction of good and evil men in the community. We find in the prophets almost the very words of the Psalms, or, by turning prophetic into psalm language we get certainly the situation underlying the Psalms. And it is difficult to conceive any state of society in ancient Israel in which it could be otherwise. Compare the modern condition in the East. (3) The oldest historical books show : (*a*) how the nation grew out of the family, and the family out of the individual—the history is full of *biography;* (*b*) how the individual may bring harm on the community ; (*c*) how the individual may act as intercessor for others ; and (*d*) generally how the individual is in direct relationship to God.—All this sufficient to confute the view, held since Vatke, that the individual did not count for anything, and to show that such a sweeping distinction between pre-exilian and post-exilian religion is untenable . Pp. 291-318

CHAPTER XIII.

DAVID THE PSALMIST.

The ground now cleared for putting the question, Whether we know of individuals in pre-exilian times high enough in spiritual tone to write psalms and situated similarly to the psalmists? (1) The individual prophets are the best instances of good men, alone against a multitude, and standing in direct relation to God. Amos, Samuel, Moses, all exemplify this and use language like the Psalms. Jeremiah a conspicuous example, but not essentially different from other prophets. From him and others we have language, and even *pieces* quite like the Psalms. But (2) the prophets did not stand alone. Cases of Jeremiah, Isaiah, and even Elijah. A prophet's life not spent in giving public addresses. We know they prayed *for* the people. Did they never pray *with* them ? (3) Therefore the difference between prophetic and psalm religion is more one of form and audience than of substance. As to the objections to Davidic psalms : We must allow for the versatility of David's muse, and we must acknowledge the possibility of various elements in his character. Parallels in both lines are abundant in literature and

CONTENTS.

history. The "tradition" in regard to David implies the existence of such qualities and such a variety of qualities in the historical David, as (a) formed the empire he left, and (b) impressed the heart of Israel in such a way as to give the tradition that precise shape. He was already idealised in his lifetime. Cheyne's explanation of "Davids" examined. An unbiassed reading of the documents and a fair interpretation of the Psalms make Davidic psalmody credible. The events in his life are sufficient to enable us to say, Here was a man capable of producing songs like some of those in the Psalter. Illustration from one day in his life. The varied experience and the long years through which his character was matured . . . . . . Pp. 319-351

CONCLUSION.

The aim of these pages is to vindicate for the Psalms an earlier date and a higher position than some critics assign to them. The argument is general, because broad issues are in question. Interesting as it would be to know the individual authors, perhaps even if we could recall the singers, they would not greatly satisfy our curiosity. It is the mood, not the surroundings, that explains the poem, and the great thing is that there *were* singers of these moods. The disparity of explanation of psalms by various expositors is proof that to the writers the occasion was not the principal thing, but something so universal that it was bound to repeat itself, so broad that it could not be confined by precise words—the eternal conflict between good and evil, as old as the dawn of conscience, and ever going on. But the psalms are not *descriptions* of that conflict, but the sighs or shouts of the combatants. Dean Stanley's observation of the ivy-like character of the Hebrew lyric poetry, clinging to the epic trunk of history. But the history is religious; and to take away religion from the lyrics is to denude the trunk of its clothing, and even to deprive the history of its living sap. Prophetic-religion and Psalm-religion cannot be separated, and our estimate of the one controls our estimate of the other; but without the existence of pre-exilian psalm-religion the whole history becomes an insoluble riddle. Songs, no doubt, modified in course of transmission. Compare the history of the Hebrew Prayer-Book and of lyric poetry in general. So also late and early may lie side by side. Psalmody, however, once started, became the outlet for the expression of all that was best in Judaism. As God was never without a witness, so were His people never without a song
Pp. 352-360

THE POETRY AND RELIGION
OF THE PSALMS.

CHAPTER I.

INTRODUCTORY.

THERE are three aspects in which the religion of a people may be regarded. In the *first* place, it may be contemplated as a thing objectively put before the people who profess it, in the form of certain truths to be received, and a number of duties to be performed. Whether the people act up to its requirements or not, the religion as a whole is there, existent as a system, whose history and characteristics may be studied. In the *second* place, we may contemplate religion in action, either practised in formal observances and exemplified in the daily life, or, better still, stirring the emotions and sentiments of the heart and finding expression for itself in the language of devotion. In the *third* place, it may be observed as an intellectual movement, the spirit seeking to understand the problems which press for solution as to the causes of things, the obligations of duty, the world unseen. In the first case, we may say we have God speaking to man with authority, seeking to reach man's conscience and control his will; in the second case, we have man speaking to God, the human heart answering the divine message; while, in the third, we may say we have man speaking to himself, seeking to give account to himself of the mysteries which perplex him.

The religion of the Old Testament presents itself in all these phases; and we may even distinguish three sets of the Old Testament writings as characterised by the respective phases which they embody. In the Law and the Prophets, we have God's call to man, characterised, in the former, by a system of rules to be observed in the life, in the latter by the enforcement of eternal principles on which God's claim to man's obedience is rested. In the second place come the Psalms, which are the expression of man's religious feelings in their struggle to reach God and to find peace. "The psalmists," says Reuss,[1] "seek God, and know where to find Him; the prophets, for the most part, address men who have forgotten Him." And, lastly, we have what is called the

[1] Das Alte Testament (1893), Band v. p. 36.

Wisdom literature, the nearest approach which the Old Testament exhibits to philosophising or speculation, the distinctive examples of which are the Proverbs, and more particularly the books of Job and Ecclesiastes. Here, however, the writers do not set themselves to elaborate either a philosophy or a theology, but concern themselves with ethical problems as to the mystery of suffering in the world and the duty resting on man as the subject of divine government.

From several points of view the phase of religion exhibited in the Psalms is of special interest.

1. These sacred songs touch our common human nature very closely and at many points. We see here the religious sentiment in actual exercise under all vicissitudes,—breathed forth in humble prayer or grateful praise, impeded in its current by suffering or sorrow, agitated to its depths by temptation, passion, or persecution, or hurried along by exuberant hope and triumphant expectation. And the expression of these varying moods of the religious spirit is so simple, the terms are so general and comprehensive, the situations of the poets apparently so unencumbered with local or temporary details, that it is not difficult for a reader at any time to place himself in sympathy with them. As we read the Psalms, we feel that people who had any religion worthy of the name might have been uttering the same things from the beginning, and may go on

saying them to the end of the world. So it has come about that these old songs of Israel, at whatever times they may have been written, and whatever occasions may have called them forth, have become, in a sense that is true of no other religious compositions, the devotional handbook of the world. The Psalms have proved how genuine and true their religious tone is by the way in which they have lent themselves to the expression of the finest spiritual experience. As that experience deepens it finds outlet for itself in the more general and comprehensive, the more simple language. When "good books" and manuals of devotion lose their freshness and relish, when the best compacted arguments fail to bring conviction to the mind and satisfaction to the spirit, when signs and wonders produce no faith, the heart responds Amen to the simple words of the Hebrew poets and finds peace. Such a psalm as the twenty-third is so general in its expressions that it may be sung in unison by the oldest and the youngest around the family altar; yet it is so suggestive and satisfying that, when all other words put together fail to express the emotion of an overflowing heart, it comes to the believer's aid and furnishes relief. One of the first to be learned by the child, it is the sweetest music that can fall on the ear of the aged Christian who has fought the good fight. Dr John Ker, in his pleasant little book, 'The Psalms in History and Biography,' after giving instances from the times of persecution in Scotland of the use of this psalm for heartening, mentions also that Edward Irving when on his deathbed repeated it in Hebrew, and that the dying words of Sir William Hamilton were, "Thy rod and Thy staff they comfort me."[1]

2. The Psalms have also a special interest to the Christian theologian. Augustine made the remark, which has been often repeated in different forms, that Christianity was as old as the world; and Tertullian put the same truth into the startling words, that in the Old Testament history Christ was schooling Himself for incarnation.[2] It is accordingly of the deepest interest to the Biblical theologian to group and systematise, with due regard to proportion and historical emergence, the truths that are contained in both dispensations. It is evident that our appreciation of Christianity will be more clear and intense the more we can perceive a positive preparation for it, and a laying of its foundations in the antecedent religion of the Old Testament. If Christianity is in any appropriate sense as old as the world, we ought not only to observe adumbrations of it in all the best of the ancient religions, but also to find these most

---

[1] It is an ingenious conjecture of a recent commentator on Shakespeare that even the dying Falstaff was thinking of the 23rd Psalm when he "babbled of green fields" (King Henry V., Act ii. sc. iii.)

[2] De Carne Christi, vi.

manifestly displayed in the religion of Israel, with which it is so closely connected in historical sequence. And, further, if Christianity is both the last and the best of religions—the absolute truth—we ought to find in the antecedent religion germs at least of ultimate truth, which are independent of local occasion, and retain their vitality through all lapse of time.

Now, just as the religion of the Old Testament, as a thing attained, reaches its culmination in the Psalms, so the points of contact between the Old and New Testaments increase when we look at the Psalter in relation to the new dispensation. The connection here lies deeper than in mere references in the New Testament to individual passages in the Old, or in the fulfilment of Messianic prophecies or accomplishment of types. For religion, from our present point of view, is not a speculative but an active thing; Scripture is not so much an embodiment of so many truths made known for man's instruction, as a record of a movement of man's spirit by the spirit of God for a practical end, man's salvation. Accordingly, the religion of the Old Testament appears not as a problem which man seeks to solve for himself, nor as a series of questions propounded by God to man's intellect, but as a course of discipline to prepare man's soul for the good that was in store for him. In this way the Old Testament was the schoolmaster to lead to

Christ, by quickening in man the sense of sin and the desire for renewal; in other words, it is not merely nor even principally a record of revelation, but a record of the process of redemption. From this aspect, the points of contact between the Old and the New Testaments are seen not only to increase in number but to gain in significance. And so we can understand how the New Testament writers, to whom this view was paramount, refer so frequently to the Psalms, although there are fewer direct Messianic references in the Psalms than in the prophetic Scriptures. It is said [1] that there are in all two hundred and eighty-three quotations from the Old Testament in the New, and that of these a hundred and sixteen are from the Psalms.

It is therefore not by accident or out of simple convenience that the Psalms are bound by us in one volume with the New Testament as if they were New Testament Scripture. The Psalter has indeed become a New Testament book and come to be incorporated into the liturgies of nearly every branch of the Christian Church. "It was the first book which the early Church put into the hands of her young converts, the primer of her religious teaching; and no man could be admitted to the highest order of the clergy unless he knew the Psalter by heart. It was used for singing in the first assemblies for

---

[1] Van Dyke, The Story of the Psalms, *ad init.*

Christian worship,"[1] and it has ever continued to be used, sometimes as the sole book of praise, and always as the best and most enduring of all.

3. In a wider field, to the scientific inquirer into the history of religion, the Psalms present a very interesting subject of study. For the question occurs, Whether the three phases of religion of which we have spoken are evolved in historical succession, or whether they may not have emerged simultaneously, or at least may not have in a measure run a parallel course before assuming a formulated shape in writing? Though we have specified different books as examples of the different tendencies, a hard-and-fast line cannot be drawn among the books of the Old Testament in this respect, for there are reflective or speculative psalms, and there are subjective devotional elements in the Prophets. It would seem that the reflective phase came somewhat late to its fuller development among the Hebrews; but then it is to be noted that speculative problems such as early exercised Greek philosophers seem scarcely to have troubled the Hebrew mind; for, as Matthew Arnold has pointed out, while the Hellenistic tendency was towards speculation, the Hebraistic was towards practical righteousness. So that it would not be safe to lay down any *a priori* dictum as to what must be the order of development in

[1] Van Dyke, *ut sup.*

these matters. But as regards the devotional phase of religion exhibited in the Psalms, it is a question not only of great interest but of vital importance in connection with the history of the religion of Israel, whether such a kind of religion came comparatively early to maturity; for on the answer to this question depends the estimate that we shall form of the greater part of the pre-exilian history.

We do not require at this point to raise the deeper antecedent question as to the origin and earliest phases of the religion of Israel, nor to pronounce an opinion as to whether the Law preceded or succeeded the Prophets. Both of these taken together may be said to represent generally the objective phase of the religion. The prophets, however, are on all hands regarded as teachers of a purer and more spiritual religion; and the question to which we restrict ourselves in the meantime is—Whether, concomitant with their teaching, there existed among the people, in narrower or wider circles, a religion such as the Psalms express, or whether this latter phase is of slower growth and the product of a later time? The question will, in fact, occupy much of our attention in the sequel. Lest, however, any bar should be placed upon its consideration by some preliminary assumption as to the course of development which the religion must have run, one remark may be made at this point. It is this. The prophetic teacher himself is the human medium of the divine authoritative teaching, and we can hardly suppose a prophet raised up to declare such truths as the Hebrew prophets proclaim, without being himself imbued with the truths he enforces, and animated by them as living principles. The prophetic message is not like what Mohammed called his Qor'an, a *tanzîl*, something handed down in a concrete form from heaven—not like the tables of stone given to Moses on the mount. It was a continuous though varied message, addressed by living men of the time to men in special circumstances, reiterating the same fundamental truths in application to the changing events of history. The earnestness and force with which each prophet delivered his word—nay, the persecution and opposition he encountered in the delivery of it—are proofs that he himself was a witness and example of the truths he made known. The word was not only in his mouth, but it was a burning fire in his heart (Jer. xx. 9), impelling him, not less than did the divine command, to deliver his message.

Now, if we are to believe the prophets themselves, they were not isolated witnesses, but rather connected representatives of a purer religion than that which commonly prevailed in the nation. And if it was their personal religion that gave them the power to stand forth as unshaken witnesses, then there was a line of good as well as true men, and the prophets were not only the *light* of the world but also the *salt* of the earth. Of course we cannot thus summarily draw the conclusion that psalm composition was contemporaneous with prophetic teaching; but it is important to make it clear at the outset that we have no right to assume that it was not. And the reason for touching on the point now is, because the main problem connected with the Psalms lies just here. The vital question in Old Testament criticism is not, Who wrote such and such books? but, Do they give a fair representation of the history of the religion as it was made known and received? In regard to the Pentateuch, for example, the essential question is not, Was Moses the author of the book? but, Was Mosaism, and was the patriarchal religion which preceded it, such as the Pentateuch represents them to have been? And in regard to the Psalms, more fundamental than the question, Did David write all the Psalms? or, How many of them did he write? is the question, Was there a religion such as the Psalms express, from David's time onwards? Were there men in Israel, expressing in songs like these their trust in God, their feelings of sin and misery, their hope of the ultimate triumph of good over evil?

Now, the tendency of modern criticism is to represent the earliest phases of the religion of Israel as of a crude, unrefined character, and to bring lower and lower down in date the beginnings of the religion in a purer and spiritual form. And it will be at once apparent that the Psalms must be involved in such a rearrangement. If it was not, say, till the eighth century before Christ that the prophets began for the first time to teach, as a new and strange thing, an ethic monotheism, we need not look for psalms breathing a spiritual religion at that period, much less in the time of David, two centuries earlier. It will be found, accordingly, that the view taken of the Psalms has undergone modification in accordance with the modified view of the Old Testament history of religion as a whole.

But just because the problem of the Psalms is thus part of a greater problem, it must be approached independently and without prepossession or assumption of what is still matter of dispute on the broader field. The Psalms may, in effect, contribute their share of evidence for the settlement of the greater question, and ought to be regarded as independent witnesses. It is illegitimate, for example, to say: The pre-prophetic or the prophetic religion was of such and such a character, and these Psalms, exhibiting a far higher type of religion, must therefore be later than the pre-prophetic or the prophetic period. Neither can the assumption be allowed that David's personal character and the circumstances of his age were so far below the level of the religion of the

Psalms that he cannot possibly be regarded as the author of any of them. There has been far too much assertion of this kind, which owes its acceptance more to the confidence with which it is reiterated than to the solidity of the arguments on which it is supported. It may please those who are wedded to a hard-and-fast theory of development to arrange the facts of religious experience as a naturalist arranges specimens in a cabinet; but the actual course of history shows how artificial is such a process of systematising; and those who believe that

> "If there be
> A devil in man, there is an angel too,"

will see nothing incredible in the idea that side by side with ignorance and superstition there may have existed a simple and pure faith, and that the solution of the over-perplexed problem of Old Testament religious history is to be sought, not in a dead uniformity of evolution, but in a contemporaneous movement of good and bad, such as all ages have witnessed, and such as is going on in the world around us.

If there is any force in these remarks, it will appear that, although it is not a matter of entire indifference who wrote the books of the Old Testament, yet the inquiry into this subject should be allowed to fall into its proper place. When we have before us a mass of ancient literature, a great proportion of which is entirely anonymous, it becomes a very difficult and delicate task to assign the various portions to their respective dates and authors. Such an inquiry cannot be confined to the books themselves which are in dispute, but must proceed on broader historical evidence. And in prosecuting it we shall, no doubt, have at many points to confess our ignorance or our inability to determine many things in detail. We may not, for example, be able positively to prove the authorship of the Pentateuch, or even to fix the dates and origin of its different parts; or we may not be able to tell what psalms, or how many, were written by David, and who were the authors of the rest. Still, on the line of cautious historical inquiry, we may make it probable that the position and work of Moses were such as are assigned to him in the Pentateuch; and that, without a Mosaic period such as is described in the Pentateuch the succeeding history is not intelligible. So, in regard to the Psalms, if by any argument we can make it appear probable that there was from David's time such a set of circumstances and such a religious consciousness and experience as find expression in the Psalms, —even though we may not be able to determine the precise occasion and circumstances in which the individual pieces were composed,—we gain a historical foothold for further inquiries into the literary history of the collection. But on such a line of investigation it is evident that we must not attempt to begin with David, but be content if we can end with him.

And yet, as has just been said, the authorship of the Old Testament books, and particularly the authorship of the Psalms, is far from being a matter of indifference even to the reader unskilled in technical criticism. Indeed to him it is in an important respect more vital than to the critic. There is some justification for the alarm that is manifested by ordinary readers of the Bible in the face of the apparent havoc that is being made in these days among the books which they have been accustomed to revere so highly. And generous allowance should be made for what may be called the criticism of religious sentiment. If a poet can best understand and criticise poetry, religious experience may claim to be heard in settling the primary reference of compositions that take strong hold of the religious consciousness. It may be true, as a recent writer has said,[1] that the value of the 51st psalm "To him who reads it in the inner chamber, 'having shut to the door,' is the same, whether it expresses the passion of penitence which shook David's soul after his great sin, or the collective confession of the Jewish Church-nation." Yet I doubt if the general concession which underlies this statement will sat-

[1] W. T. Davison, The Praises of Israel, p. 32 f.

isfy the mind of the devout Christian. Much as the psalm has been prized for its own sake as the expression of sincere repentance, the reader would like to feel assured that he has before him the confession of one of like passions with himself. And its power to give comfort has been enhanced by the reflection at every turn that if David, or an individual precisely situated as David was, after so great a crime as he is supposed to be confessing, could take heart of hope to believe in God's forgiveness, the same mercy will not be withheld from any other penitent suppliant.

To the philosopher, investigating the history of "ideas" in the dry cold light of speculation, it may seem a matter of no consequence that Abraham be explained as a creation of legend, and Moses and David turn out not to be so much names of historical individuals as symbols of tendencies and periods in history. But for the plain man, to whom religion is not an object of abstract study but a vital concern of practical life, these are not altogether matters of indifference. A very great part of the Old Testament is biography, religion exemplified in the lives of individuals; and it is this that not only constitutes to a great extent the literary charm of the books, but explains the powerful hold they take upon the heart, and accounts for their influence as a religious education. Just as in any perplexity or sorrow we are helped more by the sympathy of one who has gone through the same experience himself than by any amount of commonplace maxims, however sound; so, in turning to the Bible for consolation or guidance or encouragement, we wish to get into contact with persons and not merely to find ideas. The great Teacher Himself enforced His lessons by concrete examples, and moved men's hearts by an exhibition of the individual and the minute. The care of the divine Father for the sparrows and for the lilies of the field touches a more tender chord than the contemplation of the starry worlds. And though, abstractly considered, they both teach the same lesson, we derive more comfort from the experiences of an individual than from the records of Church history. We wish to feel kindred with men of flesh and blood who had like passions with ourselves, and we love to believe that the religion which is our own stay and support was the stay and support of men like ourselves before us, that the God in whom we trust has been the dwelling-place of His people in all generations.

The foregoing remarks will indicate what is the purpose of the following pages. No attempt is to be made to determine the authorship of individual psalms, nor will the main attention be concentrated on the Psalter itself. The inquiry will be of a more general kind. First of all, an attempt will be made to trace the existence of the Psalter or of a Psalter, and generally the practice of psalmody, as far back as the evidence from different sources will warrant. It will then be necessary to take a general survey of the Psalter itself, and make an appreciation of its internal character and contents. And finally, an endeavour will be made to determine how far it is possible to find room in pre-exilian times for such a religion as is expressed in the Psalms. If it can be shown to be probable that the practice of psalmody goes back to Hebrew antiquity, that the general situations of the Psalms agree with the situations of early time, and that the tone of religious experience expressed in them is not too high for those times, we shall not only be vindicating for the Psalter its right place among the Old Testament books, but showing also that the earlier Old Testament religion was a richer and fuller thing than many in modern times are disposed to allow.

We must, however, begin with a rapid survey of the opinions that have been held regarding the Psalms in ancient and modern times, that we may see how the various problems in the inquiry have emerged, and estimate precisely the present position of the question. This will be the subject of the next chapter.

CHAPTER II.

HISTORICAL SKETCH OF PSALM CRITICISM.

In endeavouring to determine the place of the Psalms in the religion and history of the Old Testament, we naturally inquire in a preliminary way what attempts have been made in this direction in ancient and modern times.

The earliest of all the indications of opinion on this subject is furnished in the titles and superscriptions which are found in the Hebrew text. The most cursory English reader cannot but have noticed the headings, "To the chief musician, a psalm of David," and so on. Being found in the Hebrew Bible, they are, of course, retained in the Revised Version; but are to be carefully distinguished from those summaries of contents found in ordinary English Bibles, which come only from the translators. If these headings are, as is usually admitted, later than the Psalms themselves, they must represent the belief, resting on tradition, or based on a view of the contents of the Psalms, as to the persons who wrote them. It is a question when these headings were affixed to the Psalms. According to Reuss they are the work of Jewish scholars, but of unknown date; yet in no case much older, and possibly even later, than the Christian era.[1] The superscriptions are, at all events, older than the LXX. Version; for the Greek translators had them before them, and clearly did not, in some instances, understand their signification.

This view is also found expressed in the Talmud in the famous passage[2] in which the authorship of the various books of the Old Testament is formally stated—viz., that the Psalms come from the persons whose names are attached to them in the headings. It is, indeed, not very clear what is meant in that passage by the expression that David wrote the Psalms "at the hands of ten elders"[3]—viz., those whose names are mentioned besides his own. At any rate, the view which prevailed in the middle ages, following Jerome and Eusebius, and which has found expression in the commentaries of Aben

[1] Das Alte Testament, Band v. p. 38 f.

[2] Baba Bathra, fol. 14. A translation of the passage is given by Ryle, 'The Canon of the Old Testament,' Excursus B.

[3] Or, as Driver translates, "at the direction of." Dalman, however, explains the expression as meaning "in the name of," and for Talmudic usage in support of this rendering appeals to the Mishna Bab. Mez., vii. 9, and Gemara Gittin, 67 b. See 'Der Gottesname Adonaj,' p. 79, note.

Ezra and David Kimchi, is, as just stated, that the names attached to the Psalms denote authorship. As to the psalms which bear no name, the tendency was to assign them all to David, or to ascribe anonymous psalms to the author last named in a preceding one—a method favoured by Jerome and Origen.[1]

This mode of representing David as having composed the Psalms " at the hands of," or " in the name of" others, passed practically into the habit of ascribing the Psalter as a whole to David. And one need not be surprised that this became the current mode of speaking of the book of Psalms. We find it formulated in the Talmud;[2] and, in the New Testament books, "David" seems to stand as an equivalent for the book of Psalms.[3] Such a mode of speaking of the Psalter was natural before literary study, not to say criticism, had come into operation. The Old Testament books were handed down from ancient time, each with a great name attached to, or associated with it—probably the name of the first or greatest individual who had literary connec-

---

[1] See Baethgen, Psalmen, Einl., § 4.

[2] By R. Meir in Pesachim, 117 a.

[3] "As He saith in David" (Heb. iv. 7) refers to Psalm xcv., which in the original is anonymous. So in Acts iv. 25 the 2nd Psalm, which is also anonymous, is quoted as the words of David. It is only inferentially that we can class the Chronicler as holding the same view. There is no doubt that he refers to David's time the full practice of psalmody. But the passage (1 Chron. xvi. 7 ff.) does not positively assign to David the psalm there given. But more of this in the sequel.

tion with it—and the book was then spoken of as his work. So we have come to speak of the "Books of Moses," the "Psalms of David," and the "Proverbs of Solomon." Closer study may enable us to rectify such designations; and the books themselves sometimes declare that they are not in all parts from one writer. Yet we should neither, on the one hand, overlook the elements of truth involved in these representations, and scout all tradition as worthless; nor should we, on the other hand, hold the early writers who employ such language as committed to, or binding us to, positions in literary criticism that are not warranted by the general language which they employ and the popular view which they present.

The early Church Fathers, as they received the Old Testament canon from the Jews, received from them also the traditions as to the origins of the books, and so they usually proceed on the assumption that the Psalms were all written by David. When other names occurred in the headings, they were explained as the names of persons to whom David delivered the Psalms to be sung or set to music, or else as names of persons concerning whom, or in whose name, he wrote. As to the contents of the Psalms, it was supposed that David wrote many of them prophetically, so that it did not excite surprise that in some of them reference was made to the time of the Captivity or the return from it, or that others could be referred to the times of the Maccabees, or others again to the wars of the Romans against the Jews. This mode of interpretation was quite common among the Jews also, as the Targums abundantly show.[1] Of course, when in the heading there was mention of the occasion of the composition of a psalm by David (for it is only in "Davidic" psalms that such notices occur), the references were by most of the Fathers accepted, and the psalms explained accordingly.

A notable exception, however, to this mode of explaining the Psalms meets us in the school of Antioch, particularly in the treatment of the psalms by Theodore of Mopsuestia,[2] the great exegete of that school. Differing as the theologians of Antioch did from those of Alexandria on the great doctrinal questions that were then discussed, they differed no less in exegetical methods. Just as the Alexandrians, in their views of the two natures of Christ, almost merged the human in the divine, while the tendency in Antioch was to make the two natures almost distinct; so in exegesis the prevailing tone among the Alexandrians was allegorising, to the exclusion of the primary reference, while the Antiochians looked for the primary reference and the

---

[1] Not only the late Targums, but even Targum Jonathan, as, *e.g.*, on Hannah's song. See the Cambridge Bible for Schools, 1 Sam. Appendix III.

[2] Born at Antioch about 350, died at Mopsuestia in Cilicia Secunda A.D. 428 or 429.

historical setting and unfolding of Scripture, and thus indeed anticipated modern critical study. Of this school Theodore, though not the earliest, is the most distinguished representative; and when we remember that he was a contemporary of Chrysostom and of Jerome, and when we compare, as we are now able to do, his exegetical method and results with the conclusions of modern scholars, we shall see that he is eminently entitled to be called the exegete of the ancient Church.

By virtue of his critical talent, which manifests itself with particular distinctness in his Commentary on the Psalms, Theodore takes a position quite unique in the whole of antiquity. The manner in which he expresses himself in regard to the inscriptions of the Psalms, and his strict following up of the historical references, at no point tolerating allegory, that enemy of all sound exegesis, exhibit him as a stranger in his immediate surroundings, and as belonging to an epoch later than himself by many centuries. With this critical faculty, moreover, he combines an eminent ability to penetrate into the thoughts of the poet, to trace their inner connection, to enter into the feelings of the psalm-singers, and finally to simplify and accommodate all this to the readers of his Commentary.[1]

Theodore, like others of his time, ascribed all the Psalms to David, taking the common view that, in many of them, the Psalmist spoke prophetically. "In the Compendium of Isagogic of Junilius Afri-

---

[1] Baethgen in Zeitschrift für die alttestamentliche Wissenschaft, hereafter for brevity cited as ZATW, for 1886, p. 262.

canus, which reflects the theology of the schools of Antioch and Nisibis, the Psalms are reckoned among the prophetical writings."[1] The two main things to be noted in regard to Theodore's position are : (1) his setting aside of the titles as of no value in indicating the reference of the Psalms, and (2) his endeavour, by an examination and exegesis of the Psalms themselves, to determine the circumstances to which they referred. It is to be remembered that, apparently, he was not much of a Hebrew scholar,[2] and that the basis of his exegesis was the Greek LXX., in which there is a considerable divergence in the matter of the headings from the Massoretic text; and Baethgen suggests that it was perhaps owing to Theodore's influence that the Syrian Church discarded the Hebrew titles altogether from the Psalms, substituting for them an entirely new set of superscriptions.[3] No doubt, also, his view of prophecy as operative in the Psalms was a very mechanical one, for David is represented by him as speaking " in the person of " (ἐκ τοῦ προσώπου) this or that individual, and with reference to definite concrete events and situations. But the very crudeness of this view of prophecy aided Theodore in his search for precise historical occasions or correspondences between the Psalms and the situations for which

---

[1] Baethgen, as above, p. 266 f.   [2] Ibid., 265 f.
[3] Baethgen, Psalmen, Einl., § 2.

they were composed.[1] In this way it is that he anticipated modern criticism; for it will be found that psalms which he, on his method, regarded as prophetically referring to certain times, are by modern writers assigned to these times for their actual composition.

Theodore, as is well known, was condemned for heresy by the Fifth Council of Constantinople in A.D. 553, one of the grounds of his condemnation being that he had explained reputed Messianic psalms " in a judaising manner"—*i.e.*, in fact, that he had referred them to events in Jewish history. And it was no doubt on this account, and owing to the suspicion attaching to the school of Antioch generally, that his exegetical method was not carried out in the ancient Church, and his exegetical labours lay so long neglected. It is not indeed till the Reformation period that we find a positive advance on his view in regard to the Psalms.

It is, in fact, to Calvin that we are indebted for the first attempts at what may be called the historical criticism of the Psalms. Discarding the mechanical view of prophecy in regard to the Psalms, which had hampered Theodore, he repeatedly draws a distinction between the modes of prophetic and poetic diction. Prophets speak of future things; but the Psalms should be interpreted as referring to, and therefore giving evidence of the

[1] Baethgen, ZATW, 1886, p. 268.

circumstances and situations of, the poets who composed them. Thus, in commenting on Ps. cxxxvii. ("By the rivers of Babylon," &c.), he says: "This is not the way the Prophets speak of future events; here the discourse is evidently of a thing known and experienced." So on Ps. cxxvii. ("Except the Lord build the house," &c.), which is inscribed "to Solomon," he says: "The Jews without reason refuse to ascribe this psalm to Solomon; for the expression in the heading is exactly similar to that which assigns other psalms to David." So in regard to Ps. xc., which is entitled "A prayer of Moses the man of God," after saying that it is doubtful whether the psalm was actually composed by Moses or adapted for popular use by some one of the prophets out of traditional matter, he has no hesitation in accepting it as the work of Moses himself. Again, on Ps. lxxxix., which is inscribed to Ethan the Ezrahite, after discussing who Ethan may have been, he adds: "As for those who will have it that the people are here warned by the spirit of prophecy in regard to future calamities, they are easily refuted by the contents of the psalm, in which the writer, whoever he was, clearly laments the change that took place after the revolt of Jeroboam." Again, to take one more example, on Ps. lxxix. ("O God, the heathen have come into Thy heritage," &c.), which is one of the Asaphic psalms regarded as Maccabaean by those who admit that there are such in the Psalter, Calvin remarks :—

> This psalm, among others, clearly proves itself to have been composed after the death of David. There is no reason for the objection urged by some that the spirit of prophecy here predicts future misfortunes of the Church, in order that a coming generation might be prepared to bear the calamity. For prophets are not wont in their predictions thus to speak historically; and whoever will read the psalm with unbiassed mind will clearly perceive that it must have been composed either when by the Assyrians the temple was burned, the city laid waste, and the people carried into captivity, or when by Antiochus the temple was polluted amid much slaughter. The contents will suit either time.

From which it appears (1) that Calvin did not place reliance on the inscriptions, but sought to determine the reference of a psalm from its own contents, and (2) particularly that he regarded the Psalms as severally the reflection of the times and circumstances in which they were produced. He is not, indeed, quite consistent with himself in his treatment of the inscriptions. For whereas he allows to David all the psalms assigned to him in the titles, and others besides (as Ps. cxix., for example), he has no hesitation in making Asaphic psalms late, some of them as late as the Maccabees (*e.g.*, Pss. lxxiv., lxxvi., lxxix.), though Asaph is a contemporary of David (see 1 Chron. xvi.) And even in his treatment of Davidic psalms, when he finds that the internal situation does not agree with David's circumstances, he falls back on the old method, and says that David composed the psalm as a mirror for future times, as, *e.g.*, Ps. cxxiv., and Ps. lxix. 35 ff.

Rudinger, who had been Melanchthon's friend and colleague at Wittenberg, and went over to the Moravian Brethren, may be described as Calvin's exegetical successor. It was while he was among the Moravian Brethren that he wrote his Latin paraphrase of the book of Psalms, which appeared in 1580 and 1581, and was after Calvin's exposition the most important exegetical work of the sixteenth century.[1] In general we may say that he carried out Calvin's method more consistently than the reformer had done. Finding things in individual psalms which did not agree with the titles attached to them (as, *e.g.*, in Pss. xc. and cxxiv.), he puts the question, "If some of these titles are false, why should we believe the rest, especially as the LXX. has quite a different set of titles from the Hebrew?" And thus, from examination of the Psalms alone, he sought to assign them to different periods, from David to the Maccabees.[2]

Rudinger's investigations proceeded mainly on

---

[1] Ehrt, Abfassungszeit und Abschluss des Psalters, &c., p. 3. On Rudinger's application of the Psalms, in a corporate way, to the Church, see Smend's article on the Ich der Psalmen in ZATW, 1888, p. 57.

[2] It may be mentioned that Rudinger positively assigned twenty-

what may be termed historical considerations, and less on inner exegetical grounds; but his position was practically that maintained by the majority of succeeding expositors who sought to determine the historical occasions of the Psalms.

The seventeenth century was a time of dogmatic rather than of exegetical activity;[1] but the eighteenth century shows a greater historical interest in the Psalms. And, although the prevailing spirit (represented, *e.g.*, by J. H. Michaelis) inclined to a Messianic and typical interpretation, and thus favoured the old view of the Psalms being prophetically written by David, yet there were others, notably Venema (Comment. in Psalmos, 1762-67), who boldly assigned the Psalms to the times to which their contents severally related.

It is with De Wette (born 12th January 1780, died 16th June 1849) that a decided turning-point is reached in the interpretation of the Psalms, and what we may call the modern method sets in. De Wette was the first, says Delitzsch, to clear away the rubbish under which exposition had been buried, and to introduce into it taste, after the example of

five psalms to the Maccabaean age—viz.: i., xliv., xlix., lvii., lx., cviii., lxvi., lxviii., lxxvi., lxxiii., lxxiv., lxxix., lxxvii., lxxx., lxxxviii., lxxxix., xc., cxix., cxx., cxxi., cxxiii., cxxv., cxxix., cxxx., cxxxiv. In regard to two others, xxvi. and xxviii., he leaves it open as to whether they are Maccabaean or not.

[1] The chief work on the Psalms in that century, the Commentary of Geier (1668, 2 vols. 4to, and later, 1709, fol.) has furnished dogmatic and homiletical material for succeeding expositors.

Herder, and grammatical precision, under the influence of Gesenius. Former scholars had agreed that a greater or less number of the psalms ascribed to David were written by him, and they usually proceeded on the principle of not assigning psalms to other writers unless on clear grounds, such as the indubitable mention of, or reference to, later events or situations, as the Temple, the Exile, &c. De Wette, however, pushed Rudinger's method farther. The credibility of the inscriptions being shaken by the cases in which David is said to be, and yet manifestly cannot be, the author, the genuineness of all the other Davidic psalms becomes problematical. "It is not enough," he says, "that the contents and character of the psalms merely do not contradict the inscriptions; there must be positive grounds of probability to remove the suspicion which rests upon the inscriptions. Still more precarious is it to ascribe anonymous psalms to David; the reasons that have been urged for so doing are utterly weak and unworthy of consideration."[1]

To a certain extent De Wette shows a reaction from Rudinger and Venema, who had been too positive in fixing precise dates for the Psalms. De Wette "declines altogether to dogmatise on the occasions when the Psalms were composed,"[2] though

[1] Comment. über die Psalmen, Einl., iii., 5te Aufl., pp. 12, 13.
[2] Cheyne, Founders of Old Testament Criticism, p. 38. Some of the psalms whose authorship he declines to determine are, iii., vii., &c.

he does believe David was a psalm-writer, and ascribes to him certainly Psalm xviii. It was he, however, who gave to succeeding writers on the Psalms an impulse which they followed on different lines, according as they accentuated one side or another of his critical principles.

Hupfeld (born 31st March 1796, died 24th April 1866) may be taken as the representative of the more *negative* side of De Wette's position. Indeed he glories in declaring himself an adherent of it by that epithet. His position is this:[1] Seeing that the superscriptions are not to be relied upon, we are thrown back on internal indications of date, occasion, &c. But in view of our limited knowledge of Hebrew history, the great absence of clear personal or historical traits in the Psalms (which for the most part move in a certain sphere of standing ideas and phrases), and also in view of the ambiguity of most of the linguistic and poetical phenomena, such an investigation has not got beyond a process of uncertain groping and arbitrary opinions. The conjectures of the most recent interpreters accordingly—the field being widened by the removal of the boundary-stones of the inscriptions—move hither and thither between *termini* which are more than eight centuries apart, in such a manner that the same psalm is by one ascribed to David, by another to the Maccabaean

---

[1] Stated in the Einleitung to his Comm. on the Psalms, § 6, with Anmerk. 27.

or even a later period. "I hold it," he says, "to be unworthy of serious research to give oneself up to such childish play at hypotheses, and consider it a duty to restrain oneself within the limits which are fixed, and resolutely to forego every reference to historical events which rests only upon uncertain guesses."

In thus stating his position he has an implied controversy with his contemporaries, Ewald and Hitzig, whose position will be stated presently. He says that the exercise of what they claimed to be *positive* criticism is in his opinion less excusable in regard to the Psalms than elsewhere, "because the Psalms, by virtue of their general human and poetical import—which is intelligible in itself, and for us has its value for edification only because of its general character—can dispense with a [precise] knowledge of their historical relations more readily than any other Scripture." Proceeding on such lines, Hupfeld is content to leave a large proportion of the Psalms undetermined as to their authorship and occasion. He seems to take a delight, in his introduction to each psalm, in collecting together the various opinions—very various oftentimes—that have been held as to the date and occasion; and then concludes by waiving them all aside, and giving a general statement of the import of the psalm and the situation of the unknown writer. The dates of some, of course, within somewhat broad boundaries, as post-exilian or pre-exilian, he considers evident enough ; but he refuses to make any as late as the time of the Maccabees, and this chiefly on the ground that the collection was closed before that time.

The more *positive* side of De Wette's criticism was, as has just been indicated, carried out by Ewald and Hitzig, with whom may also be classed Köster.[1] Although not disposed to rely on the titles as giving proof of authorship, they assumed that the ascription of psalms to David, to such an extent that the whole Psalter was regarded as his work, could not be a baseless tradition, but must rest upon some foundation of fact—in other words, that he must be assumed to be the founder of psalmody, and that the Psalter must contain at least a kernel of Davidic psalms, which they set themselves, each in accordance with his own method, to determine.

Hitzig (born 23rd June 1807, died 22nd January 1875), after stating the well-authenticated facts relating to David's poetical talent and musical skill, and rejecting the supposition that all David's psalms should have been lost, concludes that it was only possible for the whole Psalter to be ascribed to David on the supposition that *some* at least were his work ; and he sums up the position as follows : " Finally, in individual cases, since the traditional

---

[1] Köster, Die Psalmen nach ihrer strophischen Anordnung übersetzt mit Einleitungen u. Anmerkungen. Königsberg, 1837.

statements [of uncertain date] are not to be relied upon, criticism must decide independently the question of authorship; and it has decided that a portion of those psalms which in the superscriptions are assigned to David, certainly came from him."[1]

Ewald (born 16th November 1803, died 4th May 1875) took substantially the same position with regard to David's influence, and the existence of Davidic psalms; and both these writers accepted a number—although a limited number—of psalms as authentically David's, Ewald ascribing to him eleven, and Hitzig fourteen.[2] There was this difference in the method of these two critics—the mark of Davidic authorship insisted upon by Ewald was more a literary one, Hitzig's criterion was mainly historical. Ewald said: "A poet of such eminence and consciousness, of such fortunes and experiences, so unique among the whole people, must reveal himself clearly in every song and every sentence." Hitzig said in substance: "Those songs alone are to be assigned to David which can be referred to the precise situations in which the history shows that he was placed." Each of them, however, gave

[1] Die Psalmen (1863), Erster Band, Einl., p. xiv f.
[2] The fourteen psalms ascribed by Hitzig to David are all those between Psalms iii. and xix., with the exception of v., vi., and xiv. Ewald, in addition to eleven entire Psalms—iii., iv., vii., viii., xi., xviii., xix., xxiv., xxix., xxxii., ci.—assigns to David also the fragments: lx., 8-11, and lxviii., 14-19. See Cheyne, Origin of the Psalter, p. 208, note c.

weight to the other's contention — *i.e.*, Ewald to the historical criterion, and Hitzig to the literary.

Starting as they do at the same point, and acknowledging at the outset practically the same number of Davidic psalms, both proceeding, moreover, on the same principle of positive criticism, Hitzig and Ewald arrive at very different conclusions not only in regard to the actual Davidic psalms, but in regard to the great bulk of the collection. On the one hand, Hitzig, after the Davidic psalms, assigns a very considerable number to Jeremiah (twenty-seven according to Ehrt), three to Isaiah, and four to the Deutero-Isaiah; but then he assigns all the psalms from the lxxiii. onward to the Maccabaean period, with the exception of a few smaller psalms of Book III., which were composed immediately before the outbreak of the persecution.[1] So confident is he in his historical insight that he arranges these later psalms into seven different periods, from the time of Antiochus the Great (B.C. 224-187) to that of Alexander Jannæus (B.C. 104-78). He claims[2] to have shown that the Psalms move step by step in pace with the progress of the history, so that, as has been said,[3] on Hitzig's view the first book of the Maccabees would furnish the scholia for a historical interpretation of the Psalms from Ps. lxxiii. to cl.

[1] Ehrt, Abfass., &c., p. 8 f.
[2] Hitzig, Psalmen, vol. ii., Einl., p. xi.   [3] Ehrt, p. 10.

Ewald, on the other hand, after declaring that it is of the utmost consequence to determine the historical occasion of the Psalms, confesses that it is impossible always to be precise as to the day and date of each, owing to the lack, *e.g.*, of proper names and definite historical references. He arranges and comments upon the Psalms, however, in groups according to their chronological succession, viz. :—

I. Psalms of David and David's time.
II. After David (viz., to the close of the monarchy).
III. Psalms of the Dispersion.
IV. Psalms of the restored Jerusalem.
V. Last psalms.

In his last group he includes twenty-four psalms, which he places in the middle of the fifth century B.C.—in fact, about the time of Ezra.[1]

Our object is not to present all the various views that have been held by the many writers who have given themselves to a study of the Psalms. It is proper, however, to mention as reactions against the critical movement, both in its negative and its positive side, the position taken by Hengstenberg, Hävernick, Keil, &c., who even endeavoured to show (by the example of Arabian poets) that the inscriptions of the Psalms were added by the psalmists themselves, and that the contents of the Psalms did not in any case

[1] Dichter des Alten Bundes, Erster Theil, Zweite Hälfte.

disagree with the titles and occasions as set forth in the headings. Perhaps no one now will seek to defend the authenticity of the titles. The exposition of the Psalms, however, by Hengstenberg is still of value to the Christian theologian, as a devout attempt to look at these sacred songs in connection with the sacred history and the life of the Church. The same may be said, and much higher praise must be given to the Commentary of Delitzsch, who may be taken as the representative of the attempt to combine literary criticism with an adherence, as far as possible, to tradition. He agrees with Ewald and Hitzig in assigning a number of psalms to David, but would increase the number to somewhere about forty-four. He is, however, willing to allow Jeremiah to have been the author of some psalms; and, though he does not regard with favour the view that there are Maccabaean psalms, he does not deny its possibility.[1] Delitzsch's position is virtually assumed by Strack and F. W. Schultz. Köhler also ascribes not a few psalms to David.

We have next to look at the view of Justus Olshausen (born 9th May 1800, died 28th December 1882), whom we may regard as representing another development of the critical position of De

---

[1] Delitzsch's characterisation of the literary features of the Davidic psalms, after the manner of Ewald, may be seen in his Comm., vol. i., Introd. iii.

Wette.[1] At all events De Wette gave a hint of a line of thought which he carried out systematically and rigorously. De Wette had remarked that, in very many of the psalms, the persecution which is represented as endured by the poet is described always in very similar terms, and in explanation of this he put forth the consideration that national misfortune characterises the whole course of Israel's history. Wherever, therefore, persecutors are referred to in the Psalms, he understood the reference to be to the heathen nations. The point to be noted is that De Wette considered *national* misfortune to be the background of these plaintive songs; although he still regarded the speaker in the Psalms as an *individual*. Rosenmüller caught up the idea, and revived in a way the old method of referring the Psalms to the Church. But Olshausen appropriated it in a more critical manner, and straightway characterised the Psalter as the book of praise of the Church of the Second Temple, the speaker being the Jewish Church personified.

Olshausen's view led him to an extreme position

[1] Smend points out this connection in his article on the "Ich," ZATW, 1888, p. 58. Proximately of course Olshausen, as well as von Lengerke, may be described as following out the view of Hitzig (see Delitzsch, Comm., i., Introd. iii.) Olshausen assigned the composition of the latest psalms and the compilation of the Psalter to the time of John Hyrcanus (B.C. 135-107); while Hitzig comes still farther down, ascribing some psalms and the arrangement of the whole to Alexander Jannæus, son of John Hyrcanus.

in the dating of the Psalms. Taking the persecuted "I" to be the Jewish Church of the Second Temple, he perceived that the persecutors were not always heathen, but even more frequently were the godless part of the people. In his endeavour to understand such a schism in the Jewish Church, he felt compelled to come down to the time of the Syrian persecutions, the "godless" among the people being the Hellenising party; so that, in fine, the Psalter, in his view, was mainly composed in the Maccabaean age.

It was perhaps this extreme that made Olshausen's view, as first published, unpopular, or at all events prevented its gaining ground; though, as we shall presently see, he has only anticipated some of the conclusions of the most recent time.

We are thus brought to the period of contemporary criticism, and to the phase of speculation which may be said to have been inaugurated by Reuss of Strassburg (born 18th July 1804, died 15th April 1891). He has the honour of having given the start to the theory of Graf, and to have taught it before Graf himself published it—the theory, viz., that the Prophets precede the Law, and that the Pentateuch is the law-book of the restored post-exilian community. Closely connected with that position, and in fact flowing from it, on the principles of this school of criticism, is the position, taught also by Reuss, that the Psalter comes after the

Law. Reuss, in fact, as he claims priority in enunciating the Grafian hypothesis, claims also to have been the first to express the doubt whether there are any Davidic psalms.[1] In the same manner he is to be classed along with Olshausen in the view of the Psalms which has just been explained; for, more than fifty years ago, he laid stress on the personification that runs through the Psalms, and referred a very large number to the Church and not to any individual speaker.

The leading representatives of the modern school of advanced criticism agree in the main with the conclusions which have just been mentioned, though emphasising different details according to the varying bent of their speculations and the lines of reasoning which they employ. Wellhausen's dictum on the subject of the Psalms is quoted again and again by different writers, as giving a summary statement of the present attitude of criticism: "As the Psalter belongs to the Hagiographa (*i.e.*, the last division of the Old Testament canon), and was the praise-book of the Church of the Second Temple; as also the inscriptions imply the arrangements of musical service described in the books of Chronicles, the question is not whether it contains any post-exilian psalms, but whether it contains any that are pre-exilian."[2]

---

[1] Reuss, Geschichte der heil. Schriften A. T., p. 186.
[2] Bleek, Einleitung, 4te Aufl., § 251, note.

Stade, who has written a voluminous History of Israel from the advanced critical point of view, maintaining that the pre-prophetic religion was based upon nature-worship, and that even the prophetic religion was of late and tardy growth, of course brings the Psalms down to a post-exilian period. "That the Psalms are a product of post-exilian piety appears pre-eminently from the faith in God which they exhibit, — a faith which in every article bears the post-exilian stamp; and the same views pervade the whole book." The Psalter, he says, we are entitled to take generally as the source of information regarding the world of religious thought among the Jews between the time of Ezra and that of Alexander the Great, wherever there is no definite reason for thinking of a later origin. And since it expresses the hopes, prayers, fears, anticipations of the corporate Jewish Church, "the Psalter is the Messianic book of the Old Testament."[1]

Duhm, again, approaching the question from the side of the development of religious thought, carries out Olshausen's line, and seeks[2] to determine the dates at which such expressions as the "pious" or "holy" ones and the "wicked" stand for representative parties in later Judaism.

Smend, however, has recently taken up Olshau-

---

[1] Stade, Geschichte Israels, Band ii., pp. 213, 215, 216.
[2] Theologie der Propheten, p. 20, note.

sen's view where that writer left it, and sought to carry it out without his strong Maccabaean bias. He thinks that Olshausen was wrong in assigning most of the Psalms to the Maccabaean era, because there were parties and animosities among the postexilian Jews from the first. The special task, however, which Smend has taken upon himself is to exhibit the principle of personification in the Psalms. He has examined all the psalms in which an "I" is the speaker, and has come to the conclusion that in all these, without exception, it is the Church personified, and not any individual, that speaks.[1] Smend's view of the whole subject of Israelite religion, early and late, of which his view of the Psalms is a part, is elaborated in his more recently published 'Lehrbuch der Alttestamentlichen Religionsgeschichte,' 1893.

Another modern writer, Giesebrecht, has approached the subject from the linguistic side, and maintains that the majority of the Psalms can be proved on this ground also to be postexilian.[2]

Then we have the elaborate work of Prof. Cheyne, 'The Origin and Religious Contents of

[1] Smend, Ueber das Ich der Psalmen, ZATW, 1888, pp. 49-147; along with which is to be taken his review of Nowack's edition of Riehm's Psalmen in Theol. Literaturzeitung, 2nd November 1889.

[2] ZATW, 1881, p. 276 ff.

the Psalter' (Bampton Lecture for 1889). Beginning his critical studies, as he tells us himself, in the school of Ewald, he has passed latterly into that of Kuenen and Wellhausen;[1] and he has, in regard to the Psalms, reached a position even in advance of most Continental critics. Not one of the Psalms, he tells us, can be assigned to pre-exilian times, except a part of Ps. xviii., and even that is as late as the time of Josiah. He makes no secret of his view as to the pre-prophetic religion, and says in effect that the religious tone of the Psalms is far above what could have been reached by David or long after David's time. Though he does not go so far as Smend in the theory of personification, yet he sees a collective reference not only in the Psalms but in other parts of the Old Testament, and generally regards the Psalter as "a monument of Church consciousness."[2] But the distinguishing feature of his work is the critical method by which he reaches his conclusions as to the dates of particular psalms or small groups of psalms. Starting with a psalm, or with several that give tolerably clear indications of their date and occasion, he lays it down as "a canon of criticism that when certain psalms, all of which agree in some leading features, and positively disagree in none, have come to us from ancient

---

[1] Origin of the Psalter, p. 191, &c.   [2] Ibid., pp. 265, 277.

times in one group, we are bound to assign them to the same period, though it is only in one instance that we can from internal evidence speak positively as to their date."[1] Provided with this critical canon, he exclaims: " A truce then to the inconclusive vagueness of De Wette and Hupfeld," and proceeds with the utmost confidence in his processes till he leaves even Hitzig behind in the definiteness of the dates to which he assigns the Psalms or psalm-groups.

The object of the foregoing review has been to exhibit the various steps by which the problem of the Psalms has been brought to its present position, not to enumerate all the leading writers or commentators. The problem is still under lively discussion. Besides the new edition of Hupfeld's Commentary by Nowack, published in 1888, we have the Commentary of Baethgen,[2] which, in a calm and impartial tone, takes account of the positions of other modern writers, and is particularly valuable for its notices of the views of Theodore of Mopsuestia. Special mention should also be made of a dissertation by Sellin,[3] with the view of proving that the first book of the Psalter

---

[1] Origin of the Psalter, pp. 18, 19.

[2] Die Psalmen (1892) in Nowack's Handkommentar zum Alten Testament. A second edition has appeared (in 1897).

[3] Disputatio de Origine Carminum quæ primus Psalterii liber continet (1892).

contains pre-exilian psalms. The same writer has more recently published [1] the first two of a projected series of treatises on the Old Testament Religion, in which in a more systematic way he adduces proofs that in pre-exilian antiquity the individual, as well as the nation, stood in direct religious relation to God,—in other words, that there was an individual as well as a national religion. Lastly, we have a special treatise by Beer,[2] intended to distinguish the psalms which have an individual reference from those that were composed in the name of the Church.

[1] Beiträge zur Israelitischen und jüdischen Religionsgeschichte, Heft i., 1896; Heft ii., Erste Hälfte, 1897.
[2] Individual- und Gemeinde-Psalmen, 1894.

CHAPTER III.

THE PROBLEMS OF THE PSALMS.

THE foregoing review of the past course of Psalm criticism brings into prominence the leading problems that call for solution, and suggests an inquiry into the method that ought to be employed in the discussion.

It is evident, first of all, that we cannot accept the inscriptions as authoritative or reliable indications of the authorship and occasions of composition of the psalms to which they are attached. These headings have a historical value of a certain kind, and furnish important evidence as to the Psalter as a whole—an evidence at which we shall have to look in the sequel. In the present connection we speak of them merely in so far as they profess to give information as to the authorship and occasion of the particular psalms to which they are prefixed. There is nothing to lead us to suppose that they were written by the authors of the respective compositions. On the contrary, everything tends to prove that they were appended at a later time—how late we cannot precisely tell—either on some traditional grounds or as a crudely critical inference from the contents of the psalms in question. That they must belong to a period antecedent to the time of the LXX. translation appears from the fact that the translators evidently had the Hebrew headings before them. But it is equally evident that the translators either possessed them in a varying form or considered them of so little historical value that they permitted themselves to alter or add to them,—a course they would scarcely have followed had they regarded these headings as an integral part of the text.[1]

Another inference we may safely draw from the attempts of critics to determine the dates and authorship of the Psalms is: that it is impossible to start with a limited number of acknowledged Davidic psalms and make them a standard of comparison for others. The actual number of psalms allowed to David by different critics sufficiently indicates how unsubstantial are the grounds on which the conclusions are reached. Hitzig and Ewald each enumerated about fourteen (which were not, however, the same in each enumeration); Delitzsch increased the number to forty; Schultz

[1] An exhaustive statement of the inscriptions, and of their renderings in the Versions, is given in Baethgen's Psalmen, Einl., §§ 2, 3.

reduces it to ten; and Baethgen limits it still further to a few at the beginning of the Psalter. It is evident that a canon of literary excellence, by which Ewald was mainly guided, is always liable to be variously applied according to the taste of the individual critic. And in any case we must, first of all, obtain some undoubted production of David before we can set up a standard of comparison. And though Strack, for example, has advocated this method as the only safe process of literary criticism, and proposes to start with the 18th Psalm as beyond all controversy Davidic, recent criticism has shown that not even this lyric can be taken as a basis of comparison; for it is declared to be, if even pre-exilian at all, not earlier in date than the time of Josiah.

It is proper to remark here, however, that if this much has to be conceded on the one side, there must be a corresponding concession on the other. That is to say, if we are not allowed with Ewald to set up a high literary standard for Davidic psalms, and to reject all compositions that do not come up to it, neither should we allow ourselves to pronounce psalms to be non-Davidic on the ground that they are too high in literary merit or religious character. For this would be simply the setting up of another standard of comparison even more shadowy and subjective than the other.

Again, the method of determining the dates

and occasions of psalms from some supposed references in them to the times and circumstances of the author has not yielded encouraging results. The confidence which individual critics have expressed in their conclusions in this direction has generally been confined to themselves; for different critics have with equal certainty assigned the same psalms to very different persons and occasions, as a glance at any comprehensive critical commentary will show. The considerations which restrained Hupfeld from a positive determination of the occasion of individual psalms on this line still retain their weight. The references in these lyrics to the situations of the writers or the circumstances of the times are in the nature of the case very general, and therefore capable of application to various times. And even where there seems to be a correspondence in the psalms with recorded events in the national history, and a reflection of known situations of certain writers, it is to be remembered that our acquaintance with long tracts of the history is exceedingly meagre, and that the situations and experiences of writers repeat themselves at different times. For this reason it is comparatively easier to find suitable occasions for many psalms in the later periods of history, of which we have full records—as in the first book of Maccabees and the pages of Josephus—than in the pre-exilian period, where details fail us. And even where such historical identifications are claimed by critics to be made out, it will be found that all they amount to is perhaps the conviction that such and such a psalm *might* have been composed at such and such a time. There are, indeed, certain psalms, as we shall see, that proclaim themselves to be post-exilian; there are a few others so strongly marked that even conservative critics admit the probability of their being as late as the Maccabaean period. But it may be safely said of a very great majority that, had their own testimony to the time and circumstances of their composition been definite, it would have been recognised long ago.

The canon of criticism laid down by Prof. Cheyne promises at first sight to furnish a better principle of procedure; and no doubt in such a direction lies the only hope of being able to determine the relative dates of the Psalms. But the rule he lays down in regard to "groups" must be applied with great caution, and his canon can only be accepted with important reservations.

Psalms that "have come to us from ancient times in one group" can at most attest only the time from which they existed *as a group*. The date of the component elements remains still to be determined. We have before us the striking example of the Twelve minor prophets. These have existed " as a group" from ancient times; perhaps the very first notice we have of them in history is a reference to them as a collection, known as "the Twelve." Yet that group contains what are now believed to be both the earliest and the latest written prophetical works, separated by many centuries—pre-exilian and post-exilian being placed side by side. Now, each of the psalms is primarily a separate composition, as independent in its origin, for aught we know, as each book constituting the "group" of the minor prophets. One member of any group may, for aught that the existence of the group tells us, have been composed and used long before the origin of other members in the same group. In a word, the presence of groups of psalms in the Psalter furnishes only a relative evidence bearing on the history of the collection, but affords no proof of the dates, relative to one another, of the individual psalms.

But the canon under consideration stipulates that the psalms in each group shall "all agree in some leading features and positively disagree in none"; and it is claimed that, under these conditions, if we can determine the positive date of one of the group, all the members of the group must be assigned to the same period, "though it is only in one instance that we can from internal evidence speak positively as to their date." Let us consider what this involves.

It implies obviously the setting up of a standard

of some kind, according to the "leading features" of the psalms to be compared. But who is to fix that standard, and how is it to be applied? Is the standard to be a literary one, or is it to be determined by historical indications or by religious tone? Manifestly there will be varieties of opinion in regard to any one or all of these as to what constitutes a "leading feature" for the matter in hand —viz., the origin and composition of the Psalms. And there is likely to be as little unanimity as to whether a number of psalms—occurring in a group or otherwise—come up to, or do not deviate from, such a standard. In point of fact, is it not just the uniformity of tone and absence of definite indications—the want, in short, of common "leading features"— that make it a matter of so much difficulty to decide the dates of these compositions? Take, for example, a group of psalms which have evidently been long associated — the Pilgrim Psalms (cxx.-cxxxiv.) The points of essential agreement here are few and secondary as compared with the points of diversity. For some reason, valid to the collectors, these psalms have been classed together under one common title, and so have "come down to us from ancient times in one group." But that title, "Songs of Degrees" or "Songs of Ascents," which is the expression of the fact or belief that they had "one common feature" at least, though apparently intended to be significant, is at the present day variously interpreted, and may adapt itself to one of several "features" having no necessary connection with date. So that it is quite legitimate and even reasonable to conclude that the individual psalms of the group may belong to different situations and times, and that the inclusion of the whole into one group may fall comparatively late, and have been occasioned by secondary and accidental considerations. How very arbitrary this method may become appears when we look at its operation. Prof. Cheyne, for example, with great confidence sets down the four criteria of a non-linguistic kind for the detection of Maccabaean psalms : (1) The presence of some fairly definite historical allusion ; (2) a uniquely strong Church feeling ; (3) a special intensity of monotheistic faith ; and (4) an ardour of gratitude for a wonderful deliverance. But he has no sooner announced these criteria than he shows that one of them — the last — will not apply to some of the psalms which have usually been regarded as having a special claim to be classed as Maccabaean—viz., Ps. xliv., lxxiv., lxxix.[1]

Moreover, should it be found that several psalms placed in one group *do* agree or do not positively disagree in their main features, this is no proof that they all belong to the same time and the same author. For, in the first place, it may have been

[1] Origin of the Psalter, p. 95.

precisely on the grounds of such resemblances that psalms of very different ages were grouped together by some later collector; and, in the second place, we cannot so circumscribe the poetical and religious activities of the writers, nor so mechanically divide off the history into periods, as to say that similar occasions may not arise at very different periods, and modes of thought and phases of feeling may not recur at far remote intervals.

There might be some hope of successful results from this comparison of groups, if the groups themselves were historically attested and well defined, for then we might say for certain that all the members of a particular group were at least limited in their dates by the date of that collection; and we could at least, in such circumstances, arrange the Psalms relatively if not absolutely. But when the admission comes into play that groups may have been broken up, at or before the final redaction, and when, on the strength of some internal resemblance, one member of a group here is found to have affinity with one or two members of some other group there, and forthwith these outlying members are brought together into one sphere of time, it is manifest that the principle of grouping is a speculative one, and the results are dependent on the judgment of the critic. In fact, it comes finally to this, that instead of groups, in the sense of attested collections that have come down together, we are presented with groups that are formed on grounds of internal criticism. Before acquiescing in a canon of criticism so sweeping as this, we should do well to imagine its application to any other literature—the attempt, for example, to arrange chronologically in "groups" the productions of some lyric poet, secular or sacred, on the ground of some leading feature common to all of them. And the case before us is much harder, when we have, for aught we know, productions of ages far apart and of men of most varied attainments and situations. Neither individuals nor nations have the habit of exhausting a subject at one time and never recurring to it.

Amid all this uncertainty, one thing becomes clear, that in the final appeal we must fall back upon each individual psalm for indications of its date and authorship. Whether these indications will suffice to establish a safe conclusion is another matter; but it is evident that here, as always, exegesis must be the basis of criticism.

Since, however, the present trend of criticism is towards a late date of the Psalms, it is proper now to consider the various lines of argument on which that conclusion is reached. For there are a few broad principles, which are either tacitly or overtly assumed as proved, on grounds not always strictly exegetical, and which, if accepted at the outset in the sense in which they are put forward, would no doubt warrant us in relegating the Psalter to a late date. The chief of these are—

1. The Psalter stands in the third division of the Canon, and was the praise-book of the Second (or post-exilian) Temple.
2. The language of the Psalms is incompatible with pre-exilian origin.
3. The historical allusions and the situations implied in the Psalms do not agree with pre-exilian but do agree with post-exilian times and circumstances.
4. The stage of religious consciousness that is reached in the Psalms is too advanced for pre-exilian times.
5. The speaker in the Psalms who utters thanks or supplicates divine aid is not an individual but a personification, the Church of the Second Temple.

In regard to these various positions it is necessary here to make a few remarks.

1. On the position that the Psalter was the praise-book of the Second Temple, the remark is obvious that this assertion, made in this axiomatic tone, proves no more as to the age of the Psalter than the statement that the Psalms are the only praise-book of a certain body of Presbyterians, and does not at all warrant the inference that the whole of the Psalms were composed after the Exile. At the most the fact—if it be a fact—can only guar-

antee the inference that the Psalms were regarded as suitable for and introduced into the worship of the Second Temple. But whether the whole or any number of them were earlier or later than the Captivity is a matter for independent investigation. The fact that the Psalter stands in the last division of the Canon, along with books which are confessedly late, cannot be urged in proof of the post-exilian date. Least of all can this fact be insisted upon by those who are also adherents of the prevailing theory as to the dates of the Pentateuch and the prophetical books. For these critics maintain that many of the prophetical books are older than the Pentateuch; yet the Pentateuch was the first to be codified, the first also to be set apart and used in the public service of the Second Temple. If, therefore, prophetical books were in existence before they were canonised Scripture and publicly read in the Temple worship, why should we be required to admit that psalms were only written after the Exile, because they are included in the third division of the Canon? The very fact that the Psalter consists of psalters within the Psalter, as we are continually told—that is, that it is composed of different minor collections—would lead to the conclusion that it is of gradual growth; and, as the "Twelve" minor prophets is a collection containing both the very earliest and the very latest prophetical books, it remains a matter of investigation, not to be settled by off-hand statement, whether the Psalter is in whole or in part a pre-exilian or post-exilian production. In fact, the assertion itself, that the Psalter was the praise-book of the Second Temple, is misleading and requires qualification. For, in the first place, those who make the assertion do not mean by it that the whole collection was prepared and ready for use as soon as the worship of the Second Temple was inaugurated; on the contrary, they maintain that it only began to grow in post-exilian time. And, in the second place, the assertion, even if admitted, would not prove that no part of the Psalter was employed in the worship of the First Temple. Indeed, if it were established that psalms or a psalter was employed from the first inauguration of worship in the Second Temple, we should be led to look to an earlier time for the composition of such psalms. But even if it were ascertained that psalms were not in use in the First Temple, that would not amount to proof that the Psalms, or many of them, were not composed in pre-exilian times. As a matter of fact, there is no evidence that the Psalter as a whole ever formed part of the liturgical service either of the Second Temple or of the synagogue. We may legitimately infer, as we shall see by-and-by, from statements in the books of Chronicles, Ezra, and Nehemiah, that at the time these books were written psalmody was known and certain psalms employed in public worship, but that is a very different thing from the use of a complete collection like the Psalter. There are also indications in a few of the headings [1] that certain psalms were appropriate for certain days or occasions; and such indications are more numerous in the Versions and in the Rabbinic literature.[2] But these would rather tell against than for the regular use of the Psalter as a whole. Not even does the Jewish Prayer-book incorporate the entire Psalter. In a word, the Psalter is not so integral a part of the liturgy of the Jewish synagogue as it is of the service of the Church of England.

Let us take the parallel case of the book of Proverbs, which also stands in the third division of the Canon. Suppose it was proved that that book was composed or redacted at a comparatively late post-exilian period, this would be no proof that all its contents were of post-exilian origin, or that none of the smaller collections which it contains belongs to an earlier time. Much less would it prove that the practice of speaking in proverbs was entirely unknown to Hebrew antiquity. Therefore the portentous *dictum* as to the Psalter being the book of praise of the Second Temple should not be put forth as a starting-point in this discussion. It proves nothing as to the

---

[1] See Ps. xxx., xcii. There are more in the LXX.

[2] See Beer, Individual- und Gemeinde-Psalmen, p. ii. ff., for a list of these.

main point in dispute, at what time the composition of psalms commenced.

2. The argument from the language of the Psalms is somewhat technical, and involves a consideration of many minute details. There are, however, some facts of a more general kind which call for mention, regard to which will indicate the nature of the linguistic argument and the limits within which it has to be prosecuted.

(*a*) In the first place, it is only natural that in the Psalms we should find distinctive linguistic peculiarities. In all languages there are words and expressions which are either confined to poetry or affected specially by poets. These may be archaic or they may be simply peculiar to poetical composition in general; and since, as is well known, songs and ballads are among the earliest efforts at literary composition, we may be prepared to find in the poems of any age the archaic forms and special phraseology which have become associated with this kind of composition.

(*b*) In the next place, Hebrew poetry was liable in a pre-eminent degree to a variation in the phraseology, resulting in a special enrichment of the poetic vocabulary. The parallelism, which is the outstanding feature of Hebrew poetry, demands in many cases the repetition of the thought in varying expression, and in every case leads to some modification of the expression in one member of the verse to correspond with a variation of the thought in another. So marked is this characteristic that an attentive regard to the parallelism often helps the expositor over a difficulty that arises from the obscurity of an expression in one clause, a clearer expression of the thought being usually found in the other. It will be evident that in this manner Hebrew poetry attains a richness of vocabulary and a variety of diction which is not found in prose, the poet being obliged to ransack the literary stores of all ages and adopt decadent or unusual expressions, as well as to coin new phrases or give special turns to existing words, in order to bring out the modifications of thought and the niceties of distinction which compositions of this kind demand.

This being so, it is far from safe to argue from a word or phrase which may occur in one member of a parallelism, without taking into consideration its correspondent in the other. Equally unsafe is it to reason from an expression of a peculiar kind which may be found in two different psalms, that both compositions belong to the same age; for the two occurrences may arise from a similarity in the thought of the two writers, or from the choice by a poet of a peculiar word or words in the service of his art.

When a comparison of this kind is carried out in conjunction with the assumption of the late date of a number of other books, no doubt a formidable array of instances can be produced, and very short work is made in determining the dates of particular Psalms. Thus, for example, it is argued [1] that such Psalms as viii., xix., and xxix. are post-exilian, because they refer to the first chapter of Genesis, and the word "firmament" occurring in Ps. xix. is only found in late books, such as Ezekiel and Daniel. But if we are to assume that so simple a cosmogony as that of Ps. viii., and so obvious a parallel word to heaven as firmament, with all the other words and ideas which Giesebrecht, *e.g.*, pronounces late, were unknown to the Hebrews till the period of the Exile, we run the risk of not only attenuating the ideas of the time, but even of depriving the people of a working vocabulary.

(*c*) It is to be observed, in the third place, that the argument from language does not amount to the plea that the linguistic style of the Psalms as a whole indicates a late period of the language. There are some books in the Old Testament which, as it has been said, must be pronounced late if there is any history of the language at all. And it may be granted that some of the Psalms [2] bear such marks of lateness from beginning to end. But the attempt to prove this of the Psalms as a whole ends in absurdity. Nay, so far is it from being the case, that a critic so competent as Reuss, in arguing

---

[1] Beer, Individual- und Gemeinde-Psalmen, p. lvii; but compare Cheyne, Origin of the Psalter, p. 468.

[2] *E.g.*, Psalm cxxxix.

for a late date of the Psalter, feels called upon to meet the objection that the language of the Psalms is good, pure, classical Hebrew. Except in places where it may be supposed the copyists have not correctly preserved the text, he says, the language is so simple that the Psalms may be given as exercises in reading to beginners.[1] But this purity of language he does not accept as a proof of early date; his explanation being that the psalm-writers affected the language of the Law and the Prophets, to which the people were accustomed, very much as in modern times the liturgical and devotional compositions used in Christian Churches have an archaic cast, in keeping with that of the sacred books with which the worshippers are familiar.[2] Whether his reasoning be valid or not, it is sufficient to prove how dubious the argument from the language of the Psalms becomes. And it is not to be wondered at that Giesebrecht, who has set himself[3] to prove the lateness of the Psalter from the language, finds so many marks of late date, and these in so many of the psalms, that it becomes difficult to conclude what style he would allow to be pre-exilian at all. On the whole, his contention is hardly approved of even by those who

[1] Reuss, Das Alte Testament, Fünfter Band, p. 46.
[2] At the same time, however, he concludes the lateness of such a psalm as cxxxix. from the decadent phase of the language which it exhibits.
[3] ZATW, 1881, p. 276 ff.

on other grounds are disposed to bring down the Psalms to a late date. In the words of Professor Driver,[1] the essay "contains much that is superficial and crude"; and Professor Cheyne [2] characterises it as "a suggestive but too indiscriminate collection of the evidence for a late date of the Psalms."

Neither of the two preceding arguments, therefore, constitutes a preliminary bar to the supposition that the Psalter may be, in greater or less part at least, of pre-exilian origin. As to the other arguments which have been mentioned, it will be found that they raise wider issues than a simple exegesis of the Psalms, involving, in fact, the whole question of the pre-exilian history and religion. When, for example, it is asserted that the historical allusions and situations of the Psalms do not agree with the circumstances of pre-exilian times, there is involved a certain theory of the early history, and a judgment on the credibility of certain of the historical books. Or when, again, it is maintained that the tone of religious experience in the Psalms is too high for pre-exilian times, and that the speaking "I" in the Psalms is Israel personified, there are involved the deeper questions of the so-called pre-prophetic religion of Israel, the origin of the prophetic conceptions, the extent to which these conceptions influenced a wider circle, and the whole

[1] Introduction, p. 361, footnote. Compare 6th edition, p. 383.
[2] Origin of the Psalter, p. 461.

contrast between pre-exilian and post-exilian times. In short, as has been already indicated, the problem of the Psalms is part of the larger problem of the Old Testament religion in its widest acceptance.

No doubt, if these underlying assumptions were admitted, the question of the Psalms would become simple enough, and would settle itself as a matter of course. Seeing, however, that they are subject of controversy, and that an independent consideration of the Psalms may help to throw light on those very points, we cannot admit them at the outset as postulates. They will have to be faced as we proceed, but, in order to make our inquiry as little controversial as possible, it will be better to approach the subject in another way.

What it is proposed here to do, therefore, is, in the first place, to look for any historical evidence, outside of the Psalter, of the earliest existence of a psalter or of the practice of psalmody; and then to consider what may be gathered from the Psalter itself as to its origin and collection. If these two lines of proof show with certainty, or with great probability, that the Psalter originated in pre-exilian times, it will then be proper to examine the literary, historical, and religious features of the Psalms, and consider whether there is room and place in pre-exilian antiquity for the manifestation of these features, and to what times and occasions the manifestation of them may be ascribed.

CHAPTER IV.

EXTERNAL EVIDENCE.

ANY available evidence as to the date and origin of the Psalter must be derived—it need hardly be said—either from the Psalter itself or from other ancient documents. We have already seen that the notices found in the headings of the Psalms, being later than the Psalms themselves and of unknown origin, cannot be summarily taken as authentic information on the subject; and we shall see by-and-by that evidence of another kind drawn from the Psalms themselves requires to be very carefully handled, and has, in fact, been found to lead, in different hands, to very different conclusions. The references in the Psalms to historical occasions and prominent characters are either so scant or so general and indefinite that (as has been shown in chap. ii.) both Ewald and Hupfeld confess their inability to do more than fix boundaries somewhat wide and elastic. Others, however, have not been so diffident, as we have also seen; and, in point of fact, it is the internal evidence from the Psalms that is chiefly relied upon by the more recent school of criticism for a determination of the literary history of the Psalter.

It is important, therefore, to remember that there is another line of evidence, drawn from external sources, which has been too much overlooked. This kind of evidence, if it does not furnish precise results in detail, is valuable as being more tangible and substantial so far as it goes, and therefore it affords a guide in our endeavours to estimate internal evidence, and lays down wholesome restraints within which that evidence must be arranged. Critics are too much inclined to undervalue this kind of evidence, either by questioning the facts themselves or refusing to draw from them the inevitable inferences. And yet even a few hard, positive, historical facts—which require to be accounted for, and thereby suggest underlying or antecedent facts—are much more reliable evidence than a series of inferences drawn from what may be a disputed interpretation of sporadic phrases in the Psalms themselves.

The external evidence, to which we now turn, is pretty considerable in amount; it forms a well-connected chain, each individual link of which may be put to a severe test; and if I mistake not, it is not reconcilable with, at least, the more advanced modern position which makes the *whole* Psalter post-exilian. For we have to bear in mind, in approaching it, that Prof. Cheyne, for example, makes the very earliest psalm in the collection (with the exception of Psalm xviii., which may partly belong to the age of Josiah) as late as the completion of the Second Temple (B.C. 515), and brings down the latest to the time of the death of Simon Maccabæus in B.C. 135—assigning twenty-seven psalms altogether to the Maccabaean period (B.C. 170 to 135). And we have to consider how such a position can maintain itself in presence of certain well-known literary and historical facts.

The most satisfactory mode of prosecuting a historical inquiry of this kind is to commence at some date at which there is no doubt of the existence of the Psalter, and to work our way backwards to earlier dates, according as we find indications either of a completed psalter or of its process of growth. If we had positive information of the final closing of the canon of the Old Testament, we should have an undisputed starting-point of this kind, however late it might be; and we naturally inquire, first of all, whether that date can be determined.

It used to be considered a sufficient answer to those who maintained that there are Maccabaean psalms in the Psalter, to say that the thing was impossible, because the Canon was closed before the time of the Maccabees. This was on the supposition prevalent at the time that the Old Testament collection was virtually completed by Ezra and Nehemiah,—a position which cannot, however, be taken for granted, and which, indeed, a closer study of the whole question shows to be untenable.

It is a very difficult matter to determine the date of the final closing of the canon of the Old Testament. We have no historical account of any formal act, which can be interpreted as an authoritative setting apart or sanctioning of the books of the Old Testament as a whole, as the sole Scripture acknowledged by the Jewish Church.[1] We may take it as established that the three component parts of the Hebrew Bible, Law, Prophets, and Hagiographa, indicate three successive stages in the gradual formation of the Canon; and we know that, in the time of Ezra and Nehemiah, the first portion, the Law, was brought into special prominence in connection with the public worship. But we find at no subsequent period such a formal

[1] The assembly at Jamnia (held about A.D. 90), at which Graetz thinks the Canon was fixed, is not to be regarded in this light. The discussions which then took place touched rather the claims of certain books to be in the Canon than the fact of their being already included in it. And, in the present connection, it is to be observed that the Psalter was not one of the questioned or disputed books, which were Ecclesiastes and Canticles, and, to a certain extent, Ezekiel. But all the books mentioned were already *in* the Canon, as the references in the New Testament and Josephus sufficiently prove.

act of the nation or of any council as would amount to the stamping of the other portions with public authority. This much is quite clear, from the references in the New Testament and the often-quoted words of Josephus, that by the first century of our era the Old Testament was of the same compass as the present Hebrew Bible, and was then regarded as of undisputed authority and of long standing.[1]

On the strength of these references it is generally admitted on all hands that, in the first Christian century at all events, and presumably at some undefined time before it, the Old Testament canon had its present compass. It may not be superfluous, however, to draw attention to the general character of these references. They do not attest the compass or magnitude of the individual books. The New Testament references to the Psalms, for example, though numerous, do not entitle us, in the strict letter of the matter, to say that any psalm now in the Psalter was there in its present form at that period. This remark is made in order to show the kind of evidence that, in the nature of the case, is forthcoming. If it is so general at the time when no doubt is entertained as to the compass of the Canon, we may be prepared for an equal vagueness at an earlier time.

---

[1] The passages relied on are such as Matt. xxii. 29, Luke xxiv. 44, John vi. 45, Acts vii. 42, xiii. 40, xviii. 24, 28, &c. Josephus, Contra Apionem, i. 8.

When, however, we speak of the Canon and the closing of the Canon, we must beware of being led astray by the use of a phrase. The Canon was not some repository into which books were placed as soon as they were written. Nor was it a theoretic standard of a certain class of books which the Jews set themselves in advance to produce or collect. The word itself is much later than the thing; there must be books before there is a canon. All that we know on the subject leads us to the conclusion that at certain periods certain books had attached to them such regard, and were found of such utility for the instruction and worship of the people, that they were brought into connection with the temple or synagogue service, and in a public and official manner acknowledged as of ultimate authority. Such books would presumably be old enough to have a prescriptive claim to recognition, or be known or believed to be the work of men who were universally looked upon as organs of divine revelation; but we have no right to assume that the oldest books would be the first to be thus treated —in other words, to be first formed into a canon, in the sense in which we have explained it. It is quite conceivable that books known or reputed to be old and sacred would be in the possession of the people, and yet for some time not included among the books that were thus officially set apart for use in the worship of the Church. And, conversely, the time at which a book or assemblage of books was brought into such use would be no test of their supposed antiquity, and of the intrinsic value they possessed in the eyes of the people. The position of the Prophets in the Canon furnishes the best example of what I mean. It is generally admitted that the Pentateuch was in the first place what we may call the only Bible of the Jews, being the Canon set up by Ezra and Nehemiah. Nevertheless the books of most of the Prophets were at that time in the possession of the people; they were known to be old, were regarded as the work of God's messengers, and were even appealed to by the very men who brought the Pentateuch into its prominence.[1] Yet it is believed that a considerable time elapsed before the second division of the Canon, the Prophets, was placed side by side with the Law, and made equally with the Pentateuch public authoritative Scripture.[2]

The bearing of this on the Psalter will be apparent. The Psalter stands in the third division

[1] See, *e.g.*, Neh. ix. 26 ff.

[2] The view generally entertained at the present time is that the first Canon, embracing the Pentateuch alone, dates from about 440 B.C.; the second, embracing the *Nebiim* or Prophets, from some time in the third century; and the third, or *Ketubim*, a century later. See Ryle, 'The Canon of the Old Testament,' and the article "Canon of the Old Testament" in the new edition of Smith's 'Bible Dictionary,' vol. i. p. 500.

of the Canon, the division which, as such, was last added to the Bible. But we have no right to assume that the Psalter, as a book or collection, was not known or not recognised as Scripture till after the Law and the Prophets were formed into the Canon of the time. Just as the second division of the Canon contains works which are among the earliest of the written books of Israel (many maintain that most of the Prophets were written before the Law), so the third division may contain works older than some in the second division. Nay, the Psalter in particular is a work of such a nature that it might be easily preserved by itself and employed by itself, either in public or in private, even while the Canon was in process of formation, and thus be practically canonical—in the sense of being read and reverenced as a sacred book—before the division of which it forms a part was formally and as a whole joined to the rest of sacred Scripture. Indeed there are indications, if I mistake not, that not only were there three different stages in the process of the formation of the Canon, but that the individual books within the divisions gained prominence in public regard also by different degrees. The collection of the twelve minor prophets, *e.g.*, contains, along with the very earliest written prophecies, the books of Haggai, Zechariah, and Malachi, which are the very latest. It is not, however, to be supposed that such a book as Isaiah, to say nothing of earlier ones, remained without such regard and veneration as made it in the eyes of the people holy Scripture, till the books of Zechariah, &c., were composed. Again, in the Talmud we read of certain of the books of the third division being read solemnly in the presence of the high priest on the night before the great day of Atonement; and the five rolls were set apart for five special occasions—all this showing that the regard which led to canonicity might vary in individual cases, and so a book be virtually canonical before it was placed in a canonical collection. And in fact there is nothing to hinder us from supposing that a collection of psalms— whether of the same compass as the existing Psalter or smaller — may have been in recognised public use in the worship side by side with even the earliest canonical Scripture.

Even, therefore, if we knew the date of the final closing of the Canon, this would only give us a fixed point, after which we could not suppose the Psalter to have been incorporated into the collection; but it could not determine the dates of what, presumably, may have been smaller collections of psalms, much less the dates of the composition of individual pieces. Since, however, it is maintained in modern times that the great bulk of the Psalms was not only incorporated into a psalter, but actually composed later than the Exile, we must consider how this position appears in the light of certain important literary facts.

1. The Psalter is not only in the completed Canon of the Hebrew or Massoretic text, but is found also in the Greek or Septuagint Version, and must therefore have been completed some time before that translation was made. Although we know pretty accurately the date of the commencement of this translation, the reign of Ptolemy Philadelphus (B.C. 284-247, when the Law at least would be translated), we have no direct information as to the time covered by the execution of the whole, or the date of its final completion. We may assume, however, that the third division, in which the Psalter is found, is somewhat later than the first: and we may also assume that this third division would not be translated until it was part and parcel of the recognised Hebrew Canon; for the Greek Version corresponds to the *completed* Hebrew Psalter, even to the division into five books with the doxologies, which are admitted to be features later than the Psalter itself.

We have indeed a pretty good indication that some of the psalms, at all events, were old before they were translated by the LXX. It is as clear as possible that the musical or liturgical headings prefixed to some of the Hebrew psalms (and these occur only in the earlier books) were unintelligible to the Greek translators,—a certain indication that those psalms at least do not belong to near the period when the LXX. Version was made. An argument of some value may indeed be drawn from the whole treatment of these headings. It has been already mentioned [1] that the Septuagint shows considerable variations from the Massoretic text in the superscriptions; and this was, as early as the time of Theodore of Mopsuestia, taken to be a proof that the headings were not originally an integral part of the Psalms. That is very likely, but in the present connection it tells in favour of the antiquity of the psalms to which they are attached. The variations between the Hebrew and Greek prove, first of all, that the titles are later than the Psalms. But they *are* variations—*i.e.*, the titles of the Hebrew psalms were present in the copies used by the LXX. translators. Yet, as we have just said, portions of these titles were unintelligible to the Greek translators. Therefore we infer that the titles belong to a time considerably remote from the date of the Septuagint; and much more remote, therefore, are the psalms themselves to which the titles are attached. It is worthy of remark in this connection that there is no allusion to these titles in the books of Ezra, Nehemiah, and Haggai; and only in the Chronicles is there one reference—viz., 1 Chron. xv. 20, 21, where the terms *Alamoth* and *Sheminith* occur. This argument will not, of course, apply to the whole Psalter. It would remain possible for some or many psalms

---

[1] Chap. ii. p. 25, chap. iii. p. 48.

to belong to a period much more near to the LXX. translation. In any case we argue, on the one hand, that even the latest of the psalms were in the collection some time before the whole book of Psalms was translated — and the language of the translation leads to the supposition that all the Psalms were translated at one time; and, on the other hand, certain of the psalms, at all events, belong to a period much more remote.

Now, before proceeding, it is proper to notice how Prof. Cheyne, for example, meets these facts. The case is this. Certain psalms which he maintains were composed in the Greek period are provided with musical or liturgical headings which are unintelligible to the LXX. translators of a not much later time. Prof. Cheyne admits the facts, though he does not "feel the objections to be important," and believes that "thoroughly decisive answers must be wanting until some private journal of the actors of history is discovered." All the explanation he has to offer is, that the Jewish scribes themselves may have forgotten the meaning of the headings at the time when the temple with its music was reorganised, and the Psalter re-edited by Simon.[1] On which it may be remarked—(1) that Prof. Cheyne himself confesses[2] that we have "no ancient record" of this reorganisation of music and editing of the Psalter by Simon, about B.C. 142. So far as I can see, it

[1] Origin of the Psalter, p. 458.   [2] Ibid., p. 11.

is merely an assumption in the interest of a theory. (2) Even supposing such a reorganisation to have taken place, it is not at all likely that the recollection of the older arrangement, which after all was quite recent, would so soon have disappeared. (3) If the Jewish scribes themselves may have forgotten the meaning of the titles by the time of Simon, is not this a proof that the titles were old, and therefore the Psalms still older? Are we to suppose they would make use of antiquated and unintelligible musical headings for psalms which belonged almost to their own day? Prof. Cheyne himself admits[1] that "there may have been an earlier version of the Psalter in its incomplete form" current in Egypt before Simon's edition. The point here contended for is, not that there are no Maccabaean psalms in the collection, nor that "the complete Greek Psalter was in existence much before the Christian era,"[2] but that the treatment of the headings to a certain number of psalms in the earlier part of the collection shows that by the time the translation was made these headings were old, and consequently the psalms themselves older.

2. We have next to look at the evidence borne by some of the extra-canonical books which are included in the Alexandrian collection.

(*a*) The books of the Maccabees belong to about 100 B.C.; the first book, which brings down the

---

[1] Origin of the Psalter, p. 12.   [2] Ibid., p. 458.

history to the time of John Hyrcanus (B.C. 135-105), being written, apparently, under the immediate impression of the events which it records. Now this book contains an undoubted quotation from the Psalms, introduced by the introductory formula with which Scripture is quoted: "According to the word which one wrote, The flesh of Thy saints have they cast out, and their blood have they shed round about Jerusalem, and there was none to bury them" (1 Macc. vii. 17), which corresponds so closely with Ps. lxxix. 2, 3, that the quotation is not denied. The writer who makes the quotation is speaking of the time of Judas Maccabæus, and of the massacre of Jews committed by Alkimus and Bacchides (B.C. 162), and he quotes the psalm as Scripture fulfilled in that occurrence. The remarkable thing is that the psalm quoted is one of those which, if there are Maccabaean psalms at all, are to be referred to that period. And Prof. Cheyne, admitting the quotation, takes the psalm as referring to the very events (if I understand him rightly) of which the writer of the book of Maccabees regarded it as an apt description. If this be so, then we must suppose that the psalm, within twenty years of the date of its composition, was included in the Psalter (for Simon's completion of the collection is dated B.C. 142), and then about forty years after that date it was referred to by the writer of the book of Maccabees apparently as ancient Scripture. Some will hesitate to believe, without further proof, that things moved so rapidly. And, in this connection, a point occurs which is worthy of consideration. In the LXX. translation of the Psalms, as is well known, the titles vary from the Hebrew in the matter of the author's names to whom the psalms are assigned. Not only is Jeremiah mentioned, but even Haggai and Zechariah, as authors of some psalms. It is very remarkable, however, that they assign none to the Maccabaean age; although, had psalms been composed so abundantly as is alleged at that time, it could scarcely have been beyond their knowledge, the more especially if an earlier version of the Psalms was current in Egypt before Simon's time. Prof. Cheyne's explanation of this fact seems strangely unsatisfactory. "Of course," he says, "the Egyptian Jewish community received no information on the subject of Maccabaean psalms. It was not the interest of the Jerusalem editors to publish the recent origin of a portion of the Psalms."[1] What "interest" the Jewish editors at Jerusalem had in concealing the origin of psalms which they regarded as good enough Scripture for themselves does not appear. But surely, if the LXX. translators took so much interest in the matter for themselves, that they thought it worth while to note that certain psalms had a tradition attached to them which the Jerusalem Jews had

[1] Origin of the Psalter, p. 458.

not communicated, and if they were aware of psalms being composed as late as Zechariah, it is a most extraordinary thing that they give no hint of any psalms belonging to a period which, as is alleged, was so fertile in this kind of composition.

(b) In the second book of the Maccabees there is a passage of some value, as bearing on the general subject of the collection of the Canon. It occurs in the letter prefixed to the book (ch. i. 1-ii. 18) purporting to have been sent by the Jews of Palestine to their brethren in Egypt, in the year B.C. 144: "And the same things also were reported in the records, namely, the memoirs of Neemias;[1] and how he founding a library gathered together the books concerning the kings, and prophets, and the works of (τὰ τοῦ) David, and epistles of kings concerning holy gifts. And in like manner also Judas gathered together all these books that had been scattered by reason of the war we had, and they are with us." Now even if we reject the authenticity of this letter as a letter, we have at least the date of the book in which it is contained, and an evidence of what was commonly believed at that time in regard to certain books. Some would go so far as to say we have here evidence that Nehemiah collected the second division of the Canon ("the books concerning the kings and

[1] The reference seems to be to some apocryphal book or books.

prophets" being the former and later prophets), and that even a part or the whole of the third division is referred to in the words, "the works of David, and epistles of kings concerning holy gifts" (viz., the Psalms, and such documents as those that form part of the books of Ezra and Nehemiah)—the reference to Judas being an intimation that the final closing of the completed Canon was accomplished by Judas Maccabæus (B.C. 166-161). That is perhaps too much to infer with confidence from such a passage. On the other hand, Prof. Cheyne goes too far when he says[1] that this account of the completion of the library of national records by Judas is less credible than the reorganisation of the music and editing of the Psalter by Simon, of which there is no ancient record whatever. But, at all events, we have here an enumeration of books by designations that are worthy of attention. The order in which they are mentioned certainly corresponds to the order of the books of the Canon subsequent to the Law; they are spoken of as well-known public documents "all with us"; "the works of David" can hardly be anything else than some collection of Psalms, and we know of no other than the existing Psalter; the designations apply to the existing canonical books, and we know of no other books preserved at that time that would be similarly designated.

[1] Origin of the Psalter, p. 11 f.

The very want of precision in the description may be an indication that the books were well known and easily recognisable by the titles given.

At the very least we are entitled to assume that there is here expressed the belief that the Psalter, or a Davidic Psalter, was in existence in Nehemiah's time : certainly a proof that such a thing existed in the days of this writer ; and we are entitled to demand from those who would make the whole Psalter post-exilian, and a great part of it the work of Maccabaean times, an explanation of what these τὰ τοῦ Δαυείδ were, and why they are so named.

3. A more precise indication is furnished by the book of Ecclesiasticus or Ben Sirach.[1] To this book, which was originally composed in Hebrew, is prefixed a short preface by the grandson[2] of the author, who translated the book into Greek. He tells us the year in which he himself came into Egypt, which on any explanation cannot be later than B.C. 132 ; and this would fix the date of his

---

[1] The book is entitled in the original Greek Σοφία Σειράχ.

[2] The expression ὁ πάππος μου is generally taken in its literal sense of grandfather. On this view the Simon the high priest, of whom the author gives a glowing description in chap. 1. 1-21, would be Simon II., son of Onias. The editor of the Complutensian Polyglott, however, gives the more general designation ἔγγονος, "forefather," and this would admit a reference to Simon the First, surnamed the "Just," and would place Jesus the author as early as B.C. 250. This view is indeed taken by Horowitz in his 'Das Buch Jesus Sirach,' Breslau, 1865. Ehrt, Abfassungszeit, &c., p. 127.

grandfather somewhere about B.C. 200. Much later it could scarcely have been, for the book has no reference to the stirring times of the Maccabees, which may be said to have begun in B.C. 175.

The editor, in excusing the imperfection of his own translation, makes the remark that even "the Law itself and the prophecies, and the rest of the books, have no small difference, uttered in the original"; from which it is not too much to infer that by this time there were some books — apparently a completed collection, "the rest of the books"—not only regarded as of a character to be ranked with the "Law and the Prophets," but already current in a well-known Greek translation; and the language of the editor would lead us also to infer that this book of his grandfather's stood on a lower level. No doubt the expression is general, "the rest of the books," for it does not specify the number nor the names; but, on the other hand, in saying "the rest of the books" (τὰ λοιπὰ τῶν βιβλίων), the writer leads us to suppose that the compass of the collection was limited and definite, and the collection well known. It is also to be remembered that the third division of the Canon has never received a more precise designation than "writings," its contents being somewhat varied; and that at a period when the whole Canon was certainly closed, this division was spoken of in similar general terms.

Moreover, the editor, after referring to the many things handed down to us through "the Law and the Prophets and the others that followed them," immediately after says that his grandfather had given himself "to the reading of the Law, and the Prophets, and the other books of our fathers."

We have thus three times in the compass of the brief prologue a reference to the Old Testament books, which is, to say the very least, most intelligible on the supposition that the Canon, if not by that time absolutely complete, was made up of three parts, corresponding in their general description to the three parts in which it now appears. Short of an actual enumeration of the various books composing the Canon we could not, in the circumstances, look for more.

When we turn to the book itself, we do not find definite references to the books by name. The author magnifies the "Law" as the foundation of wisdom, using the term apparently in the wide sense of "Scripture," in which we find it employed also in the New Testament (*e.g.*, John x. 34, xii. 34, xv. 25 ; 1 Cor. xiv. 21). But even this vagueness might be construed to mean that there was in his time a well-recognised canon. In one passage (xlix. 10), in which he enumerates the great men of earlier times, he speaks of the "twelve prophets," an evidence that the "minor prophets," usually called the twelve by the Jews, were by that time a collected *corpus*, and that the author, though speaking of men, was thinking also of books.

As to evidence of the existence of particular psalms, Ehrt maintains that quotations are found in Ben Sirach from all the five books of the Psalter,[1] and, among others, from psalms that are usually spoken of as Maccabaean. He also thinks that the language in which these psalms are quoted in Ben Sirach indicates that the editor took them, not directly from the Hebrew, but from the LXX. version,—another proof, if it can be established, that the Psalter was by his time translated into Greek. Prof. Cheyne, however, says[2] that "Ehrt's list requires sifting," and he himself finds very few allusions to pre-Maccabaean psalms. Dillmann also finds no testimony in the book of Sirach itself to the Psalter, Proverbs, and Chronicles.

As to whether we have in all this sufficient proof that the Canon was completed and closed by the time of Sirach, there are of course differences of opinion. No doubt there is an absence of detailed enumeration of the books and of clear quotations to such an extent as would afford certainty. On the other hand, the books, especially those in the third division of the Canon, are spoken of in the same general terms at a later time when certainly the Canon was completed. Though it need not be

[1] Abfassungszeit und Abschluss der Psalters, p. 126.
[2] Origin of the Psalter, p. 456.

contended that in the time of Nehemiah, or soon after it, the Canon was closed in any such formal manner as would imply a determination to add no more to it, yet there must have come a time after which it was felt that the number of sacred books was completed. And it is a circumstance of considerable weight that the book of Sirach itself, though written originally in Hebrew, and altogether unobjectionable in its contents, was never received into the Canon; and that both its author and its translator refer to the canonical books in terms of high veneration, as if these belonged to another category.

But, however that may be, the facts are sufficient to bear out the conclusion in support of which they are now adduced. There were, besides the Law and the Prophets, other books ranked along with them as well-known sacred books in the time of Sirach: there was a third division of the Canon, whether fully completed or not. The reference in 2 Maccabees is sufficient to prove that in this collection "the works of David" were included—in other words, that a collection of psalms, reputed to be Davidic, was then well known as one of the sacred books.

We have now to endeavour, if possible, to reach a still earlier time, and see whether it bears any anterior testimony to a psalter or psalmody.

CHAPTER V.

EXTERNAL EVIDENCE—*continued*.

WE have found in the extra-canonical books, to which we have referred, sufficient evidence that at their date the Psalter was part of the Canon, or, at all events, that a collection known by the name of David was of practically canonical standing. The next witnesses to be examined are the canonical books other than the Psalms. And the evidence for which we may look will be of either of two kinds—viz., *general*, asserting or implying the existence of a collection of psalms; or *particular*, containing actual quotations from the Psalms. Evidence of the former kind, being less technical and less susceptible of double application, deserves the first consideration.

Let us begin with the books of Chronicles. These books are usually dated about the commencement of the Greek domination in Asia—*i.e.*, B.C. 330,[1]

---

[1] Not earlier, but not later, in the opinion of Dillmann. Herzog-Plitt, Realencyclopaedie, vol. iii., Art. "Chronik," p. 220 f.

and thus take us 130 years farther back than the extra-canonical witnesses have brought us. Their date is determined mainly by certain genealogical lists (1 Chron. iii. 1-24). In these tables the genealogies of the Davidic and high-priestly families are, we may assume, brought down to the author's own date at the very latest. They thus furnish a point of time *before* which the composition is altogether impossible (unless, indeed, we suppose them to be the work of a later interpolator), but *after* which the composition is extremely improbable, as the author would, for completeness, give the names of the living representatives of the two lines. He reckons in all six royal generations after Zerubbabel,[1] and five generations of high priests, which would cover a period of from 150 to 200 years. Now the death of Zerubbabel took place in the reign of Darius, after 516 B.C.; so that the terminus here given would be the close of the Persian or the beginning of the Greek period. The last-named high priest, whom we may take to be a contemporary of the author, is named (1 Chron. iii. 24) Jochanan, and, according to Josephus,[2] his successor, Jaddua, was still alive at the beginning of the Greek period (say B.C. 330).

---

[1] The kingly genealogy (enlarged by the LXX. to a few generations) is (1 Chron. iii. 17-24) : (1) Zerubbabel, (2) Chananiah, (3) Shechaniah, (4) Shemaiah, (5) Neariah, (6) Eljoaniah, (7) Hodajahu.

[2] Josephus, Antiq., xi., ch. 7, § 2.

THE CHRONICLER. 91

Seeing, however, that it is customary, at the present time, to question the historical accuracy of the Chronicler as a late writer, we must consider how far his testimony is reliable for our present purpose. In reading the books of Chronicles it is to be borne in mind that, by the time they were written, the national independence of Israel had passed away, but that the national religion, with its outward observances, remained as a uniting bond of the people. Accordingly a writer, composing the history of his nation at that period, especially knowing as he did that the national history had already been written from another point of view (in the books of Samuel and Kings), and perhaps just because it had been written in its more political aspects, and in a more specifically prophetic spirit, would take another attitude and dwell upon the continuity from early times of those features of the national life which now survived and seemed to be the chief remaining hope of national existence in the future.

No doubt the tone of the whole book of Chronicles is in marked contrast with that of the books of Kings. The history of the northern kingdom is entirely passed over, as the record of an apostasy, and the writer follows the fortunes of the house of David with unconcealed partiality. Moreover, his interest in the priestly and Levitical element is so marked that the conjecture is not unreasonable that he was himself of the tribe of Levi or of the family of the priests. Indeed the whole tendency at the time was sacerdotal, and the men who were at the head of affairs were of the priestly caste. But we are not on this account to conclude that the writer is simply transporting back to earlier times the arrangements existent in his own day. The more closely the books of Chronicles are examined, the more forcibly is the conclusion pressed on an unbiassed mind that the writer is honestly giving an account of what was matter of tradition in the circle to which he belonged. There is nothing at all incredible in the supposition that the priestly tradition retained many things in memory which find no place in the historical books of Samuel and Kings, which were written from the prophetical point of view; and there are some features about the books of Chronicles that go to confirm our belief in the honesty of the writer and the credibility of the matters he relates. Thus :—

(*a*) His introduction of lists, genealogies, &c., into his narrative is a presumptive proof that he drew from available written sources, and that he was careful, almost to punctiliousness, to be accurate in details. If he was so careful in matters that are verified by his lists, we may conclude that he had a good authority for other matters of fact which he states. We can allow for a writer's partiality in the way he uses his facts and marshals his details, without questioning the accuracy of either.

(*b*) In many places he gives us the narrative that is found in the books of Kings in the very words of that book. It is believed that both writers drew from one common source; but at all events, the Chronicler, when he found details already related, and considered them necessary for his purpose, shows his want of bias by faithfully transferring them to his pages. If his dominant tone is priestly, the prophetical element also finds place.

(*c*) He is not an indiscriminate *laudator temporis acti*. In regard to some reigns, he pronounces the same unfavourable decision that we find in the books of Kings; and the good kings, whose acts are not so fully narrated in those books, naturally come in for his special commendation. He loves to dwell on the personal virtues and religious services of those kings especially who exerted themselves to undo the ungodly work of their predecessors, and took active measures to beautify the Temple or to foster and adorn its worship. His veracity is thus confirmed, as far as it can be, by the parallel narrative; and for his additional details we may well believe that he had sufficient authority, or else he would not have entered so minutely into particulars, and made such striking distinctions.

On the whole, we may take the narrative of the Chronicler as a true picture of the circumstances of his own time, when he is dealing with these; and, in regard to events and circumstances of the past, his manifest simplicity and honesty guarantee the conclusion that he is stating what was matter of common belief in his day, and matter which was based on the best and only evidence available at the time. And for our present purpose this assumption is sufficient. Even if it be asserted that the Chronicler transports himself to earlier times and transfers his own local and temporary circumstances to the past, this implies, first of all, that the circumstances of his own time were such as he describes, and, secondly, that he had some sufficient reason for ascribing these things to an earlier date. It seems to me that we must, at the very least, give him credit for believing, and expressing the current belief, that these things were of old standing. It is simply incredible that arrangements fresh in the memory of men, or whose origin was matter of recent tradition, should be summarily assigned to a far distant age by a writer who expected that his work would receive acceptance; and those who are ever talking of writers transporting themselves to a past time are bound to give some intelligible reason, in the shape of historical facts in the past, to account for so anomalous a procedure.

Now, in turning to the books of Chronicles for information as to psalms or psalmody, we meet with constant references, on occasions of public ceremony, to the singers and performers on instruments connected with the Temple. Thus, as in the book of Samuel, David is described as playing before the ark (1 Chron. xiii. 8, xv. 25 ff.; comp. 2 Sam. vi. 5 ff.), and under his reign we find several other references to his provision of music, and his arrangements for the musicians who were "set over the service of song" (1 Chron. vi. 31, xv. 16). In one place we are told he asked the chief of the Levites to appoint singers, &c. (xv. 16); the description and arrangements of the singers are given more than once (ix. 33, xv. 16-22, xxv. 1 ff.); the number of Levites who praised the Lord with instruments is said to have amounted in David's old age to 4000 (xxiii. 5). Amidst these details, we almost hear the refrain of the songs that were sung, when mention is made of "Heman and Jeduthun, and the rest that were chosen, who were expressed by name, to give thanks to the Lord, because His mercy endureth for ever" (xvi. 41). Thus we are clearly given to understand that the service of praise, with song and instruments of music, in an orderly manner, dated from the time of David; and this we may take, at least, to be the general belief of the time.

So when we come to the succeeding reigns, as dealt with in 2 Chron., the same thing is observable. We have praise, with David's instruments of music, at the dedication of the Temple by Solomon (2 Chron. v. 11-14, viii. 14). In the reign of

Jehoshaphat we find the Kohathites singing at the head of the army as it goes out to battle, and playing on the return march (xx. 19 ff., 28). There is music and singing at the proclamation of Joash (xxiii. 13). And at Hezekiah's cleansing of the Temple it is related that "the song of the Lord began also, and the trumpets, together with the instruments of David. And all the congregation worshipped, and the singers sang, and the trumpets sounded: all this [continued] until the burnt offering was finished" (xxix. 25 ff., also ver. 30). So at Hezekiah's Passover "the Levites and the priests praised the Lord day by day, [singing] with loud instruments unto the Lord" (xxx. 21); and part of Hezekiah's reform was to arrange the work of the priests for offerings, &c., and "to give thanks, and to praise in the gates of the camp of the Lord" (xxxi. 2). Finally, at the beginning of the reformation under Josiah "the overseers of them were . . . of the sons of the Kohathites, to set it forward [marg., 'preside over it']; and [other of] the Levites, all that could skill of instruments of music" (xxxiv. 12). At the great Passover in Josiah's reign "the singers the sons of Asaph were in their place, according to the commandment of David, and Asaph, and Heman, and Jeduthun the king's seer" (xxxv. 15). And at Josiah's death "Jeremiah lamented for Josiah: and all the singing men and singing women spake of Josiah in their lamentations, unto this day; and they made them an ordinance in Israel: and, behold, they are written in the lamentations" (עַל־הַקִּינוֹת) (2 Chron. xxxv. 25).

It is not enough to set all this aside with the remark that the Chronicler is "a saintly man, but a prejudiced historian."[1] The Chronicler makes no secret of his prejudice or prepossession in favour of the worship; but these notices in regard to historical times are too varied and circumstantial to be the work of pure invention. There can be no doubt that there were guilds of singers, just as there was the line of priests, in the Chronicler's day, who traced their descent back to the early Davidic times; and in such guilds and families might have been quite easily preserved the traditions of the sacred functions in which they engaged before the Exile, though the author of the Kings, writing from another point of view, has not put them on record.

Coming upwards in time, we look next at the books of Ezra and Nehemiah. In their present form these books are by many regarded as being of the same date as the Chronicles, and supposed to have been reduced to their final form by the author of those books. However that may be, both books manifestly contain portions (written in the first person) which must have come from the hands of Ezra and Nehemiah respectively; and, besides, there are certain lists and summaries contained in

[1] Cheyne, Origin of the Psalter, p. 101, note e.

both books which must have been drawn from written sources. The books refer to the time of the return of the exiles and the reconstitution of the new state; so that, even if we suppose the author of the Chronicles to be the writer, he cannot in this case be projecting his own circumstances into a remote past, for the reference is to times comparatively recent, for which there was a sufficiently good tradition, as well as actual memoirs of the men concerned in the events. There is also this to be said, that any references of the kind of which we are in search are the more valuable because they are, so to speak, incidental and indirect, and cannot be ascribed to priestly prejudice or prepossession.

First of all we come upon a list, preserved both by Ezra and Nehemiah (Ezra ii.; Neh. vii.), of "the children of the province, that went up out of the captivity of those that had been carried away, whom Nebuchadnezzar the king of Babylon had carried away, and came again to Jerusalem and Judah, every one unto his city"—*i.e.*, those who returned first (B.C. 536) consequent upon the edict of Cyrus. In this list are mentioned, after the Levites, who were seventy-four in number, "the singers : the children of Asaph, an hundred twenty and eight" (Ezra ii. 41);[1] and in the enumeration of the totals at the

[1] The list as found in the book of Nehemiah, though giving most of the numbers in identical terms, makes the singers of the children of Asaph 148, and the total number of singing men and singing women 245 (Neh. vii. 44, 67). For a similar discrepancy compare 2 Kings viii. 26 with 2 Chron. xxii. 2.

end of the list, it is said, "they had two hundred singing men and singing women" (Ezra ii. 65). This notice is important, as showing, by the connection, that these singers were not of a secular class. They are mentioned along with priests and Levites, and it is not as if other lists of secular guilds and crafts were given, for there are none such; although even the numbers of the beasts of burden are carefully specified. Prof. Cheyne's remark, therefore,[1] seems somewhat gratuitous: "Ordinary singers were not much thought of: Neh. vii. 67 classes them with slaves." But when he goes on to say, "Even the Temple singers were not quite equal to the Levites in Zerubbabel's time" (Ezra ii. 40-42; Neh. vii. 43-45), we may set over against his remark what we are told of the ceremony of the laying of the foundation of the Temple in Zerubbabel's time: "They set the priests in their apparel with trumpets, and the Levites the sons of Asaph with cymbals, to praise the Lord, after the order of David king of Israel. And they sang one to another in praising and giving thanks unto the Lord, [saying], For He is good, for His mercy is for ever towards Israel" (Ezra iii. 10, 11).

So much for the time of the first return. When we come to Ezra's own time, we find that among those who returned with him to Jerusalem were "singers" (Ezra vii. 7); and in the decree of Artaxerxes carried by Ezra to the governors—which we

[1] Origin of the Psalter, p. 213, note n.

may assume to be an authentic document — it is particularly mentioned "that touching any of the priests and Levites, the singers, porters, Nethinim, or servants of this house of God, it shall not be lawful to impose tribute, custom, or toll upon them" (Ezra vii. 24)—in other words, they were privileged as sacred officials or guilds.

Turning now to the book of Nehemiah, we find some incidental references of the same kind. Thus he says at the conclusion of his arduous work in building the wall, after he had "set up the doors, and the porters and the singers and the Levites were appointed," he handed over the charge of Jerusalem to a governor (Neh. vii. 1); and at the great assembly in the seventh month, when the people solemnly separated themselves and took the covenant, the singers as a class are mentioned among those who "sealed" (Neh. x. 28). In the same chapter there is a significant indication of the official character of these singers, and of their forming an integral part of what we may call the staff of the Temple, where mention is made of "the chambers where are the vessels of the sanctuary, and the priests that minister, and the porters and the singers" (Neh. x. 39).

The eleventh chapter of Nehemiah tells us how, in order to swell the population of Jerusalem, one out of ten was taken by lot from those dwelling outside, and lists are given of the different families and classes brought into the city. Among the Levites is mentioned "Mattaniah the son of Micha, the son of Zabdi, the son of Asaph, who was the chief to begin the thanksgiving in prayer" (xi. 17). "The Nethinim dwelt in Ophel" (ver. 21), and "the overseer of the Levites at Jerusalem was Uzzi, . . . of the sons of Asaph, the singers, over the business of the house of God. For there was a commandment of the king concerning them, and a settled provision for [marg. A.V., 'a sure ordinance concerning'] the singers, as every day required" (Neh. xi. 22, 23).

A great public occasion was the dedication of the wall of Jerusalem which Nehemiah had built at the cost of so much labour. On that occasion he tells us (xii. 27 ff.) "they sought the Levites out of all their places, to bring them to Jerusalem, to keep the dedication with gladness, both with thanksgivings, and with singing, with cymbals, psalteries, and with harps. And the sons of the singers gathered themselves together, both out of the plain [marg., 'circuit'] round about Jerusalem, and from the villages of the Netophathites; also from Bethgilgal, and out of the fields of Geba and Azmaveth: for the singers had builded them villages round about Jerusalem." And finally, when everything was put in permanent order about the Temple, overseers being appointed to look after the provisions that were brought in for the offerings and for the ministrants, we are told that "Judah rejoiced for the priests and for the Levites that waited [marg., 'stood']. And they kept the ward of their God, and the ward of the purification, and so did the singers and the porters, according to the commandment of David, and of Solomon his son. For in the days of David and Asaph of old there was a chief [another reading, 'there were chiefs'] of the singers, and songs of praise and thanksgiving unto God. And all Israel in the days of Zerubbabel, and in the days of Nehemiah, gave the portions of the singers and the porters, as every day required: and they sanctified for the Levites; and the Levites sanctified for the sons of Aaron" (Neh. xii. 44-47).

Now all this tells us little or nothing about psalms or a psalter, but it tells us a great deal about sacred music as part of the recognised public worship. Here we have a class or guild of singers mentioned in connection with the priests and Levites, and always mentioned in connection with public ceremonies of a liturgical kind. They come from the Captivity, and are as well marked a class as the priests and Levites, important enough to receive immunities from taxation and other undefined privileges. It is absurd to think of their having arisen in the time of the Captivity; they are, like the other officials, survivals of the old Temple worship, and they come to put into exercise their well-understood gifts. They are engaged in antiphonal singing, the very words that are given as the refrain of one of their songs agree with the refrain of several of our psalms; and when we turn to these psalms we find they are well suited for the occasion, consisting as they do of reminiscences of the whole course of Israel's wonderful history (see esp. Ps. cxxxvi.)[1]

The canonical books at which we have looked are all without question post-exilian; and any evidence which they have furnished is pretty precise in its date, fixing, at all events, the lowest limit within which we are confined for the existence of those things mentioned or implied.

There is, however, one other book in the Canon whose date is not so precisely determined, but which must also be referred to in this connection, —the book of Jonah. In the second chapter (verses 2-10) there is a prayer of Jonah, which is made up of passages from various psalms; and though there are differences of opinion as to the date of this remarkable book, the fact that it forms part of the second division of the Canon attests its composition as anterior to the date of the formation of the prophetical collection (*i.e.*, anterior to the third century B.C.) We may pro-

---

[1] Ehrt maintains that Nehemiah's penitential prayer (Neh. ix. 5-x. 1) is not only after the manner of the so-called *Viddui*, which finds expression in Ps. cvi., but that it contains echoes of the oldest songs and actual quotations from some of the psalms (Abfass., p. 71, foot).

visionally place the book not later than the fifth century B.C.[1]

In this prayer of Jonah we find an unusual number of resemblances to psalms, and not to one or a few but to a number, in different parts of the Psalter. Compare, for example (in the original)—

Jonah ii.	3	with	Ps. cxx. 1.
"	" 4 b	"	" xlii. 8 b.
"	" 5 a	"	" xxxi. 23 a.
"	" 8 a	"	" cxlii. 4 a.
"	" 8 b	"	" lxxxviii. 3 a.
"	" 10 a	"	" cxvi. 17.
"	" 10 b	"	" cxvi. 18 a.
"	i. 14 b	"	" cxv. 3.
"	ii. 4	"	" lxxxviii. 7, 8.
"	" 6	"	" lxxxviii. 18.
"	i. 11	"	" cvii. 29, 30.

It can hardly be supposed that so many psalm-writers as are here represented should all have borrowed from this little book of Jonah. Much more probable is it that the writer of the book of Jonah, wishing to exhibit the feelings of one in such a situation as he describes, fell back upon the book of Psalms, quoting phrases and expressions that occurred to him—in fact, composed a prayer suitable for the occasion out of the liturgical language

[1] Ehrt, Abfass., p. 40. The date of the book is determined partly by certain linguistic peculiarities, and partly by a consideration of the tone of thought, a so-called *universalism*, as distinguished from the older particularism, that restricted God's favourable acceptance of persons to Israel. Here the divine love, without respect to nationality, is represented as the moving cause of favourable interposition.

that was familiar to him. This is made the more probable by the fact that the book of Jonah quotes or gives reminiscences of various other Biblical books.[1]

In all the preceding references to sacred music, one thing cannot escape notice, that at the time of the return from captivity, and after it, the service of praise in connection with the Temple is consistently and explicitly assigned in its origin to David and his days. This, on any explanation of it, means that the belief, at the time of the rebuilding of the city and Temple, was universal that these musical arrangements were not only pre-exilian, but very old. And yet certainly we have not here a case of transporting existing institutions to the remotest antiquity to give them the highest sanction. For whereas all parts of the Law were ascribed to Mosaic days, and the desire to magnify the importance of every detail of the ritual would be strong, there is never the least hint that this part of the service came from Moses, but an unvarying asseveration of its Davidic origin. This would be remarkable even if there were few or no references in pre-exilian books to music in the Temple, for it would be a proof of a tradition so persistent as to demand

---

[1] Compare, for example, Jonah iii. 10 with Exod. xxxii. 14, Jonah iv. 2 a with Exod. xiv. 12, and Jonah iv. 2 b with Exod. xxxiv. 6. Ehrt, p. 39, points out also parallels to the story of Elijah in 1 Kings xix. 3 ff. (Jonah iv. 3).

the admission of some definite fact at its foundation. And it becomes the more remarkable when a few unmistakable confirmations incidentally occur in pre-exilian books. Reference has already been made to the passage (2 Sam. vi. 5 ff.) relating how, at the bringing up of the ark to Jerusalem, " David and all the house of Israel played before the Lord, with all manner of instruments made of fir-wood, and with harps, and with psalteries, and with timbrels, and with castanets, and with cymbals" (R.V.) Without stopping at present to inquire what this music was or who was its author, it is evident that we have here the employment of music and song (cf. the parallel in 1 Chron. xiii. 8, xv. 25 ff.), and that of a rather elaborate character, in the service of religion and in connection with public worship.

In a quite incidental way, too, it is mentioned in 1 Kings x. 12, that King Solomon "made of the almug-trees" (probably sandal-wood), which the Queen of Sheba gave him in abundance, "pillars [or railings] for the house of the Lord, and for the king's house; harps also and psalteries for the singers."[1] Prof. Driver[2] gives it as his opinion that this passage is ambiguous, because the technical name used in Chronicles, &c., for the Temple

---

[1] The R.V. follows the Massoretic text in inserting the article, which the A.V. omitted.

[2] Introduction, p. 357, note. [In 6th Edition, p. 379.]

singers is not here employed. It may be pointed out, however, that the simple participle "singers" (שָׁרִים) would more naturally be employed at the early period when the institution of song was recent, and a more technical term (מְשֹׁרֲרִים) is in place in a book confessedly written at a much later period. Moreover, the connection in which the expression occurs is to be noted—viz., in the midst of the arrangements of the Temple and palace; and the characteristic words with which the writer concludes, "there came no such almug-trees, nor were seen unto this day," have all the flavour of a remark by a connoisseur who had seen and handled the renowned instruments which had the reputed *fecit* of King Solomon. Besides, if "the singers" were an entirely secular class, it seems somewhat undignified and incongruous to make Solomon pose so ostentatiously as their patron. Professor Driver, in confirmation of his view that sacred music is not referred to, appeals to 2 Sam. xix. 35, where Barzillai laments that he is too old to enjoy "the voice of singing men and singing women." But it is not by any means certain that even here secular or entirely secular musicians are referred to. They must have been, at all events, court or palace officials. Jeremiah, in mentioning "mourning women" and "cunning women" who are to take up a lamentation (Jer. ix. 17 ff.), contemplates a mourning of a national and religious description; and, as we shall see by-and-by, the line was not drawn hard and fast between secular and sacred poetry and music. At all events, we get in this incidental way a striking confirmation of the belief of post-exilian times that singing men and singing women were in their institution and office something very different from professors of an ordinary trade.

If it be urged that these authorities are either too late or too ambiguous to be decisive, the same can hardly be said of Amos, who was only about two centuries after the date of David, and who, quite incidentally also, confirms the tradition that ascribes the highest place in music to the poet-king. In an often-quoted passage (Amos vi. 4-6) the prophet denounces the nobles of Samaria, who "lie upon beds of ivory, and stretch themselves upon their couches, and eat the lambs out of the flock, and the calves out of the midst of the stall; that sing idle songs to the sound of the viol; that devise for themselves instruments of music, like David; that drink wine in bowls, and anoint themselves with the chief ointments; but they are not grieved for the affliction of Joseph." By a strangely perverted ingenuity of exegesis this passage has been taken to imply that David's fame as a musician in the days of Amos rested on his secular poetry and music, of which these luxurious nobles are taken to be the exact copiers. A recent writer,[1] who has no prejudice against the methods of modern criticism, objects to this interpretation of the prophet's words on the ground that the music referred to *was sacred* music, being performed in honour of Baal by these his worshippers. Without, however, pressing this point, I maintain that the passage gives no countenance whatever to the inference drawn from it. It says absolutely nothing as to the character of David's music. It simply says that those luxurious nobles, searching for the best of *everything* to consume on their own pleasures, made for themselves instruments like David's, presumably the very best of their kind, and to the accompaniment of these instruments sang idle songs on the viol. We have already seen that instruments of all kinds were used by David in connection with religious service; and if the nobles of Samaria employed the choicest music on their own pleasure, this is no condemnation of the instruments or their inventor. That Amos himself held the "traditional" view of David's character and standing is evident from another passage (Amos ix. 11) which critics cannot be allowed to excise merely because it gives too high an estimate of the Davidic house.

The passage we have been considering—on any view of it—shows that David's fame as a musician was so well established in the time of Amos as

[1] Beer, Individual- und Gemeinde-Psalmen, p. xxv.

to have become proverbial. And other passages of the same prophet have a further significance. When it is said (Amos v. 23), "Take thou away from me the noise of thy songs; for I will not hear the melody of thy viols," when it is threatened that "the songs of the Temple shall be howling" and "lamentation" (Amos viii. 3, 10), and when these words occur immediately in connection with burnt-offerings and meat-offerings and peace-offerings of fat beasts, we learn for certain that music with singing was part of, or an accompaniment of, the public worship of the northern kingdom. And when we know that that worship was set up in imitation of the Jerusalem ritual, and when we are told of David employing music at the bringing up of the ark, we cannot have stronger evidence that music from his time took a definite place in the public worship of Israel.

Let us now sum up the evidence we have found.

I. The very latest point of time in the process of collecting the Canon of which we have found mention is the time of Judas the Maccabee (died B.C. 161), who is said, in the letter prefixed to 2 Maccabees (2 Macc. ii. 14), to have gathered the books that were scattered by reason of the war. "And they are all with us."[1]

---

[1] Prof. Cheyne, as has been already noted, gives less credit to this statement than to an alleged fact, for which he confesses he has no ancient authority—viz., that Simon (who died B.C. 135) reorganised the Temple

II. It cannot, however, be declared to be altogether impossible that Maccabaean psalms may have found their way into the Psalter. Whether there are such psalms, and how many they may be, must be determined on internal grounds. All the evidence we have yet seen, though it leads to the conclusion that the bulk of the Psalter was earlier, does not actually preclude the possibility of Maccabaean psalms. The mention of Judas may be a hint that the Canon underwent a revision or was subjected to enlargement in his days. And, as Delitzsch has pointed out,[1] the period of the Maccabees was one well suited, by its patriotic spirit, to arouse the poetic activity. The Psalter of Solomon, which belongs to about the time of Pompey, gives evidence that during the time of the Maccabees "the feelings of the faithful still poured themselves forth in spiritual songs."[2] The ancient book of Jashar seems, in a

worship and edited the Psalter. And having assumed this position, he says, "We are bound to admit that Simon the Maccabee, as high priest, had power to deal as he thought best with the provisionally closed temple hymn-book" (Origin of Psalter, p. 457). A critic may think himself at liberty to assume an important historical fact of which he finds no record; but he ought to give us some proof that a high priest thought himself at liberty to deal with a public hymn-book just as he pleased.

[1] Comm. on the Psalms, Introd. iii. Among opponents of Maccabaean psalms are to be reckoned, not only Hengstenberg, Hävernick, and Keil, but also Gesenius, Hassler, Ewald, Thenius, Böttcher, Hupfeld, Dillmann, and Ehrt.

[2] Delitzsch adds that if the book of Daniel, in its present form,

similar way, to have been an open collection, for we find references to it at earlier and later periods (Joshua and 2 Samuel); and, to make another comparison, in our modern hymnals we find the most ancient hymns side by side with those composed by living authors.

III. Nevertheless, though we thus leave the door open for Maccabaean psalms, should they be clearly authenticated as such, the evidence we have seen preponderates very distinctly in favour not only of psalms, but of a definite Psalter at an earlier period. Thus we have seen—

(1) At about B.C. 100 there is found the significant reference (in 2 Maccabees) to the "works of David," a proof that something canonical to which that designation was appropriate was well known, and that what was known by this name was believed to be ancient and Davidic.

(2) The grandson of Jesus son of Sirach, about 132 B.C., testifies to the existence, in Greek translation, of sacred Scriptures enumerated under three titles which in order and significance correspond to the three divisions of the existing Canon. He tells us also that his grandfather was familiar with these.

belongs to the time of the Seleucidæ (and its prophetic character would be assured if it was issued before the reconstruction of the Temple in B.C. 165, and before the death of Antiochus Epiphanes in 164), we may argue from the history of the Canon in favour of, rather than against, the existence of Maccabaean psalms.

(3) The grandfather himself, Jesus son of Sirach, about B.C. 200, quotes unquestionably from one psalm as Scripture, proving that a psalter in which that psalm was present was canonical Scripture in his day.

(4) The LXX. Version (begun about 284 B.C.) contains the completed Psalter, divided into five books with the doxologies.

(5) The book of Jonah—not later than B.C. 300 —quotes from psalms which are now found in different parts of the collection.

(6) The author of the Chronicles, in B.C. 330 or thereabout, attests the Psalter as divided with the existing doxologies; and proceeds, throughout his work, on the supposition that all the arrangements for the musical service of the Temple date from David. However far these *actually* go back, there is no doubt that at this time they were esteemed old—very old; else they could not thus have been spoken of.

(7) Finally, the books of Ezra and Nehemiah, though in their existing form they may belong to the time of the Chronicles, yet must be taken as giving an honest and fair account of what was done by these leaders of the restored colony from the time of Zerubbabel, B.C. 536, to Ezra-Nehemiah, about B.C. 440. They tell us, among other things, of singers coming back from the Captivity, and of the rearrangement of what we are given to under-

stand had been an old order of worship. We find them even engaging in sacred song before the Second Temple was built (Ezra iii. 10, 11), thereby linking on the practice to the worship of the First Temple, and attesting that the practice was pre-exilian.

IV. The pre-exilian books themselves, though they contain far fewer references to the subject, contain nothing at variance with this tradition, but everything they say goes to confirm it. We have Solomon's manifest regard for the improvement of musical appliances; we have the account of David and the people engaging in music and song at the bringing up of the ark; and we have the undoubted fact that by the time of Amos the most luxurious of the nobles of Samaria thought it an ambition to have instruments like David's, thus proving that his reputation in this respect was established. One step more we may be permitted to go back, by recalling how the associations of prophets in Samuel's time exercised their vocation with psaltery and timbrel and pipe and harp (1 Sam. x. 5); and how closely David was associated with Samuel and others of this fraternity.[1] The very paucity of these references in the earlier books would agree, as it seems to me, with the actual course of events. Tradition

---

[1] Binnie, The Psalms, their History, Teachings, and Use, chap. iv., reminds us that Heman was a grandson of Samuel.

in the matter goes back to David *and no higher;* music takes a marked place in religious worship just in David's time; but, once introduced, it remained, and, in the nature of the case, its cultivators and official guardians multiplied, and developed the art. So that from simple "singers" there arose a guild of professional performers or musicians, who by the time of the destruction of the Temple had as definite functions as the priests and Levites, and returned from the Exile the conservators of a traditional art which they were found ready to exercise.

The question now arises, What did these singers sing, say, at the time of the first return from Babylon? One would think they must have possessed a variety both of songs and music sufficient to give occupation to a whole guild and form their professional work. We *must* postulate a number of psalms brought back from the Captivity of a kind fitted for the service of praise in the Temple; and it is very startling, to say the least, to hear, as we do from Prof. Cheyne, that not a single psalm in the Psalter —or, at most, only a portion of one—was composed before the Exile, and even it as late as the time of Josiah. If this be the case, then we must suppose that other pre-exilian psalms were lost and forgotten in the Exile, and that a new set were immediately and rapidly produced when they were wanted at the return; or, at the best, that (as a law code, for example, was drawn up in the Captivity for use at

Jerusalem) the professional singers in exile set themselves in advance to prepare songs for the restored Temple service. Could poetry be thus made to order? Could the old psalms be thus completely forgotten and lost? Are not folk-songs the most cherished and the most permanent of a nation's possessions? In regard to such possibilities, Prof. Cheyne has some very enigmatical declarations. "It would be absurd," he says, "to maintain that there were no psalms before the Exile. But it is not absurd to question whether temple-hymns can have greatly resembled those in the Psalter. There must, indeed, have been a common element in them," and so on.[1] As to the first part of this statement, it is to be observed that it has not been proved (and it would be very hard to prove) that all the psalms in the Psalter were *originally composed* for Temple purposes. In contending for the possibility of pre-exilian psalmody, we cannot allow the restricting assumption that psalms were first and solely composed for that purpose. As to the second part of the statement, if there was a common element in the pre-exilian and post-exilian Temple psalmody, we should expect that element to appear and to be emphasised in the earliest post-exilian hymns, or if not, we should be disposed to ask for some explanation of

[1] Origin of the Psalter, p. 213, note o.

its absence. On this subject we should expect the leaders of the new post-exilian community to give us some hint by way of information; for they certainly knew whether or not every psalm they employed was, as Prof. Cheyne asserts, "a new song." [1]

Now we happen to have, in the books of Chronicles, some details which, besides being interesting from another point of view, have no little significance on this very subject. They are found in the sixteenth chapter of the first book, itself a continuation of the preceding chapter, which relates the bringing up of the ark to Jerusalem, and its deposit in the tent which David had prepared for its reception. It was a time of great rejoicing, a ceremony of great solemnity; mention is made of those whom David appointed to minister before the ark; and the Chronicler goes on to give a specimen of the very words which were employed as praise on the occasion. The A.V. gives a misleading translation of the introductory verse, "Then on that day David delivered first [this psalm] to thank the Lord into the hand of Asaph and his brethren." For the meaning clearly is, as given in the R.V., "Then in that day did David first ordain to give thanks unto the Lord by the hand of Asaph and his brethren"; and—the point we are coming to—the words

[1] Origin of the Psalter, p. 194.

that follow (vers. 8-26) are found to be almost verbally reproduced from the Psalter. Thus—

1 Chron. xvi.	8-22	=	Ps. cv.	1-15.
"	" 23-33	=	" xcvi.	1-13.
"	" 34	=	" cvi.	1.
"	" 35, 36	=	" cvi.	47, 48.

Here, though, as has just been said, the words of the Chronicler may not be taken to imply that David composed the hymn on that occasion, they certainly indicate his belief that these or similar words of praise were employed. In other words, the Chronicler believed, and his readers would believe, that the Temple psalmody of David's days was like the psalms in the Psalter. Of course it is open to reply that this does not prove that the fact was so. Yet when we find that Nehemiah's prayer also (Neh. ix. 6 ff) has many resemblances in language to the very psalms quoted by the Chronicler, and when we observe the manifest endeavour to link on the worship of the new Temple to that of the past, it can hardly be denied that we have before us a historical situation which must have behind it some solid and insuperable facts.

The passage just referred to has, however, a further significance which has often been pointed out. It is pretty evident that the hymn here inserted is not intended to appear as the Chronicler's own composition. On every page of his work we can see his labour as a compiler, and he does not hesitate to incorporate whole chapters which are found in the books of Kings. A comparison of the passage with the psalms referred to [1] leads to the conclusion that the psalms exhibit the earlier texts, and that the variations of the Chronicler are his own modifications. He is quoting, therefore, from existent psalms; and, having begun, he goes on fitting pieces of different psalms together to produce an appropriate hymn. And the remarkable thing is that when he comes to the end of Ps. cvi., which is now the closing portion of book iv., he quotes also the doxology, which, it is generally agreed, is later than the psalm itself, having been added, like the other doxologies, at the time when the fivefold division of the Psalter was introduced and the collection finally completed. If this be so, then we shall have to conclude that by the time of the Chronicler —viz., about B.C. 300—the Psalter was virtually complete in its present form, or, at all events, that a psalter with doxologies, such as we now possess, extending at least to the close of the fourth book, was in existence. And it will be hard to believe that so much psalmody came into existence in the short time elapsing since the Captivity.

Stade gets over the difficulty here presented in a summary manner.[2] He lays little stress, he tells us, on this quotation, for it seems to him questionable

---

[1] Such a comparison is made by Ehrt, Abfass., pp. 43-51.
[2] Geschichte, i. p. 215, footnote 2.

whether this psalm-passage belongs to the original text of the Chronicler, who is in the habit of merely saying on similar occasions that there was singing, without reproducing the words that were sung. In short, the psalm-portion is to be cut out as an interpolation. Prof. Cheyne's method is different. He says [1] " it is not certain that any part of Ps. cvi. is quoted in 1 Chron. xvi. ; verses 34-36 " (which agree with the psalm and contain the doxology) " consist of liturgical formulæ which were no more composed solely for use in Ps. cvi. than the doxology attached to the Lord's Prayer was originally formulated solely to occupy its present position. There is no reason why not only the doxology in verse 36 but the preceding verses should not have been attached by the Chronicler to the psalm which he had made up simply as liturgical formulæ." But are we then given to understand that the writer of the psalm fell upon the same formulæ, or that the psalm itself is later than and based upon this passage in the Chronicles? The main point, at all events, is here evaded—viz., that the Chronicler is in general fond of quotation, and that he has already unquestionably quoted from two other psalms. Without doubt he thought it "absurd to question" whether temple-hymns of early time resembled those now found in the Psalter.

Should any lingering doubt remain on this sub-

[1] Origin of the Psalter, p. 457.

ject, it ought to be set at rest by a glance at that touching psalm of the Captivity (Ps. cxxxvii.), a piece so vivid in its details that it cannot be an afterthought, but must be accepted as fresh from the impress of a recent experience:—

> " By the rivers of Babylon,
> There we sat down, yea, we wept,
> When we remembered Zion.
> Upon the willows in the midst thereof
> We hanged up our harps.
> . . . .
> How shall we sing the Lord's song
> In a strange land?" &c.

The psalm is exilian or post-exilian in date, and possibly verses 8, 9 imply that it was written before the destruction of Babylon. The writer, at all events, may be taken as a direct witness of the things he describes. And, on reading the psalm, the first thing we naturally ask is, What were the songs of Zion which the Babylonians tauntingly asked the captives to sing? Not songs composed or learned for the first time in the Captivity, for it seemed inappropriate to sing the Lord's song in a strange land. Nor were the harps new instruments they had made to solace the hours of captivity, but their old instruments, which had been used in happier days, and now seemed fit only to be hung upon the willows. It is now no longer wonderful—though it is not a little remarkable—that the Chronicler should speak of the sacred music of the Temple in the time of King Hezekiah as the "song of the Lord" (2 Chron. xxix. 25 ff). And it is surely not too much to infer from this psalm that the reference of the Psalmist is to the same sacred songs, religious and national hymns—"songs of Jehovah" and songs relating to Zion—such as we now find in the Psalter. It seems to me that the burden of this plaintive song forbids us to accept such sweeping statements as that "the religious organisation of the people in Ezra's time was too complete to allow any considerable influence to archaic liturgical formulæ," and that "almost every psalm" sung in the newly reorganised worship "might be appropriately styled a new song."[1] Here, at least, we have a psalmist who looked back fondly to the *old* songs—songs of Zion, songs of the Lord of pre-exilic times. And we can neither believe that such a fond memory would suddenly forget, and leave in forgetfulness, all the songs of a past time at the very moment when every nerve was strained to revive the glories of the past, nor admit that psalmody of an entirely new tone and purport should suddenly spring into existence after the Exile.

Whatever arguments, therefore, may be advanced on critical methods and internal evidence as to the date of the Psalter, we must give its due weight to external testimony so repeated, so coherent, and

[1] Cheyne, Origin of the Psalter, p. 194.

concurrent as this. It is inadmissible to speak here of a vague tradition. It is unhistorical and unscientific to speak of this as a projecting of modern ideas into a past. For we cannot find a step in this chain of historical reminiscence that could be fairly described as the starting-point of something new which needs to be projected into the past. From the first return of Zerubbabel onwards there was not only the arduous work of reorganisation to be done, but all was done with a constant reference to the national past, in the endeavour to conserve all that was best in the antecedent history.

No doubt, internal evidence has also to be taken into account; and if internal evidence should prove without doubt that such and such psalms cannot belong to pre-exilian times, we must bow to the evidence. But there are two things to be borne in mind here: (1) The external evidence is so strong in favour of pre-exilian psalmody of a very considerable amount, that we are entitled to ask critical writers to point out where such pre-exilian psalms are, or to give us some credible account of what has become of them if they have disappeared. Conversely we should be disposed, in view of the evidence advanced, to look carefully and without prejudice *for* just such psalms as might be considered pre-exilian. We are by the teaching of facts told to look for them. We should give the writers the consideration due to honest-minded men, and dispose ourselves to accept pre-exilian psalms if there are no convincing reasons for rejecting them. And this we should do the more when we remember (2) how very uncertain the internal arguments are by which it is maintained that the great bulk of the Psalter is post-exilian. One needs only to open a few of the commentaries on the Psalms by those who have undertaken the task of fixing their dates. It will be found, when the external considerations are entirely left out of account, and the attempt is made from the contents of individual psalms alone to assign them to their respective dates, that the expositors differ in many cases by centuries as to the time, and fix upon epochs the most unlike for the occasion of these compositions.

We should therefore, I think, in fairness turn to the Psalter, prepared to find within it psalms that were composed in the pre-exilian period in its widest sense, and even to find psalms which, during the time the First Temple was standing, were fit to be employed, and were actually employed, in its worship.

CHAPTER VI.

TESTIMONY OF THE PSALTER ITSELF.

WE now come to look at the Psalter itself as a whole, to see what information it supplies concerning its own origin.

1. The most obvious remark to be made at the outset is that the Psalter is not the work of a day. This collection of 150 sacred songs is like some collection of pictures which the superficial observer may run through in a short time, but each of which contains material for long and patient examination. For just as each picture has its own history and its own theme, so every individual psalm is complete in itself and may be made the subject of independent study. But manifestly the whole is not some sudden creation—the product of one mind or the work of a generation. Even in regard to the prophetical books, we are prone to forget the long periods over which the ministry of some of their writers extended; and the brief indications in the

headings of the various oracles uttered regarding Tyre, Egypt, Moab, and so forth, do not, without some reflection, suggest the varying circumstances in which the prophets spoke and wrote, and the length of time through which they delivered their testimony. Years may intervene between different chapters of Isaiah or Jeremiah; and so, for aught we can say at the outset, even centuries may intervene between contiguous psalms. For these compositions seem to lie together very much as the hymns in our modern collections, in which the oldest sacred songs find place beside the compositions of living writers. It is not even apparent at first on what principle they are arranged,[1] or whether there was any one guiding principle of arrangement at all. In any case, the very number of them, and their manifest variety, taken along with what we know of prophetic literary composition, make it abundantly plain that we have before us the product of different times, and probably the de-

---

[1] Delitzsch, in his early work, 'Symbolæ ad Psalmos illustrandos isagogicæ,' sufficiently established the existence of one literary nexus— viz., the occurrence in contiguous psalms of the same or similar striking phrases. But it is evident that such a conjunction would be made mainly for mnemonic reasons, and, instead of helping to determine the dates of contiguous psalms, would rather suggest that regard was *not* had in the arrangement to chronological order. It has been pointed out that in the collection of the Twelve minor prophets, something of the same kind has been done, the closing words of one prophet suggesting the succession of another whose book opens with a similar expression.

posit of a very prolonged activity in this domain of literature.

2. In the next place, we immediately come upon the fact that the Psalter as it now exists is made up of five books. And there are some features of these several books which show conclusively that the fivefold division was not a dividing into five of a number of isolated productions, nor a division made of what was in the first place one whole, but that the whole was made up of originally smaller collections. The books are of unequal length; and, in particular, the name of God varies in a remarkable way in the different books. Moreover, as we shall see, psalms that seem to have been regarded as coming from a common source are separated from one another in different books in a striking manner. There is also the well-known fact that the same psalm is virtually repeated in different books.[1] These features, and others, are not consistent with the supposition that 150 separate and unconnected productions were arranged at one point of time into five books, nor scarcely with the idea that five separate and contemporaneous collections were merged into one. We may not be able to infer that there were precisely five successive and separate stages of collection (for the fivefold division seems to have been adopted to correspond to the five books of the Pentateuch); but it seems matter

[1] Compare Ps. xiv. with liii.

beyond doubt that different collections have been placed together, and thus that the completed Psalter is a composite work, whose completion was a gradual process.

Now this has a certain significance for our present purpose. For before different collections could have been brought together, they must have been some time at least in existence as separate collections; and not only so, but before each separate collection could come into existence as such, the individual psalms of which it is composed must have been there, and deemed suitable and worthy to be so collected. All this would throw back the date of composition of the psalms some considerable time before the date of the completed collection, even if the separate smaller collections were contemporaneous. Much more, if the several smaller collections were successive in time, which is certainly on every account most probable,[1] the space between the composition of the earliest psalm in the collection and the date of the completed Psalter must be considerable. We must first have a time in which psalm composition began; at all events, we must have a time to which the oldest psalms in the collection belong; we must then allow space for the stock to grow by the rise of new composi-

---

[1] To mention only one fact, it is not so likely that the two recensions of one psalm, xiv. and liii., existed side by side contemporaneously, as that one was a later modification of the other.

tions. Then we must have a time at which, for some purpose, it occurred to some one to form the first collection, and so on for successive collections; and, finally, we must allow space and occasion for the gathering of all the existing collections, or for incorporating the last collection with the completed Psalter.

Of course it might be maintained that the process was very rapid. That is a matter for proof; but in any case we must assume such a process, according to all the analogy of such compositions; and we must keep such a process continually in mind if we would arrive at any reasonable and intelligible explanation of the history of the Psalter.

It seems to me that the advocates of the late origin of the Psalter have not given due weight to this consideration, or else they have not produced satisfactory evidence of such quickened activity in literary production as would result in a completed psalter so extensive and so multiform as the existing collection. And, instead of strengthening their position, they weaken it by maintaining that any psalmody that may have existed before the Exile was entirely different in character from that which lies before us, and by refusing to accept as genuine productions of pre-exilian times those hymnic passages that are found in historical and prophetical books. For thereby they burden themselves with the assumption that not only the collection of the first group of psalms was posterior to the Exile, but that even the first stimulus to this kind of composition, or at all events the first attempts at it, did not emerge till that late time.

3. Moreover, we find not only this arrangement of the whole Psalter in five books, but we discover evident traces of smaller collections underlying the several books. The headings or titles of the psalms, although, as we have seen, they are not to be accepted as decisive of the dates and authorship of the psalms to which they are prefixed, have a certain positive value for us at this stage of our inquiry; they are evidence at least that the psalms have passed through various hands, and that, for some reason or other, they were not regarded as all belonging to one category. We may or may not believe that all or any of the psalms ascribed to David were written by him; but we have here proof that some distinction was understood to subsist between those psalms and others differently named, or left unnamed. It can hardly have been a mere arbitrary work of the collectors that has ascribed a certain number of psalms to David, another number of psalms to the sons of Korah, others to Asaph, and so on. And the collocation of the different groups is noteworthy. By far the greatest number of so-called Davidic psalms are found towards the beginning of the Psalter, and the Korahite and Asaphic psalms lie closely together. Besides those

SMALLER COLLECTIONS.

which bear names, we find, placed closely together, small collections of psalms beginning or ending in the same way, as the so-called *Hodu*[1] and *Hallelujah* psalms.[2] And there is the remarkable collection of fifteen psalms (Psalms cxx.-cxxxiv.), each one of which is inscribed a "Song of Degrees" (or more probably "Song of Ascents"), all lying in succession.

All this looks, again, as if the process of collecting the Psalter was a gradual one. And it is to be observed that the various groups that have been mentioned seem to be anterior to the divisions into books. Whether originally they were formally embodied into collections, or merely preserved orally with their distinctive designations traditionally associated with them, they seem to have belonged to their several categories before they were transferred to or incorporated in the different books; and it is now generally believed that it was by a dislocation of these groups, anterior to or on the occasion of the division into books, that groups of psalms with a common heading got separated. The division into books, in fact, seems to be a more artificial and editorial arrangement than the association which unites these smaller groups. For several of the latter—such as

---

[1] The *Hodu* psalms, beginning, "O give thanks" (הוֹדוּ), are Pss. cv.-cvii.

[2] The *Hallelujah* psalms begin and end with "Praise ye the Lord," and are found in minor groups—viz., cxi.-cxiii., cxv.-cxvii., cxlvi.-cl.

the *Hodu, Hallelujah,* and "Ascent" psalms—have certain marks of affinity in the nature of the subject and the literary form. The Korahite and Asaphic psalms also have well-marked characteristics of their own; and even the Davidic psalms—at least those in the opening part of the Psalter—have common features.

Such a diversity implies, on any view of it, a considerable lapse of time and variety of situation. We can hardly suppose that one person would set himself deliberately to compose any one set of compositions corresponding to any one of these collections; much less that several individuals would at the same time produce several such collections. There must be individual compositions before there are sets or collections of kindred compositions; and the natural supposition is that it was the existence of the individual compositions, with a resemblance in their subject-matter, or a similarity in their literary form, that led to their being grouped together.

So then, underlying the completed Psalter we have five books, which must have taken time in their formation; and under these books we have groups of related psalms, which, whether in written or in oral form, must have had some common tradition associated with them before the formation of the several books; for though grouped pretty closely together, they do not correspond with the divisions of the books. These several collections also required time for their formation. And behind, and underlying all, we have the individual psalms, which must have existed before they could be placed in groups. And seeing that they are varied in literary form and in subject-matter, we are necessarily brought to the conclusion that psalm-composition was a manifold thing, practised long and in varied circumstances. The Psalter itself tells us plainly that it has had a long history; and it is hard to believe in the face of these literary *facts* that the very earliest stages of that history began with the foundation of the Second Temple.

4. Now if we could assume that the books of the Psalter were arranged in chronological order, so that the successive books represented the psalm literature existing at successive periods, and that the smaller groups were in a similar way chronologically arranged, we might be able to work our way back from the latest to the earliest collection, and thus determine the dates, at least of certain *groups* of psalms, within approximate limits of time.

This, however, we are not at liberty to do. We have no positive information as to the mode in which the collections were brought together, or how they were treated in the course of the final arrangement of the Psalter. There are, moreover, indications of a negative kind which forbid our concluding that the arrangement, either of books or of groups, is chronological. Thus we find psalms ascribed to David in all the five books of the collection, though the preponderating number is found in the two earliest (viz., thirty-seven out of seventy-three in all). So also book ii. begins with Korahite psalms and ends with Asaphic ones: while book iii. begins with Asaphic and ends with Korahite psalms; the two psalms that open the collection are anonymous, while one in the fourth book is ascribed to Moses. Whatever may be the precise significance of all these facts, we can hardly, in face of them, assume that a particular psalm in any one book determines the date, even approximately, of the whole book. The same remark applies to the collections; an examination of individual cases makes it probable that psalms bearing the same title belong to very different periods; and the mere fact of different psalms with a common heading ("David") standing in all the five books, would of itself suggest such a conclusion.

There is one characteristic notice at the end of Ps. lxxii. which at first sight promises to give us a fixed chronological point—viz., the statement with which, as it now stands, the psalm closes: "The prayers of David the son of Jesse are ended." This notice, it will be observed, coincides with the close of the second book of the Psalter; and the only intelligible explanation of it is, that at the time it was appended there was a completed collection that could be thus described as the prayers of David the son of Jesse. In other words, it seems to be a colophon attached to a primitive Davidic psalm-book. Could we be sure that no alteration or subsequent rearrangement has taken place, we might therefore conclude that the psalms of the first two books at one time formed a collection by themselves, and then we might infer, from the name given to the collection, that this Davidic psalm-book was the earliest collection. This, however, we are not entitled to do. But we may with tolerable confidence conclude that the earliest psalms in the collection have found their place, for the most part, near the beginning. It is indeed quite possible that compositions which were early were not included in the first collection, but were afterwards taken up (somewhere after Ps. lxxii.) when an enlargement took place or a new collection was formed. So it is quite possible that psalms which were later in origin may, in the subsequent rearrangements that took place, have been inserted among earlier ones. Still, it is in every way most probable that the earliest in date would be allowed to stand in the first portion of the collection, if they were once in it, and that the bulk of the first collection would be the relatively earlier psalms. The mere fact of the colophon being allowed to stand at the end of Ps. lxxii. is an indication that there was a disposition not to disturb the arrangement that was found existing. It may be remarked also that the psalms in the earlier part of the book are in literary form very different from those at the close, being more rugged and broken, more intense in feeling and enigmatical in expression, contrasting with the even flow, transparent lucidity, and uniform tone of those towards the end. The latter have all the marks of being composed with a direct view to liturgical use, which is not by any means the case with the former.

To sum up: the whole appearance of the Psalter, with the headings of the different collections, suggests the inference which many critics draw, that there was, first of all, a limited psalter, known by the name of "David" (of which there remains a trace at the end of Psalm lxxii.); that there arose also collections known by the names of "Asaph" and the "sons of Korah"; and that by the addition of these, and similar collections, the original book was enlarged till it grew to its present dimensions. As to the precise sense in which the original titles of these collections were bestowed, we are not required to maintain that they actually denoted authorship. In regard to the psalms of the "sons of Korah," for example, instead of supposing that a psalm was a joint production of a family, we more naturally think of the psalms so designated arising in the circle of the guild or family so named, and being preserved among them. And it may be the same with the name of David; the earliest psalms being his, the collection as it grew retaining his name.

5. Proceeding a step farther, we have to consider whether we can determine, even approximately, the earliest and latest dates of psalm-composition. It is only an approximation that can be expected, on this kind of evidence; for any collection or group that might be selected as a starting-point has, as has been pointed out, its own history and process of growth, and we cannot be sure that it has remained undisturbed during subsequent processes of collection. For the precise determination of the date of any psalm, if such a thing is possible, we must, in the long-run, depend upon a careful exegesis and examination of its contents. That this is a matter of no little difficulty, however, is sufficiently attested by the very divergent opinions that have been held by competent critics who have relied on this kind of proof. The contents of many of the psalms are of such a nature that it is impossible, from their subject-matter, to infer their dates. In many of them there are no references whatever to historical events; and in most of them there is no reference to persons, such as would enable us to assign them to any precise occasion or even definite epoch.

Accordingly, almost all who have made the attempt to determine the dates of the psalms have taken advantage of the existing minor collections or groups as starting-points for the inquiry. There is, however, a variety in the manner in which the groups have been apprehended. A recent writer,[1] for example, takes as his basis the first and second books, on the presumption, reasonable in the circumstances, as we have seen, that the oldest psalms are to be found there; and endeavours to show that most of the psalms of these books may reasonably be assigned to pre-exilian times. This mode of arguing has, at least, the merit of proceeding on historically attested groups, and ought to give surer results than the method of grouping psalms according to their tone or contents. To this latter method the objection is obvious, that there may be a variety of individuality in writers who are contemporary, and that modes of thought and expression, and even external historical situations, are liable to recur at different periods.

There are, however, psalms in the collection which bear unmistakable evidence of comparatively late date, and can be assigned to a comparatively restricted period. Thus Ps. cxxxvii., which has been already referred to,[2] bears every indication of having been composed very soon after the return

---

[1] Sellin, Disputatio de Origine Carminum, &c., 1892.
[2] See chap. v. p. 121.

from Babylon, or perhaps before the humiliation of that great Power had taken place.

So no doubt there are others referring to that time of suffering, and celebrating the glorious deliverance that followed; although it is remarkable that so few positive references are made to Babylon, as contrasted with the references to Egypt and the Exodus.

Of course, as opinions now go, such a date as we have spoken of would not be regarded as late. On the contrary, it would be comparatively early, and modern expositors find what they consider conclusive references to much later times. It must, however, be admitted as remarkable that the references are not so obvious as, for example, those we have alluded to. Even to the revolt of the Maccabees, if we admit that there are Maccabaean psalms in the Psalter, there are not many references, nor are these so precise as we might have expected to occur in sacred songs inspired by that memorable struggle. There are, no doubt, a few psalms which from a very early period have been regarded as relating to that time; and, as has been already said, there is nothing in the history of the Canon, as we now know it, to preclude the admission of such psalms into the collection. The psalms in question are: in the first rank, as bearing marks which have led many in former and modern times to declare them indubitably Maccabaean, Pss.

xliv., lxxiv., lxxix., lxxxiii. ; and, in a second rank, another four that closely resemble them in subject-matter—viz., lx., lxxx., lxxxv., cxxxii.

Although in these psalms, particularly in the four first mentioned, there are expressions and references which all admit would well suit the Maccabaean period, and which some maintain would suit no other period, yet it cannot be said that the references are of that precise, express kind which we have seen in an immediately post-exilian psalm; and there have been and still are writers who refuse to assign any of the psalms to the Maccabaean age. It comes finally to be a matter of detailed exegesis; and while a great deal depends upon the interpretation of individual expressions, or of the general tone of the psalm under consideration, the conclusion arrived at is also very much determined by the critic's estimate, in advance, of the capabilities and situations of the various historical periods to which the psalms are assigned, the facts being liable to be controlled by the bias of the critic.

We have seen, however, undoubted evidence of post-exilian psalmody, and have admitted the possibility of Maccabaean psalms being in the collection. Can we in a similar way fix an approximate date for its commencement?

Here again we are confronted with the task of exegesis of individual psalms. For there is the same absence, at this extremity, of such definite, precise mention of facts, places, or persons as would enable us to fix the actual dates. No doubt a number of interpreters recognise in certain details of the earlier psalms what they consider indubitable references to the life and circumstances of David; and no doubt others would admit that certain psalms *might* have been written by him. The mere fact, however, that prominent critics refuse, on internal grounds, to assign any psalms at all to David, indicates that the alleged proofs of Davidic authorship are not so cogent and irresistible as of themselves to set the matter at rest.

We are compelled, therefore, to abandon the shorter road and betake ourselves to a more circuitous one, in order to determine, if possible, how far back we may place the earliest compositions in the Psalter.

We have seen enough, at all events, to encourage and even compel us to look to pre-exilian times for such a commencement. For just as all the external evidence available pointed back to pre-exilian and even Davidic times for the beginning of sacred song, so our rapid survey of the Psalter itself suggests the same thing. We have seen one undoubted post-exilian psalm; but it stands well down in the collection, and there are good reasons for the conclusion that the earliest compositions will be near the beginning. Moreover, this post-exilian song seems to have been composed when the misery of the Exile was still fresh in memory. But the song, besides being far down in the collection, is a finished production, giving evidence of long practice in the art; and it even refers to the harps and songs of Zion as well known in exilian times. Accordingly, as we cannot suppose the art to have arisen in Babylon, we are shut up to the pre-exilian time for its commencement.

Of course it is only a presumption that we have, so far, reached, to the effect that psalmody such as the Psalter exhibits was practised in pre-exilian times, and that the earliest compositions will be found in the first part of the collection. Apart from the positive evidence on which it is based, the strength of the presumption may be estimated by the alternative that has to be faced—viz., that all pre-exilian psalmody has been lost, or, if there never was any, that the earliest attempts at a new and special kind of literary composition were of the most finished quality, as well as very considerable in quantity.

As for the attempt, on grounds of internal criticism, to determine with precision the occasions upon which the Psalms were composed, and to classify them into historical periods, however fascinating the exercise seems to be to many minds, I must frankly confess I have so little confidence in its success that I feel constrained to follow another line of proof. The actual historical references are confessedly so rare or so indecisive that in a great many cases we have to content ourselves with a conclusion of a general or negative kind, to the effect that such and such psalms *may* belong to such and such a period, or that there is nothing in the situation and contents of such and such others to forbid our assigning them to such and such a time. With regard to many psalms, probably, we shall be obliged to give up the attempt to determine their date altogether. It would manifestly be rash to assign such psalms as give no hint of their date to the period which, on subjective grounds, we consider most appropriate; for it is to be borne in mind that a psalm may have arisen in some period of which the historical books tell us little, and in circumstances which they have never mentioned. Summarily to say that a psalm belongs to a certain time, of which we happen to know the circumstances, is not legitimate, since it might, for all we know, be as suitable to a time of which we know comparatively little. Nay, though it may seem paradoxical, it may not be safe to assign a psalm to circumstances which it seems to suit best. I am speaking here of psalms which contain no indubitable positive references to historical events which might enable us to allocate them. There are many such in the Psalter; and, in dealing with compositions like these, which are general and germinal in their statements, we are to remember that a general truth is always receiving particular confirmation—always repeating itself in new circumstances—that a germinal truth is always finding fit and fitter illustrations as history goes on. No doubt many of those psalms, like all popular lyrics, would be sung often from time to time, and on every occasion be found suitable to the circumstances of those using them. In a sense it may be said that all great truths are prophetical; the more fundamental they are, the more will they find recurring illustration and exemplification as history is unfolded. Even on a much lower plane than that of prophecy, is it not the case that many of the common maxims or classical quotations which have become a world's property receive from time to time a fuller meaning, and more striking applicability, than attached to them when they were first employed?

In view, therefore, of the admitted want of positive historical references in the psalms themselves, and at the same time resting upon the presumptive historical evidence before us, we may proceed to an inquiry as to whether there is room in pre-exilian history and religion for compositions such as lie before us in the Psalter. Here will arise such questions as, whether in that period there is proof of such literary and poetic attainment as would make psalm-composition possible, whether there were circumstances that would furnish a stimulus to such composition, and whether the historical situations, the religious sentiments, spiritual attainments and aspirations of the period, were likely to find reflection or embodiment in the psalms.

The object is not to prove that all the psalms are pre-exilian. There will not even be an attempt to begin with a limited number of psalms for which a pre-exilian date may be claimed. But the endeavour will be made to discover what the early times were capable of furnishing, in the way of lyric poetry and of religious sentiment expressed in lyric form. Should it be found, on this line of inquiry, that there is *room* in pre-exilian times for such compositions, especially as are contained in parts of the Psalter that are presumably of earliest date, it will then be open to those who feel competent to the task to assign, on critical grounds, various psalms to specific times and circumstances.

CHAPTER VII.

POETRY IN PRE-EXILIAN TIMES.

WE come now to consider the question whether the pre-exilian period affords sufficient room and occasion for the production of such compositions as the Psalms. Let us, first of all, recall the presumption at which we arrived on the grounds of external evidence—viz., that we are entitled, and even required, to look to this period for the beginnings of the psalmody which meets us in full operation in the early post-exilian period. The return from the Captivity of official "singers" in considerable numbers, the provision made for their support and the grant of immunities to them along with other sacred officials, the express mention of solemn liturgical music at the laying of the foundations of the Second Temple, not to speak of the proof of its existence in full operation at the time the Chronicler wrote, the graphic reference to the harps on the willow-trees in the time of the Captivity, and to the incongruity of singing the Lord's song in a foreign land,—all these amount to a mass of very strong presumptive evidence, that the practice of psalmody was well developed in pre-exilian times.

In the next place, let us consider what in the circumstances we may expect to find. We need not, for example, look for another psalter, or formal collection, larger or smaller, similar to the collection before us. Into this collection have evidently been gathered a very varied number of sacred songs belonging, on any reasonable hypothesis as to their origin, to different times. So that, if we leave the supposition open that psalm-composition began in pre-exilian times, it will not be surprising if the whole, or the most of this class of literature, should be embodied in the one collection.

There are, indeed, in some of the pre-exilian prophetical books, compositions of a hymnic and even of a liturgical and musical kind. And these to an unprejudiced mind would be evident proof that this kind of composition was in exercise before the Exile. Thus, for example, the 18th Psalm is found, slightly varied, in the book of Samuel (2 Sam. xxii.), which also contains the song of Hannah (1 Sam. ii. 1-10). In addition to which it may here suffice to mention the song of Hezekiah (Isa. xxxviii. 9-20), and the prayer of Habakkuk (Hab. iii.), which have all the characteristics of psalms, to say nothing of other hymnic passages found up and down the prophetical books. Unfortunately the advocates of the post-exilian origin of the Psalter object to our citing such passages as evidence, maintaining that they have been interpolated into the prophetical books at a later time, when psalm-composition was in vogue. Unfortunately, I say, not for those who believe that the prophetic writers were capable of producing such psalms, for the exception that is taken to them is entirely of a subjective kind, but unfortunately for the theory of the post-exilian origin of the Psalter, because, in addition to the objections urged in the preceding chapter, suspicion cannot fail to arise when, at a crucial point of evidence, the theory of interpolation should need to be resorted to in order to evade the force of a very strong objection. We must therefore allow these hymnic pieces to stand as authentic parts of the books in which they occur, until better proof of their interpolation is produced than the fact that they are inconvenient for a theory.

Instead of beginning, however, with a comparison of single pieces such as these are (although the comparison is very interesting and very instructive), let us fall back upon our more general line of investigation. The evidential value of these pieces will appear as we proceed.

The three main lines of inquiry suggested by all that has preceded are these :—

I. Whether, in pre-exilian times, the poetic

faculty was so well cultivated that lyrics like those of the Psalter were possible.

II. Whether the pre-exilian period furnishes occasions sufficiently varied and sufficiently outstanding to explain national and social references in the Psalms.

III. Whether, in pre-exilian times, the religious consciousness had attained a development sufficient to produce religious lyrics like the Psalms.

In the present chapter we shall confine ourselves to the first of these questions; and, first of all, we would draw attention to the favourable position in which the people of Israel were placed for the cultivation of poetry, and the abundant evidence we have that the poetic faculty among them was very strong, and that it was actively cultivated from a very early time.

No country in the world presents the variety of scenery and productions to be seen in Palestine. The snows of Lebanon and the tropical heat of the Jordan valley; gushing streams in winter, parched plains in summer; cloudless and rainless skies for many months, thunder, lightning, and tempest in others—these are the normal features of its climate. Waving fields of grain on deep alluvial soil in one place, clinging vines on stony hillsides in another, the cedar and the palm, the oak, the walnut, and the pine, with the fruit-trees of the torrid zone, all find their appropriate soil and air; the shaggy bear hides in the mountain fastnesses, and tropical birds of rare plumage flit about in the groves of Jericho; almost every conceivable contrast, almost endless variety, are characteristic of the country. The very face of the land seems to spread out in rhythmical undulations of height and hollow; the seasons succeed one another in marked alternation. And yet the country is so limited in extent that from the tops of the mountain-peaks one can see almost to one or other extremity of its length, and frequently from one extremity to the other of its breadth.

What a wealth of language and of imagery must such a country have suggested! And, poor as its vocabulary is in some respects, few languages show greater variety of nomenclature for natural objects than Hebrew. And it is evident that from the smallness of the country, and the compression of so many contrasts within the limits of a few degrees of latitude, an immense variety of terms to denote natural objects would enrich the stock of the common language, and furnish material for the exuberance of metaphor which is so observable in its poetry and even in its prose. Where the face of nature was so diversified there was not only the most pleasing stimulus to the imagination, but there was every aid to the expression of mental activity in the terms of physical phenomena. Language in its very formative processes was suffused with poetic feeling. Nowhere was there monotony in the landscape. Every feature was confronted with its antithesis, so that as the imagination was kept ever on the alert, the materials were at hand to supply forms in which the changing mood might express itself. Every torrent as it made its wild music in the storm harmonised with and quickened the perturbed spirit of the poet; every mountain and hill not only fed the feelings of awe and wonder, but suggested the ideas of strength, defence, security. The shadow of a great rock in the sun-beaten expanse, the miry clay of the alluvial plain, the bleak barren land in which was no water, the shady ravines in the mountain defiles, the repose of the widespreading tree, the quiet of the homestead at evening, alternating so rapidly under the eye of the wayfarer, kept pace with the rush and play of inner thoughts and feelings, and at the same time nourished these thoughts and feelings and formed a spiritual education. And if we should find poetry thus lying at the very root of a language, in rich, varied, and suitable metaphor, we may conclude that there is a strong and true poetic instinct in the people employing it, and that they have led a long course of national life in close observance of nature's phenomena and in loving sympathy with nature's movements.

Now this is what the Hebrew language does exhibit. The distinction between poetry and prose here is shadowy, just because the language is poetical from the first; and it is this metaphorical element that enables the language with its restricted vocabulary to express ideas of the most varied description and of the most delicate kind. Words denoting the most ordinary acts, or phases of the most common life, are transferred to the expression of the variety of mood of the inner life; so that wherever the Bible goes, in whatever tongue, it speaks to human hearts the same language. To walk, to sit, to stand, to eat, to drink, to rise, to fall,—almost every movement or gesture of the body is made to denote, by the most patent transition, a corresponding phase of the mind or fluctuation of the spirit; and poetry is the handmaid of theology. Says Isaac Taylor : [1]

> Those who choose to do so may employ their time in inquiring in what other modes than those which are characteristic of the Hebrew Scriptures the highest truths in theology might be embodied, and whether the principles may not be, or might not have been, subjected to the conditions of abstract generalisation, and so brought into order within the limits of a logical and scientific arrangement. Let these philosophic divisions be pursued at leisure until they reach a result which might be reported of and accepted. Meantime it is enough for us to know that no such result has hitherto ever rewarded the labour, either of Oriental sages or of Grecian philosophers, or of the Alexandrian teachers, or of mediæval doctors, or of the great thinkers of

---

[1] Spirit of the Hebrew Poetry, pp. 4, 5. Comp. p. 6 and p. 11.

the sixteenth century, or of those of the times in which we live. Metaphysic theologies, except so far as they take up the very terms and figures of the Hebrew Scriptures, have hitherto shown a properly religious aspect in proportion as they have been unintelligible: when intelligible, they become, if not atheistic, yet tending in that direction. When this is affirmed, the inference is not—that a true theology might not be embodied in abstract terms in an upper world; but this, that the terms and the modes of human reason are and must ever be insufficient for purposes of this kind.

There was, therefore, we may take it, a strong and true poetic instinct in the Hebrew people, and there was a powerful stimulus in nature around them towards the expression of the instinct in song. And though, for reasons that are well known, there are comparatively few remains of what may be called secular poetry, or the poetry of nature, yet there are more evidences of its existence than superficial readers readily perceive. In the earlier historical books, relating to times when the people were passing from the half-settled condition, we have pictures here and there of the festive gatherings, with song and dance, which evidently made up a great part of their common life. The daughters of Shiloh had a yearly feast at a place on the north side of Bethel; and it was while engaged in the dance that they were surprised by the rude wooers of the tribe of Benjamin (Judges xxi. 19-24). The men of Shechem, in the time of Abimelech, went out into the fields, and gathered the vineyards, and trod the grapes, and made merry (Judges ix. 27); and the song of the vintage (Isa. xvi. 10) and the joy of harvest (Isa. ix. 3) were household words. Nabal at his sheep-shearing (1 Sam. xxv.), Samson at his marriage (Judges xiv.), the shepherds and warriors at the wells at eventide (Judges v. 11), all sing and make merry; and prophets speak of it as a regular thing that the harp and the lute, the tabret and the flute (Isa. v. 12), with other instruments of music (Amos vi. 5), were used at feasts. So also naturally, poetry having found its voice in song, any stirring event gave it fresh and larger utterance. The finding of a well is celebrated in a lilt in its praise (Num. xxi. 17), warlike exploits of which we have no historical record are commemorated in snatches of old song (Num. xxi. 27-30). Samson sings his exploit performed with the jawbone of an ass (Judges xv. 16). The women of Israel celebrate David's triumph over Goliath (1 Sam. xviii. 7); the victory of the ever-memorable day of Bethhoron is embalmed in the song of which we have still a fragment (Josh. x. 12); and at full length we have, in the song of Deborah, the recital of the great achievement with which her name is associated (Judges v.)

In sorrow, also, as well as in joy, did the poetic instinct find vent for itself in song. The maidens of Gilead lamented over Jephthah's daughter (Judges

xi. 40); David composed an elegy on Saul and Jonathan (2 Sam. i.), and a lament over brave Abner so foully slain (2 Sam. iii. 34).

These are but instances, most of them only incidentally mentioned, which go to prove that the poetic spirit found ready and habitual utterance in face of the more ordinary and common incidents of life. Moreover, from several of these references, and from other indications which have been already noticed,[1] we may perceive that the cultivation of music as an art or profession was an early thing in the history. Barzillai, we have seen, speaks of singing men and singing women at David's court (2 Sam. xix. 35), and though uttered at a late time, Jeremiah's words (Jer. ix. 17) plainly refer to an old-established custom, when he speaks of the "wise women" skilled in making a lamentation.

The funeral dirge, in fact, seems to have been committed specially to a professional class of singers —a custom of which there remain survivals among the people of the East to the present day;[2] and the very form in which the "lament" was cast (the *Qîna*) is found in certain elegiac pieces incorporated in the historical and prophetical books. It is referred to as early as Amos (Amos v. 1) as a

---

[1] See chap. v. p. 107.

[2] Budde has a very interesting paper on this subject, entitled "Das hebräische Klagelied," in ZATW for 1882.

well-known thing among the people of his day, and he gives us a specimen, though brief, cast in the very form in which we find the chapters of the book of Lamentations :—

"The virgin of Israel is fallen, no more to rise;
She is cast down upon her land, with none to raise her up."

Now if we turn to the Psalms we shall perceive in them all the elements and characteristics of the best Hebrew poetry. The Psalter is not, indeed, an anthology, covering the whole field of the manifold daily life which, as we have seen, furnished materials of song. Some subjects, common in national popular lyrics, are conspicuous by their absence. Others appear but in an incidental or subordinate manner. The whole collection has a specific distinctive religious tone, and of that we shall have to speak at length by-and-by. In the meantime the fact to be emphasised is that, as literary and poetic compositions, the Psalms exhibit the features, and almost exclusively the features, which are found elsewhere and even early in Hebrew poetic literature.

One essential feature of Hebrew poetry which has been already referred to—the metaphorical use of language—is strikingly conspicuous in the Psalms. Though found throughout the whole Hebrew Scriptures, as has been said, it is more abundant in the Psalms, for the very simple reason that these compositions, being the lyrical expression of the inner thoughts and feelings of the psalmist, make a demand upon the resources of metaphor which is unnecessary in the simple narratives of prose, and is not even so imperative in many of the prophetical books, although it is found even in these, as soon as the writer enters the domain of inner experience and has to express spiritual ideas. But so much are the psalmists occupied with just such ideas, that we have only to open the Psalter at any page in order to find illustrations. The very first psalm not only presents us with the striking comparisons of the righteous to the tree planted by the channels of water, and of the wicked to the chaff before the wind; but employs the best chosen though simplest metaphors—*walking, standing, sitting*—to express the various grades of conformity to evil. Throughout the Psalms it is the same: however delicate the shade of feeling to be expressed, it is swiftly and impressively brought out in a metaphor, easy of comprehension but full of meaning. However varied the experience, there is a suitable figure to denote it. At one time the psalmist stumbles and slips, his feet are almost gone; at another time he has his steps enlarged under him and stands in an even place. Now he sinks in miry clay, anon he is planted firmly on a rock At one time his God turns His face from him, at another He lifts the light of His countenance upon him. Again, his enemies tread down his life and lay his glory in the dust; but soon they are smitten, their arm broken, their teeth shattered. Insidious foes dig a pit or spread a net to entangle the innocent; but they fall into their own ditch, or are discomfited with the slings and snares of an avenging God. What could be more expressive than the care of God depicted (for it is a picture) as holding the saint by the hand, or guiding him with His eye? What more pathetic than the suppliant surrounded by floods of ungodliness, or being poured out like water? If oppression is brought to an end, it is bonds that are broken; joy is a lightening of the eyes; and the soul is bowed down in grief. The highest earthly good is to eat and drink at God's table, and final bliss is to behold His face.

Now it is to be remembered that the metaphors, so abundant in the Psalms, are precisely of the same kind as those employed in the other literature, and that they are borrowed from nature in all its vicissitudes, from the scenery of Palestine in all its variety, or based upon the occupations and experiences of a life as diversified as the historical books show the life of pre-exilian Israel to have been. We have but to suppose the attempt made to remove the whole of this rich store of metaphor from the language in order to realise how closely it is woven into the texture of thought, and therefore how necessary it is to postulate a long life for its development and cultivation. One would never expect a small colony of Jews, who had no antecedent poetic training, who were busy with the hard task of effecting a settlement in Judæa after the Exile, and at best absorbed in the ritual observances of the restored Temple, suddenly to burst into song as varied in its dress as the whole face of the country from Dan to Beersheba, and employing in its imagery a stock of metaphor drawn from long observation of nature and its phenomena. Even if it were proved that the existing psalms as they lie before us were all composed after the Exile, we should be forced to conclude also that poetic language, and the metaphorical use of language for the expression of spiritual thoughts, were long practised before they could be handled so deftly and enter so fully into literature.

It has been already observed that this metaphorical element, lying at the formative root of the language, is as striking in a translation as in the original, so that the Hebrew poetry is in its essence poetical in any tongue. It has now to be pointed out, moreover, that the same thing is true also of the *form* in which the Hebrew poetry is cast. It is well known that much of the ancient poetry of other nations loses a very great part of its beauty in passing into another tongue; so that some of the productions most highly prized in the original are flatter than ordinary prose when rendered faithfully in a translation, just because the features on which the charm of the original depends are peculiar to the original language and form. On the other hand, the distinguishing feature of the Hebrew poetry is not rhyme or assonance—which disappear in a translation or can only be preserved by art and effort—but the rhythmical balancing of parts, or parallelism of the thought,—a feature that only becomes the more striking the more faithfully the words are translated. This is the whole explanation of the fact, which often causes an expression of surprise, that the Psalms, for example, though highly poetical, exhibit their poetical character more vividly in a prose than in a metrical translation. It is simply because the prose version is more faithful to the original, transferring all the charm on which the original depended, without sacrificing anything to the exigencies of a new language and a strict metrical form. This feature of the poetry, whereby one member of a verse stands over against another by resemblance or by contrast, the parallelism being balanced often in minutest details, is so outstanding that even the reader of a translation can scarcely fail to notice it, and to conform his reading to it, for it is the natural expression of the sense. And the Revised Version, by printing the parallel members in separate lines, has made manifest even to the eye the fact that the Psalms are all in poetry. *E.g.*—

"Blessed is the man that walketh not in the counsel of the wicked,
Nor standeth in the way of sinners,
Nor sitteth in the seat of the scornful.
But his delight is in the law of the Lord;
And in his law doth he meditate day and night."
—Ps. i.

Or—

"The heavens declare the glory of God;
And the firmament sheweth His handywork," &c.

And—

"The law of the Lord is perfect, restoring the soul:
The testimony of the Lord is sure, making wise the simple," &c.
—Ps. xix.

Or—

"O Lord, rebuke me not in Thy wrath:
Neither chasten me in Thy hot displeasure," &c.
—Ps. xxxviii.

This feature is not confined to the Psalms. The Revised Version has printed also the books of Job, Proverbs, and Lamentations in parallel lines; for they are all composed in the same formal style. Here and there also, where songs occur in the historical books, they have been exhibited in the same manner. Thus, *e.g.*—

"Adah and Zillah, hear my voice;
Ye wives of Lamech, hearken unto my speech:
For I have slain a man for wounding me,
And a young man for bruising me:
If Cain shall be avenged sevenfold,
Truly Lamech seventy and sevenfold."
—Gen. iv. 23, 24.

162　POETRY IN PRE-EXILIAN TIMES.

And, even where it is not so represented to the eye, it manifests itself to the ear throughout the prophetical Scriptures, whenever these take a loftier flight :—

> "Violence shall no more be heard in thy land,
> Desolation nor destruction within thy borders;
> But thou shalt call thy walls Salvation,
> And thy gates Praise.
> The sun shall be no more thy light by day;
> Neither for brightness shall the moon give light unto thee:
> But the Lord shall be unto thee an everlasting light,
> And thy God thy glory."
> —Isa. lx. 18, 19.

Even the simple prose of the Hebrew narrative books tends to run into a balance of clauses and a rhythmical march, as if music were engrained in the very language. And at all events the snatches of old song preserved, it is believed, as the very earliest remains of Hebrew composition, show that the form, which gives its distinguishing beauty to the very highest specimens of literary art, was well marked as a characteristic from the very first.[1]

We have seen enough, therefore, to warrant the conclusion that, so far as poetic spirit and poetic expression go, there was abundant room in the very earliest antiquity for compositions of the literary standard of the Psalms. We find a language satu-

---

[1] The English reader is in a position to observe these, for example, in the books of Genesis and Numbers, as they are printed in parallel lines in the Revised Version. See Gen. ix. 25-27, xxv. 23, xlix. 2-27; Num. vi. 24-26, xxi. 14, 15, 17, 18, 27-30, &c.

rated with poetry, not indeed tricked out in gaudy artificial finery, but blooming with the flowers of artless metaphor fresh from the fields of nature, and a rhythm as finely measured as "the rapid stroke of alternate wings,—the heaving and sinking as of the troubled heart."[1] And we have a people revelling in music and song, now shouting in the vintage, now wailing by the bier, bursting into singing on every occasion when the heart is full, making the earth ring again with their piping and dancing.

Now a most important question arises at this point, and it is this—How came a people like this, a people in these circumstances, to assign precisely to David the very highest place in music and song? They had been singing and playing long before his day. The water of the Red Sea was scarcely dry on their sandals when Miriam and all the women went out with timbrels and with dances and raised the song, and a religious song too :—

"Sing ye to the Lord, for He hath triumphed gloriously;
The horse and his rider hath He thrown into the sea."
—Exod. xv. 20, 21.

They had been singing ever since, and the song of Deborah, for instance (Judges v.), is a highly finished composition. Nor perhaps would any one say that the so-called "secular" pieces, which are all that a grudging criticism would allow to be genuine

[1] Dean Stanley, Jewish Church, Lecture xxv.

Davidic poetry, his elegies on Saul and Jonathan (2 Sam. i. 19-27) and on Abner (2 Sam. iii. 33, 34), are on a higher level than other lyrics that have been preserved to us. Why then does David hold this peerless place among the singers of Israel?

The question needs to be pressed, because there seems to be a tendency to depreciate the position of David to such a degree that nothing is left by which to account for the tradition to which we are referring. That David was a musician no one denies; but this is almost the full extent of the admission in some quarters. Robertson Smith even goes the length of saying [1] that though David might have been a musician, it may appear doubtful whether the oldest story of his life set him forth as a psalmist at all. The Hebrew writers, however, whether early or late, were well aware of what their nation had achieved in the field of music and song; and yet, with wonderful unanimity, they assigned to David an altogether unique position in regard to both.

The only sufficient explanation of the fact that a musical people has given to David this distinction is that he brought music to higher perfection and applied it as it had not been applied before to the highest end, the service of praise. Prof. Cheyne, who "would not for a moment disparage the truly

---

[1] Old Testament in the Jewish Church, chap. vii.

ASCRIPTION OF PSALMODY TO DAVID. 165

noble qualities"[1] of David, cannot withhold the admission that though "his posthumous fame rested chiefly upon his secular poetry, we need not assume that all his compositions had a non-religious character."[2] But then, although he will not allow that a single word of this religious poetry has been preserved, so that we might be able to say what it was like, he goes on to make a comparison of the Hebrew *tehillah* or praise, to the *tahlîl* or shouting of the Arabs at the pilgrimage, and says of the original "singing" in the Temple, that "only by slow degrees did it rise from a shouting like that of the vintage or of the bridal night" (Judges ix. 27 ; Lev. xix. 24 ; Ps. lxxviii. 63).[3] Nay, it is not only the *primitive* Temple music that was so poor. Pre-exilian song in the mass, Professor Cheyne[4] asserts, was so rough that "as late as the fall of Jerusalem, the noise of the Chaldean soldiery in the Temple is likened to that made by the worshippers on a feast-day (Lam. ii. 7)." And "all the evidence goes to show that throughout the pre-exile period the service of religious song was not committed to any special class, but was the privilege of the congregation at large." The texts which are cited in support of this statement (2 Sam. vi. 5 ; Amos v. 21-23 ; Isa. xxx. 29) certainly go to indicate that the people as a whole took part

---

[1] Origin of the Psalter, p. 211.
[2] Ibid., p. 192.
[3] Ibid., p. 460.
[4] Ibid., p. 194.

in the musical service; but surely Professor Cheyne would not have us suppose that when "David and all the house of Israel played before the Lord on all manner of instruments—with harps and with psalteries and with timbrels, and with castanets and with cymbals" (2 Sam. vi. 5), each person played his own tune, and that they did not wait for a leader to strike up the music nor even for the king to give out the hymn. The mere mention of so many instruments in such a connection implies that there was a systematic cultivation of sacred music. Even the modern minstrelsy of the East, whatever we may say of its quality, is not produced without systematic training, and in the rendering of the popular songs there are recognised professional leaders.[1]

As to the rudeness of the pre-exilian music, it is doubtful whether even the music of the Second Temple would have sounded "polished" to Western and modern ears. In this, as in many other things, the Oriental has a very different standard from our own. Since we have never heard the music of the First Temple, however, perhaps the less we say of it the better. That it was hearty, Professor Cheyne himself proves; that it was the best the people of the time had to offer there can be no doubt. If it was at all as good as their poetry, it needs neither

[1] See the interesting details, furnished by Wetzstein, in Budde's paper, "Das hebräische Klagelied," ZATW, 1882, p. 26.

QUALITY OF PRE-EXILIAN MUSIC. 167

eulogy nor apology. As to the comparison with the Arabs, there are certain circumstances which show how far the cases are from being parallel. We know, for example, that they cultivated lyric poetry to a considerable degree even in pre-Islamic times, so that we cannot take the *tahlîl* as a standard of their early musical and poetical attainment. Moreover, though they preserve the *talbiyah* in all its primitive rudeness in connection with the pilgrimage celebrations, they have never, to the present day, employed music in their regular public worship. All this, however, does not touch the main point for which we are here contending—viz., that though the people had, ever since they entered Canaan, been singing those vintage and bridal songs which we are told were the prototype of the original Temple music, yet for some unaccountable reason they have conspired to celebrate one who was antecedent even to this rude music as peculiarly "pleasant in the psalms of Israel" (2 Sam. xxiii. 1).

Again, therefore, our train of reasoning brings us back to David. There is no ascription to him of the *origin* of music and song, for these go back into the mists of antiquity. But a people nurtured on music and song have assigned to David a unique place in this regard. The only feasible explanation is that he cultivated and adapted these attainments in such a way as to ennoble and purify the national life. He was a psalmist, and the first and greatest psalmist. The suggestion is worth considering, whether the services of David to his nation and to posterity were not analogous to those of which we have examples both in secular and sacred poetry among ourselves. Students of Burns know that many of the most popular songs which we all delight to call his were adaptations by him of words to old tunes, which either had no words associated with them, or were wedded to words entirely unfit for popular use. A closer parallel is afforded by the case of the Scottish Reformers who, " grudging the devil all the best music," rescued many of the popular and ineradicable national melodies from their association with profane and licentious songs and adapted to them sacred words, thus turning "idle songs" into psalms and hymns.[1] In claiming for David, however, this high place in national sacred song, it is not to be understood that by some sudden and violent wrench a separation between secular and sacred took place. The distinction which we usually draw here was by no means so clearly marked in Hebrew literature as it is in the different classes of modern poetry. It would seem indeed as if, among the Hebrews, all the

---

[1] " Ane Compendious Booke, of Godly and Spirituall Songs. Collectit out of sundrie partes of the Scripture, with sundrie of other Ballates changed out of prophaine sanges, for avoiding of sinne and harlotrie : " reprinted by Andro Hart, 1621, from "the first originall Copie." See additional note at the end of this chapter, p. 173.

usual channels of ordinary song had been flooded with the waves of religious feeling, so that the distinction of sacred and secular was almost obliterated. Not only is there a marked absence of grosser themes which are found so generally in earlier popular poetry, but even the innocent themes of social life and experience are treated from a religious point of view, and everything that we include in the broad designation of sentiment is tinged with religion. An Eastern proverb has it that "love of country is religion"; and among the Hebrews, instead of a sharp line being drawn between sacred and profane, the domain of the sacred was made to extend to the whole of life. So, too, as to form, melody, and musical accompaniment, there would seem to be little or no distinction between the songs prompted by natural phenomena or national or social events, and those inspired by the highest religious emotions. David brings up the ark from the house of Obed-edom with gladness, and dances before the Lord with all his might; and he justifies his conduct in words full at once of reverence for his God, and of scorn for his passionless wife (2 Sam. vi. 12 ff.) So in one of the most magnificent of the Psalms—a production so overcharged with imagery that we can scarcely follow its meaning—in connection with the goings of God in the sanctuary, we have a representation of the singers going before, the players on instruments following after, among them the damsels playing with timbrels (Ps. lxviii. 24 ff.) So, again, the prophets set forth the joy connected with God's manifested glory as showing itself in the forms of festive gladness: "Ye shall have a song as in the night when a feast is kept; and gladness of heart, as when one goeth with a pipe to come into the mountain of the Lord, to the mighty One of Israel" (Isa. xxx. 29). "Again I will build thee, and thou shalt be built, O virgin of Israel: thou shalt again be adorned with thy tabrets, and shalt go forth in the dances of them that make merry" (Jer. xxxi. 4).

It is now generally believed that we can detect a link connecting secular and sacred song in the inscriptions to those psalms which have directions for musical accompaniment or indications of the melody to which they were to be sung.[1] There seems no doubt that, obscure as these headings often are, they relate to popular airs, whose words have not been preserved, and to modes of music which formed the types after which the liturgical music was modelled. These enigmatical headings are found for the most part towards the beginning of the Psalter, and in the great majority of cases are attached to psalms which are inscribed "to David." If he did no more than originate the custom of transfiguring popular

---

[1] See, *e.g.*, in the R.V. the headings of Psalms ix., xxii., xlv., liii., lvi., lvii., lviii., lix., lx., lxix., lxxv., lxxx.

airs into sacred lyrics, it would be enough to account for the fame which tradition has assigned him. For henceforward the literature of the nation was enriched with a new class of composition without being robbed of the pleasure of old association attaching to the familiar cadences of the popular music. Here also perhaps, as in the parallel cases that have been mentioned, we may see how the old and the new would be blended so intimately that their separation is now all but impossible.

It is, however, worthy of particular notice that the religious element, though it predominated, did not obliterate the lower elements of poetical stimulus. Eichhorn, in writing,[1] more than a century ago, on Eastern poetry, gives as one reason for the inferiority of Syriac poetry to either the Hebrew or Arabic, the constraint imposed on the poets by the themes they treated, which were for the most part the doctrines of the Christian religion or the aberrations of heretics. The contrast, indeed, with the Hebrew lyrics is here very complete. The psalmists were not Jewish ecclesiastical versifiers. There is no indication as yet of such a preoccupation with the Law or the ritual as became characteristic of the later Judaism—an argument in itself that psalmody did not arise in the post-exilian legalistic Church. The Hebrew poet did not cease, because of his

[1] In his Preface to Sir William Jones's 'Poeseos Asiaticæ commentariorum libri sex.' Lipsiæ, 1777.

religious inspiration, to have a keen observation and lively appreciation of natural phenomena; nor, because he was lifted to a higher air, did he become indifferent to facts on the lower plane of daily life. His poetic instinct kept him in full sympathy with all that poetry loves to dwell on, and adorned his verse with the unadorned beauties of the choicest lyric. At the same time, however, his religious instinct kept him from losing himself in nature or boastfully exalting his nation: his faith never wavered in an unseen, omnipotent, all-ruling God, the God of nature, the God of his nation, the God of the world. So that whether the singer looked to the starry heavens, or contemplated the earth and its fulness, or sang of the quiet resting-places and domestic peace of the families of Israel, all was viewed in the light of a universal Providence, to whose power nothing was too great to be beyond control, to whose watchfulness nothing was too minute for observation. That wonderful psalm of nature (Ps. civ.), which goes the round of all the observed processes of nature as well as the employments and sufferings of men, is a psalm in praise of God from beginning to end, although it is strictly true in its delineations of outward phenomena, and warmly sympathetic with human vicissitudes. In a word, all the richness of imagery which the language had acquired, the variety of metaphor which it had elaborated, the storehouse of poetic feeling and expression which it had accumulated, are poured out as an offering to God, whose character is symbolised in the fairest of His works. The highest function of the sacred poet was to summon men to " Rejoice in the Lord " : " The Lord reigneth, let the earth be glad." " Let every thing that hath being praise the Lord."

The edition of the 'Compendious Buik' believed to have been published in 1567 is the earliest of which a copy is known to be still extant. A reprint of it, for the Scottish Text Society, has been recently edited, with Introduction and Notes, by Professor Mitchell of St Andrews. In the Introduction are given most interesting historical notices of the spiritualising of secular songs and the appropriation of their tunes. The practice prevailed not only in the sixteenth but also in the two preceding centuries, to say nothing of more modern times; and in the 'Ecclesiastical History of Theodoret' it is stated that Ephrem Syrus also adapted to a spiritual sense the secular and profane songs of Harmonius.

CHAPTER VIII.

THE NATIONAL ELEMENT IN THE PSALMS.

HITHERTO we have been speaking primarily of the literary form and poetic spirit which characterise the Psalter as a whole. We now proceed to look a little more closely at the substance and subjects of the Psalms, as distinct from the form; for here, along with the pervading poetic spirit common to all of them, and even along with a certain agreement in the tone and point of view, there is found to be a great variety of detail. Some, it is evident at the first glance, are of a more objective character than others, treating rather of national than of individual interests, addressed, apparently, rather to the ear of the people than sung for the delectation or relief of the singer himself. The themes, however, may be said to be as varied as the experiences of human life. Sometimes it is a picture of domestic quiet that the psalmist sketches in miniature compass but in clear graphic lines (Ps. cxxvii.), at other times we hear the clash of arms and the shouts of the battle (lxxvi.), and still again the low moaning of a soul in secret pain (xxxviii.)

The classification of the Psalms, however, according to their subjects, has never been found satisfactory,—and this chiefly for the obvious reason that the distinguishing quality of such lyrical compositions is rather internal and reflective than descriptive or topical. Hupfeld attempts [1] a somewhat exhaustive, but at the same time artificial, subdivision under two main heads:—

A. Of God and divine things generally (without reference to special personal or national circumstances).

B. Application of the general conception of God and His kingdom to special relations and situations.

But even these broad distinctions do not hold (to say nothing of his detailed subdivisions), for in almost all the hymns which he places in class A (*e.g.*, viii., ciii., civ.), the glory of God is always presented with reference to Israel His people.

Somewhat more satisfactory is Hengstenberg's division, which proceeds upon the varying *tone* of the psalmist's mind as exhibited in different classes of psalms. Thus:—

(1) Psalms proceeding from a *joyous* frame of

[1] Hupfeld, Die Psalmen, Einleitende Untersuchungen, i. § 1.

mind: expressing praise of God, His majesty, grace, and goodness. Such are Pss. viii., xviii., xix., xxiii., xxix., xlvi., &c.

(2) Psalms proceeding from a *sad* or depressed mind. Laments, confessions, supplications, in view of persecutions, afflictions, or misfortunes. As vi., xxxii., xxxviii., li., lxix., lxxiv., lxxix., lxxx., lxxxiii., cii., &c.

(3) Psalms of a *reflective* tone. Religious, moral, didactic psalms. As i., xv., xlix., l., lxxiii., cxix., cxxxix., &c.

Other attempts at classification are of a more general kind, as, *e.g.*—

Creation or Nature psalms;
Historical and national psalms, including kingly and Jerusalem psalms;
Psalms in praise of the Law;
Psalms in prophetical tone;
Speculative, reflective psalms;
Personal, experimental (often plaintive) psalms,[1]—

and so forth. But the general remark may be made that, with the best possible classification of psalms according to their predominant elements, the classes fade away into one another, and even within the same psalm we find varying and suddenly contrasted features; the connections of

[1] See Driver, Introduction, chap. vii.

CLASSIFICATION OF PSALMS. 177

thought being subtle, and the transitions sudden, as is the case more or less in all lyrical compositions.

Though, therefore, we cannot arrange the Psalms into strictly defined classes, it is not difficult to distinguish certain dominant notes in the grand music of the whole. We may now, accordingly, turn our attention to some of the features which stand out prominently in certain of the psalms.

And first of all, it cannot escape notice that there is a well-marked national element in the Psalms. In ancient times generally, and among Oriental peoples in particular, the nation was more important than the individual; and in a certain sense it may be said that ancient Israel exhibited this tendency even more distinctly than others. A wonderful history, and the mysterious bond that united them to their God, impressed deeply on their consciousness, and kept for ever alive in their recollection, the conviction that Israel was one, just as Jehovah their God was one. This appears in all branches of their literature; and in the Psalms it is not wanting. How far the individual and his interests bulk in the Psalter we shall have to consider more fully by-and-by. In the meantime we draw attention to the fact that the nation and its fate were never lost sight of, and that at times the predominant considerations are entirely national; so that even though they are the

M

most subjective of the compositions of the Bible, the Psalms may still be described as a conspicuous part of the national Hebrew literature.

And the national element assumes various aspects:—

1. In some psalms the past history of the nation is dwelt upon, and several of these are among the longest and most elaborate compositions of the Psalter. What may have been the exciting cause and first occasion of these national songs we may not be able to tell in every case. It may have been that in a season of national misfortune the thoughts turned fondly back to the days of old, and the singer called to mind what God did to the fathers, making to Himself a glorious name by planting Israel in the possession of the heathen. Or it may have been a signal deliverance in his own day that suggested to the psalmist the culmination of all God's goodness to the nation, the assurance that He was the same God still. Nay, it may have been some secret trouble of his own that depressed him, and urged him to use arguments with himself and with his God for interposing on his behalf. The remark of Goethe is often quoted, that the best poetry is always *occasional*. But the term must be taken in a wide sense, to embrace the mood of the singer as well as his external surrounding. The harvest comes from the seed; but if the seed is sown at the wrong time, or falls upon unproductive soil,

the harvest will fail or be poor. If the best poetry is occasional, it is not too much to say that some of the worst poetry is that which is made to demand. Some of the finest lyrics whose origin we can trace have had a very slight moving *occasion*, but the occasion has found the poet *in the mood*. And all this should be borne in mind, lest we should attempt to tie down the poet to a set of circumstances and a precise time as depicted or referred to in the poem. In any case, the presence of these psalms, and the obvious relative importance they hold in the collection, show conclusively that the national history was matter of devout contemplation in the circle of the psalm-singers, and inferentially that it was the subject of reflection among the people at large.

The psalms in which this is the predominant theme are found with various headings, or without headings, in various parts of the Psalter,—an indication that the theme was not confined to one class, nor limited to one time.[1] Moreover, a comparison of these psalms will show how variously the past history was treated, according to the mood of the singer and the immediate purpose of his song. The same facts are dwelt upon, the same episodes recounted, but in the most contrasted tones: now

---

[1] Isaac Taylor ('Spirit of the Hebrew Poetry,' p. 149) classes here seventeen psalms — viz.: xliv., xlvi., lx., lxviii., lxxiv., lxxv., lxxvi., lxxviii., lxxix., lxxx., lxxxi., lxxxiii., lxxxv., cv., cvi., cxxvi., cxxxvii.

with a background of sadness and despondency, if the times are evil; now in jubilant notes, if the prospect is hopeful; and sometimes the different strains alternate or commingle in the same psalm. One note, however, is never found. There is no boasting of national greatness, no assumption of glory to themselves or to their forefathers for all that the past had to show of prosperity. "Not unto us, not unto us," is the burden of the song, whether it is joyous or sorrowful; and even when there is the nearest approach to a bare recital of events, the inference evidently suggested is, "had it not been the Lord that was on our side."

The question for us to consider is, whether there was such a stimulus to patriotic feeling, such a variety and excitement in the national history in pre-exilian times, as might have led to the production of psalmody of this kind; or whether we have evidence in the historical books of anything of the nature of patriotic song.

Let us reflect what was the geographical and political situation of pre-exilian Israel, and what was the nature of the national life that was led before the collapse of national independence took place. Here assuredly there was no dearth of themes for the poet; for though the boundaries of Israel were narrow and their dominion insignificant compared with those of the great world-powers, they were near enough to the great movements of the time to take notice of them, and sometimes were involved in them—to their cost. Besides, they had in their own domestic history such an amount of vicissitude as to keep thought on the alert, and to sway the susceptible mind with the alternations of hope and despondency, confidence and fear.

The national life of Israel was not idyllic, though their social and domestic life partook much of that character. Like other nations whose territory is circumscribed and yet varied, they had a history more stirring than that of empires of wide extent and world-dominion. Their earliest traditions went back to events which had moulded their own growth and have fashioned the course of the world's history. The deliverance from Egypt, the wanderings in the wilderness, the conquest of Canaan,—these never-forgotten episodes were of a kind first of all to consolidate national life, and then to inspire national song, and enkindle national faith and hope. A nation that has great events to look back upon is led to look forward to great events in the future; and these habits of retrospect and prospect give a powerful stimulus to the poetic spirit. We can understand, from the cases of other nations who have had similar early histories, how, a poetic people once finding voice in an outburst of patriotic song, the music would sound down through the ages and be caught up in increased volume as succeeding days brought new occasions. And this is what, in point of fact, we find in the history of Israel.

At the very beginning of their national history stood the great deliverance from Egypt, the sojourn in the desert, the occupation of the Promised Land. And at that very time the historians have placed the song of Miriam at the Red Sea :—

> "Sing unto the Lord, for He hath triumphed gloriously:
> The horse and his rider hath He thrown into the sea."

It is a national song, a religious song; the occasion was one to rouse the most prosaic mind to poetry, and it is in every respect most credible that such a song should have arisen at such a time. And not to speak in the meantime of the so-called song of Moses and the blessing of Moses found in the book of Deuteronomy (chapters xxxii., xxxiii.), we have again the song of Deborah (Judges v.), admitted to be fresh from the impress of the great victory which it celebrates, breathing at once the spirit of corporate national sentiment and that of exultant faith in the nation's God.

These were events that could never be forgotten, and they never were forgotten. The recollection of them was the very life-blood of the nation, keeping it alive in times of direst straits, leading it into careless security in times of over-prosperity,—ever nourished and purified by the salutary teaching of the prophets. But if such events were at first celebrated in song, did the music then suddenly die away, only to be revived in post-exilian times? Was there no one among a people who were ever singing on countless other themes, to sing these old songs as the centuries rolled on? And did the singing of them, on succeeding occasions when a great victory or a signal reverse recalled to mind the old days, never quicken the poetic faculty to imitation or emulation? Are we really to believe that songs like those which are found in the Psalter (such as Pss. lxxviii., cv., cvi.), which go back to those early times, and recount God's great deeds, were never once thought of till national independence was no more and a little colony was struggling for existence in Judæa? What, then, becomes of "occasional" poetry? Why, it is just by national songs that the remembrance of national events is usually kept alive; and even if it were proved that those psalms which recount the early episodes of the history are of late composition, we should almost be bound to assume that they had been preceded by earlier songs of a similar kind which are now lost. No; if the people and the national historians loved to revert to the "covenant" by which Israel was made a nation, we may be pretty sure that the poets of the nation also caught inspiration from these cherished traditions, and found themes for their song in the unparalleled events that cluster round the covenant.

And then comes the long period of the monarchy, with its glorious victories, its startling deliverances, the establishment of the Davidic house, the building of the Temple, the rupture of the kingdom, the opening up of a new world by commerce with distant lands, the wars waged with Moab and Edom, the entanglements with Damascus, the darkening of the great cloud of Assyrian invasion, the compression of the decadent State between the great contending forces of Egypt and Assyria, the collapse of the Jewish kingdom, the smouldering ruins of City and Temple. Was there no poet to sing on any one of all these themes? Pre-exilian psalmody was, forsooth, quite different from anything found in the Psalms. Then either all this exciting history, which roused the prophets into their grandest oratory, never touched the heart of a poet in Israel—its greatest deeds and sorrows remained unsung; or, equally incredible, while snatches of songs sung at the digging of a well, and the boastful words of Samson over the slaughter of some Philistines, have been preserved, all that was sung of the nation's wonderful experiences has not been thought worthy of preservation. Even the prophets may wax as eloquent as may be, so long as they speak in the prophetic strain; but they must not throw their thoughts into the form of a psalm: the psalm-pieces which are found in their writings having been inserted, we are asked to believe, at a later period, when the love of psalms had set in. If this be so, then the editors or redactors who inserted these hymnic pieces have given proof of a wonderful insight and sense of historical proportion. For they have placed these songs just at the points where we should have expected the poetic fire to blaze up: the song of Hannah at the birth of Samuel, the father of the long line of prophets; the last words of David, when the Davidic house was to enter upon its long and checkered career; the psalm of Hezekiah, when the might of the Assyrian was miraculously broken at Jerusalem; the psalm of Habakkuk, when the Chaldean empire, the last of the invaders of Judæa, was exulting in its strength. Granting to Israel any poetic talent at all, and looking over the wide field of the nation's history, we could not fix upon more appropriate times than these for the stirring of the spirit to religious patriotic song.

From this point of view, again, we can perceive a justification of the tradition which associates psalmody, in its specific character of national religious song, with David the King of Israel.

(*a*) In the first place, David appears just at the time when the prophetic activity takes shape in Samuel. The close connection of the last of the judges, as he may be called, with the first of the Davidic line, cannot be denied. And whatever name we may give to those associations of prophets who from Samuel's time onwards appear as a prominent feature in the religious history, we cannot refuse to assign to them a strong influence in the quickening of the national consciousness and the cultivation of the national life. That these prophets were enthusiasts no one denies; indeed so marked is their enthusiasm that it is now fashionable to speak of them as fanatics. That their enthusiasm found vent in music is only what might have been expected, and is, in fact, one of their most marked characteristics. But their enthusiasm must have had something to fasten upon,—their music must have been the expression of the feelings and ideas in their mind; and, judging by the succeeding developments of prophecy, we can be at no loss in determining what it was that stirred their feelings —the past history and the future anticipations of their nation. For the period of Samuel was unquestionably one of revived national feeling, and the setting up of the monarchy marked a turning-point in national history and national life.

Now when we hear over and over again of the prophetic bands appearing with music, at such an epoch when the heart of the nation might be said to be glowing with national enthusiasm, it does not seem strange that the rise of psalmody should be placed just at this period. David's close association with Samuel, his sojourn with the prophet, and the particular favour shown by him to the priests and the manifest devotion of the priests to him,—all these considerations, combined with his undoubted poetic gift, make it no wonder that psalm-composition should be dated from him, and that he, and no second ideal David, should be spoken of as the sweet singer of Israel.

(b) Further, it seems to be a matter beyond question that with David's accession a new stage is marked in the theocratic history of Israel. The prophecy given to him through Nathan does not rest upon nothing. Without assuming something of this kind we cannot explain the tenacity with which the nation clung to the Davidic house, and nourished the belief in its perpetuity till it took shape in the Messianic hope. That this was not a late conception is seen from the way in which even the earliest of the writing prophets refer to it as a matter well known and of fundamental significance. "In that day will I raise up the tabernacle of David that is fallen, and close up the breaches thereof; and I will raise up his ruins, and I will build it as in the days of old." These are the terms in which Amos (ix. 11) refers to the hope attached to the Davidic house. They afford a proof of the character and standing of David in the national estimation, and their force can only be broken by the arbitrary assertion that they are a later interpolation in the book of Amos.

Now if from David's time such a promise was

believed to attach to the Davidic line, it is not at all incredible that this promise, or rather the expectation of its fulfilment, should find expression in national sacred song. If the belief that David's house should abide, and enjoy God's special favour, and be the means of working out God's world-purposes, existed down through the monarchy, there is no need to say that late writers projected themselves back and spoke out of the soul of David. For David could first of all speak out of his own soul, and succeeding poets, as the expectation took firmer and firmer root, could expand and enlarge the conception; so that the kingly psalms may be the fruit of the monarchical period, and yet give foreshadowings of an everlasting kingdom which was ideal and future. And this leads us to consider another aspect of these national psalms.

2. A very characteristic group of these national psalms are those which "concern the king." There are not very many in this class, but they are very strongly marked. Isolated or occasional references to the king occur elsewhere, but there is a small number of psalms that may be described as exclusively kingly.[1] These are to be found in all parts of the Psalter; and they exhibit a highly ideal cast, of which we shall have to speak presently. It is, however, here to be observed that no king is mentioned by name except David—

[1] Pss. ii., xviii., xx., xxi., xlv., lxxii., cx. are the chief.

and "David and his seed" evidently stands for the divinely constituted monarchy. This, in fact, furnishes the key to the whole of this class of psalms. Just as the psalms that recall the past history have the covenant with the fathers for their pole, so the kingly psalms have respect to the promise given to David of a sure house; and as the covenant bound the people to Jehovah as His people, so the Davidic house was the representation and the hope of outward national independence.

This has often been taken as a proof that the psalms in question are much later than the time of the monarchy, and inspired by the spirit which is manifested, *e.g.*, in the books of Chronicles, in which exclusive regard is paid to the house of David, and the northern kingdom is treated as schismatic. It is, however, to be borne in mind that the same view is taken in the books of Kings, and that the prophets also regarded the house of David as pre-eminent. Not only do we see prophetic men appearing at the time of the schism and emphasising the fact;[1] but all the prophetic writers, early and late, as they recognise a continuity in God's covenant with Israel as a whole, regard "David" as a link in the unbroken chain of divine revelation and guidance.[2] Even if it

[1] 1 Kings xi. 32-36.
[2] Hos. iii. 5; Amos ix. 11; Isa. ix. 7, xi. 1-10, &c.; Jer. xvii. 25, xxii. 1-4, xxiii. 5, &c.; Ezek. xxxvii. 24.

should be proved or conceded that these kingly psalms are all later than David, the remarkable fact remains that he and he only is expressly mentioned, and that all the glory of the monarchy, and all the expectation connected with it, are associated with his name and his line. So that it does not seem too much to conclude that, though the actual expression of the sentiment embodied in these psalms may not be his, the sentiment itself was as early as his time, and the stimulus to this expression of it in sacred song was given by his reign and his theocratic position. Thus, from another point of view, the tradition is justified which ascribes to him the beginning of national psalmody.

3. There remains another prominent feature of these national psalms to be alluded to—viz., the importance assigned to Jerusalem. This comes out in the kingly psalms; but it is not so much because it is the royal residence, as because it is the "city of the great King," in whose palaces God is known for a refuge, that Jerusalem bulks so largely in the Psalter.[1] In Salem was the tabernacle of the national God, in Zion was His seat. Thither the tribes of God went up for

[1] Isaac Taylor ('Spirit of the Hebrew Poetry,' p. 156) singles out twenty psalms which "declare their own intention as anthems, adapted for that public worship which was the glory and delight of the Hebrew people," and among which the specially Jerusalem psalms are included. They are: xxiv., xlvii., xlviii., lxxxvii., xcv., xcvi., xcvii., xcviii., xcix., c., cviii., cxiv., cxvii., cxviii., cxxii., cxxxii., cxxxiv., cxlviii., cxlix., cl.

a testimony, and from this centre, as the perfection of beauty, shone forth the glory of Israel's God. In some of these psalms we can see the crowding throngs of worshippers, and hear their joyful songs of praise. In others the holy city and its worship are seen afar off, and the devout singer longs and faints for the courts of the Lord.

It would be arbitrary to say of these psalms that they reflect the times of the post-exilian church, when Jerusalem had become all in all to the pious Jew, and the Temple was his only remaining glory. For the very pertinent question arises, What was it that induced those trembling exiles to brave the dangers of the desert, and drew them westwards to their own land where they made it their first care to restore the Temple and its worship? Beyond doubt Jerusalem was already a hallowed place in their eyes; and thus, in view of the prominence given to the city and the Temple in the Psalms, we are forced to consider what pre-exilian history and literature have to offer as an explanation.

We may at one step go back to the oracle found both in Isaiah and Micah, and believed by many critics to be derived by both these prophets from an older source:[1] "And it shall come to pass in

---

[1] According to the newest fashion, however, even this oracle is placed very late, about the time when the prophetical portion of the Canon was closed, B.C. 250. See Cornill's classification of the Hebrew Literature, at the close of his Einleitung.

the latter days, that the mountain of the Lord's house shall be established in the top of the mountains, and shall be exalted above the hills; and all nations shall flow unto it. . . . For out of Zion shall go forth the law, and the word of the Lord from Jerusalem" (Isa. ii. 2 ff. Cf. Micah iv. 1 ff.)

This already implies a long association of sanctity attaching to Jerusalem, for which there must be a sufficient occasion and definite commencement. If it was the presence of the Temple of Solomon that started the idea, then we must conclude that from at least a very early period of the monarchy Jerusalem was regarded as something far more than the royal residence of the Davidic kings: that, in the conceptions of the prophets, it was elevated, if not actually, at least ideally and prophetically, into a religious metropolis of the world.

It is customary to say that all psalms which refer to the house of God, and the dwelling-place of God at Jerusalem, must be at least later than David, since the Temple was not built in his days, and the mere presence of the Tabernacle for the Ark could not have occasioned the employment of such dignified language. However that may be, it is worth while to inquire what it was that led David to make Jerusalem the religious and political capital of his kingdom, and whether there may not be grounds for the existence of such an ancient oracle as has been quoted, and for dating the ideal importance of Jerusalem from his days.

It is noteworthy that one of the first things David set himself to do when he became king of all Israel was to make himself master of Jerusalem (2 Sam. v. 6-10). Up till that time we are not told much about the place; but it seems not a little remarkable that it was—though so central—one of the last strongholds of the native princes, and was apparently only taken with some difficulty; while, on the other hand, it no sooner passed into David's hands than it assumed a noteworthy importance.

Jerusalem was evidently a stronghold and a royal city before the time of David. Probably it had a very old and a very interesting history. If it is the same as the place called Salem in the fourteenth chapter of Genesis, as many now believe, then we obtain a very significant hint as to the reason that led to its being made the capital of united Israel.

That chapter of Genesis has been a great perplexity to the critics who have undertaken the task of determining the origin of the sources out of which the book of Genesis is composed. It refuses to be classed with any of the main sources of the Pentateuch, and is explained either as a separate composition, perhaps drawn from a native Palestinian source, and incorporated by one of the authors of the book; or, as advanced critics maintain, of later date than any of them, being a legend contrived to explain the payment of tithes to the Jerusalem priests, and to magnify the character of Abraham in a new aspect as a warrior. The critics who take this latter view, of course, place no reliance upon it as a historical document.

In that chapter it is mentioned that Melchizedek, King of Salem, priest of the Most High God, met Abraham returning from the rescue of the captives of Sodom, blessed the patriarch, and received from him tithes of all. The writer thus evidently believed that this priest-king was a man of more than ordinary importance, a professor of a pure religion, though not deriving his knowledge from Abraham's family, and apparently as such worthy to receive tithes. It is a mysterious passage, and altogether too minute and circumstantial to be a late invention. Besides, it were surely a most elaborate invention, in order to justify the payment of tithes to the priests of Jerusalem, to relate how they were paid first of all to a non-Israelite priest.

Now we have a reference to Melchizedek in Ps. cx., "Thou art a priest for ever after the order of Melchizedek." Of course, if the story in Genesis is a late invention, the psalm will be still later; but it is difficult to see any possible reference to Jerusalem-tithes or even to Abraham in the psalm. The reference is to the peculiar nature of the priesthood of Melchizedek. And merely to say that a priest for ever after the order of Melchizedek means a priest of the Most High God, as Prof. Cheyne is content to do,[1] seems very inadequate, since all the priests from Aaron's time could have been so designated. The writer of the Epistle to the Hebrews, however, gives the words another turn and a wider reference. "Without father, without mother," so he describes Melchizedek, "without genealogy, having neither beginning of days nor end of life, . . . abideth a priest for ever." He takes Melchizedek, in short, to be a type of Christ, "who hath been made [a priest], not after the law of a carnal commandment, but after the power of an endless life."

Very remarkable, certainly, are these three passages, separated, most probably, by centuries from one another. They do not merely echo or repeat one another, but each adds something to the preceding and whets our curiosity to know more. "King of Salem—priest of the Most High God"—"Priest for ever after the order of Melchizedek"—"Without father, without mother, without genealogy, having neither beginning of days nor end of life." And now, excavated from the dust of centuries, have lately been brought to light documents, older than any of them, which it is believed help to explain them all. In the first place, it has been proved that the uncouth names in this chapter are not inventions of Hebrew writers of

[1] Origin of the Psalter, p. 26 f.

legend, but that kings with the identical or closely similar names ruled over the places mentioned; and although no record has been found of the precise events related in the chapter, yet similar raids to the country of the west, and similar alliances of kings from the region of Elam, are matters of history. In short, in reading this fourteenth chapter of Genesis we are not in a region of legend, but on the firm ground of ancient history. The bearing of this on the whole subject of the credibility of the Pentateuch we need not stop to inquire.[1] But, as connected more closely with the subject in hand, we have to refer to another set of monuments recently brought to light. Among the tablets found at Tell-el-Amarna are some letters, belonging to about 1400 B.C., from one 'Abd Khiba or Ebed-Tob (as his name is variously read), prince of Jerusalem, addressed to the King of Egypt. He calls his city Uru' Salim, which is [2] explained to be "city of Salîm" or Salem; and what is most remarkable, he repeats over and over again, as a thing that was his proud distinction, that neither his father nor his mother exalted him to his dignity, but "the arm of the mighty king." This expression does not seem to refer to the King of Egypt who is being addressed;

---

[1] See Hommel, The Ancient Hebrew Tradition, chap. v.
[2] Records of the Past, Second Series, vol. v. p. 54 ff. Hommel, *loc. cit.*, p. 201.

for though the title "mighty king" (*sharru dannu*) is given to Assyrian and Babylonian monarchs in these tablets, it is not found applied to the kings of Egypt, and the context suggests that the prince of Jerusalem was appealing to some ancient and special privilege that he enjoyed over other princes. Some suppose [1] that the phrase means the oracle of the native god. But whether this be so or not, it is very remarkable to find the King of Jerusalem appealing in this reiterated way to his mysterious appointment.

There is much more here than "an interesting and valuable fact about Jerusalem," as Prof. Cheyne grudgingly describes it.[2] We have a clue to the significance of those mysterious passages in which the name of Melchizedek occurs. True, we have no mention of his name nor of his meeting with Abram. But we learn that in that remote period there was a King of Jerusalem who ruled not by hereditary succession, but by some mysterious authority which he expected the King of Egypt, his suzerain, to respect. And all this falls at a time just such as the chapter before us depicts; for the details of the invasion which it contains were not invented by the writer. The remarkable collocation of proper names precludes this supposition; and, as for the alternative explanation that

---

[1] See Sayce, *loc. cit.*
[2] Founders of Old Testament Criticism, p. 238 f.

a Jew, writing at a late period in the Exile, and desiring to give verisimilitude to a legend, embellished it with proper names procured from Babylonian scribes, it is very probable that by that time the facts would have been forgotten and their record inaccessible. The Hebrews must have learned them long, long before the Babylonian exile.

Why could not the Israelites have preserved the ancient traditions attaching to the city which became their capital? Why, indeed, might not this very tradition have had a special influence in the selection of Jerusalem for the capital, and found its way into the minstrelsy which clustered round the holy city? If there was such a sanctity attaching to Jerusalem from patriarchal times, and such a tradition of a pure religion of "the Most High God" associated with the place, we can understand David's choice of the city for his capital. For, though the Hebrews traced back their national covenant to Abraham, they proceed upon the assumption that there has been but one true religion from the beginning of the world. This is the underlying belief in all the accounts of primeval time contained in the first eleven chapters of Genesis; and a priest of the Most High God would be a representative of this true primitive faith. Abraham's faith is linked on to the one primeval religion, the order of Melchizedek is an order that is independent of time, a priesthood of that order is one that never passes away. And so the idealised king-priest of the house of David, stepping into the inheritance of the ages, taking up the honours of an indefinite past, carries them forward to an indefinite future, "a priest for ever after the order of Melchizedek" (Ps. cx.)

All this does not prove that Ps. cx. was written by David, or that it referred primarily to David in person. But it does make it quite credible that the conception involved in such psalms should have found expression in verse during the palmy days of the monarchy. And let us bear in mind what is the alternative. If psalms like this do not belong to the pre-exilian age, then they must be brought down to a period long subsequent to the captivity, the time when princes of the Asmonæan family were ruling in Jerusalem. This psalm, *e.g.*, is taken by Prof. Cheyne to refer to Simon Maccabæus (B.C. 141). But why a Levitical priest at that late period should have regarded it as an honour to be compared with Melchizedek is anything but obvious. For, though Josephus relates, as Prof. Cheyne is careful to remind us,[1] that Simon Maccabæus was made *by the people* their ruler and high priest, he does not seem to have been aware of the fact that the distinction of the Jerusalem priest-king was that he was *not* appointed

[1] Origin of the Psalter, p. 26 f.

by any such authority. In fine, if Gen. xiv. is not a farrago of outlandish names put together by a reckless story-teller, nor a legend of exilian Judaism ingeniously interwoven with painfully gathered archæological material, but gives a trustworthy picture of the times to which it relates, then the sacredness of Jerusalem was known by the time of David; and from David's time onwards such a thought might be germinating in the national consciousness of Israel. The "everlasting gates" through which the ark of Jehovah passed (Ps. xxiv.) at the beginning of David's reign were not hyperbolically so named after all; and it is no wonder that, as Prof. Cheyne reminds us,[1] Jerusalem was by the time of Isaiah called a city of righteousness (Isa. i. 21, 26), and that by all the prophets it was spoken of in terms which are not explicable merely on the ground of its being the place of the king's palace and the king's court. And the point gained is, that it is quite conceivable and credible that psalms concerning the king, and psalms celebrating the glory of Jerusalem and its worship, might have been composed and sung from the earliest period of the monarchy.

Kindred to the idea of drawing near to God in the worship of the Temple is that of nearness to God or dwelling in His house. And this idea finds expression in some of the psalms which have not

[1] Origin of the Psalter, p. 42.

inappropriately been termed "guest" psalms. The chief of these are xv., xxiv. 1-6, xxvii. 1-6, and xxiii. And the idea occurs also in brief expressions elsewhere, as, *e.g.*—

> "I will dwell in Thy tabernacle for ever:
> I will take refuge in the covert of Thy wings."—lxi. 4.

> "Thou art not a God that hath pleasure in wickedness:
> Evil shall not sojourn with Thee."—v. 4.

At first sight it might seem that it is neither more nor less than the Temple that is thus referred to as God's tent or house. But a closer examination shows that the association of thought has shifted. The idea of nearness to God, which is symbolised by worship at the sanctuary, passes into the idea of hospitality. From being a worshipper, the psalmist comes to think of himself as a guest; and the clothing of his ideas is now not the details of the Temple service, but the arrangements of a hospitable tent, or of a banquet in the house of a noble entertainer.

Perhaps, indeed, this idea of hospitality was not suggested by the Temple service, but was more primitive and elementary; although the "house" or "tent" is common to the two conceptions. The inviolability of the hospitable tent to which a fugitive or wayfarer is admitted, the idea of protection, not unconnected with that of a sacrificial meal, are old and fundamental conceptions; and perhaps we

202 THE NATIONAL ELEMENT IN THE PSALMS.

may look in that direction for an explanation of the language of the Psalms, full of confidence in security, that is employed in this connection. Robertson Smith seems to take some such view when he says [1] that Israel was Jehovah's client sojourning in a land where they have no rights of their own, but are absolutely dependent on His bounty. It is not easy to follow him when he goes on to say that this is one of the most characteristic notes of the new and more timid type of piety that distinguished post-exilian Judaism from the religion of old Israel, referring to Lev. xxv. 23; Ps. xxxix. 12 (Heb. 13); Ps. cxix. 19; 1 Chron. xxix. 15. For we might rather infer from the language of Hosea (ii. 8, 9, &c.) that the idea was old; and we are indeed told that this was part of the ruder pre-prophetic religion. Prof. Cheyne sees another reference, and connects the idea of the guest-psalms with that of forgiveness as expressed in Ps. xxxii. "Why is forgiven Israel so joyful? Because it is delivered from earthly trouble? Yes; but chiefly because it can once more fearlessly enter Jehovah's house." [2] No doubt some such reference must be assumed if these psalms are to be explained as "Church" psalms; but in unaffected lyric compositions the other reference is obvious and simple, and certainly as intelligible as it is beautiful. Prof. G.

[1] Religion of the Semites, p. 78.
[2] Origin of the Psalter, p. 236. Cf. pp. 387, 429.

A. Smith[1] has pointed out how the expressions in Ps. xxiii. 5 might be based on the idea of a fugitive from the avenger of blood, who finds asylum in a friendly tent, and has a table prepared for him in the presence of his enemies. And one would be disposed to expect such a familiar and telling image to find its way early into the figurative stock of the language of a poetic people.

In this case, again, we need not come down to a late period of history for an idea which gives colour to many of the psalms. It is indeed to be found outside the Psalter in the prose books.[2] And David, in a special manner, from his training as a shepherd, and his experience as an outlaw, would have had the idea brought home to him many a time as he saw the tents of the nomad, or was constrained to throw himself on the protection of friendly defenders in his flight from Saul.

On the whole it does not seem to demand a great stretch of credulity to believe that the pre-exilian period furnished abundant occasion for the lyric treatment of subjects connected with the national fortunes of Israel, or for songs in which the city of Jerusalem and the Temple worship

---

[1] Expositor, Fifth Series, vol. i. p. 33 ff.
[2] See Gen. xviii. 2; Judges iv. 17; 2 Sam. ix. 7 ff.; Job xxxvi. 16]; Is. xxv. 6.

should have a prominent place. And there are reasons of no little weight to lead us to suppose that some of these distinctive ideas may well have, precisely from the time of David, become themes of song.

CHAPTER IX.

SUBJECTIVE ELEMENT IN THE PSALTER.

BEFORE pursuing our present argument further, it is proper to pause here and consider the situation which has arisen. We have claimed that poetical compositions exhibiting the characteristic features of the existing Psalms may have arisen in the pre-exilian period, and also that there was no lack of occasion for them in the circumstances of the people and in the occurrences of their history in the pre-exilian time. But if this be so, it might be expected that there would be no great difficulty in detecting the occasions of the psalms, and so determining the time and circumstances in which they were composed. That there is such a difficulty, however, is sufficiently proved by the great discrepancy that exists in the periods to which different critics refer the same compositions. It is important to inquire into the cause of this discrepancy. It may be that an examination of the question will throw some light on the validity of the methods that have been employed. When whole centuries intervene between the dates to which different critics assign the same psalms, it is not inappropriate to ask whether the critics are on the right track, or are not undertaking an impossible task. When each individual is so confident in his conclusions, it is not unreasonable to suggest that the grounds of the confidence lie more in his own mind than in the facts of the case. When there is such a wide range in the possibility of reference, one is inclined to suspect that the original composers of these songs had not in view certain precise combinations of circumstances which they strove to represent objectively in poetry, but rather some general aspect of affairs such as could be treated in a more subjective tone and handed down in a form that would have more abiding application.

There are several considerations that assist us to account for what may appear a vagueness and want of precision of reference in the Psalms; these considerations will not only go far to explain the variety which prevails in critical opinions, but may guide us to a true appreciation of the character and purpose of the Psalms themselves.

(*a*) In the first place, it is to be borne in mind that our records of the period of the monarchy are exceedingly scanty, and broad and general in their statements. The accounts contained in the books of

Kings are for the most part of a stereotyped form and very limited in compass. From the close of the reign of Solomon the deeds of successive kings are repeated in slightly varied form, and long reigns are passed over in a few verses; although, when there is an exception, and the historian dwells upon more striking national events, we find either that many of the psalms would suit such occasions, or at least that vistas are opened to us of possible and probable circumstances in which others might have been composed.

If we contrast now with this brevity the fulness of detail conveyed by the authors of the books of the Maccabees or by Josephus, it will not be difficult to understand how it is possible for modern critics to find in these later writers a choice of national occurrences, and a variety of situations to which in a speculative way one might refer many of the psalms, while, it is to be confessed, the canonical books offer fewer such facilities for comparison.

(b) In the second place, it may be maintained that, even with the wide choice of historical occasions for the Psalms which the books of Maccabees, *e.g.*, present, the references to those times which critics profess to find are extremely vague and shadowy. Hitzig's attempt to set down the Psalms in regular sequence corresponding to the march of events in the Maccabaean period can hardly be characterised as successful; and I do not know that

Prof. Cheyne's attempts at precise identifications have been received by scholars with the degree of confidence which he himself exhibits. At all events, if the references are so general that two critics, so sharp-sighted, cannot agree as to details, though agreed on the general principle, surely we must allow that they are vague indeed. Prof. Cheyne himself, in allotting psalms to different periods, has to confess that as to long periods we have practically no definite historical information; and he has to characterise these periods by certain assumed tendencies or phases of religious consciousness, and then to search for corresponding tones in the Psalms.

Yet when we are brought face to face with historical periods which are crowded with events, or characterised by such outstanding incidents as could not but express themselves in sacred song, if it were practised, there is as good reason for assigning psalms to the pre-exilian period as for relegating them to post-exilian times. Critics usually adopt a somewhat high-handed manner in dealing with those psalms whose headings refer them to events in the life of David as these are related in the books of Samuel. In these cases, they say, the editors of the Psalter have simply looked about for some recorded incident that would suit the situation, and have even slavishly copied into their headings extracts from the prose books answering, in their opinion, those situations. But is not this merely doing by anticipation what the critics themselves do in the name of historical criticism? And has not the work of each successive critic practically amounted to the setting aside of the "headings" prefixed to the psalms by his predecessors? To the simple question, Do the existing headings correctly interpret the situation, or do the psalms thus applied suit the situation as well as on the modern references? — the unprejudiced answer will be that the reference is frequently as indecisive on the one application as on the other.

And then, to come to later periods in the monarchy, whenever events of an unusually exciting kind are recorded, we find no lack of suitable situations for psalms such as we now possess. The reign of Hezekiah, for example, with the marvellous deliverance from the Assyrian invasion, may well be celebrated in some of those jubilant psalms which critics now delight to refer to Maccabaean victories; and the destruction of the Temple by Nebuchadnezzar took place in circumstances which were to a great extent repeated in the time of Antiochus Epiphanes. Indeed the events of the history of Israel — as of other nations — had a habit of repeating themselves in slightly varying details at different periods; and the Hebrew psalmists, being true poets, have seen to the heart of the events, so that their songs are applicable to ever recurring situations, and never die.

A history which itself was a great drama suggests endless possibilities of poetic expression. The whole lifetime of the prophet Jeremiah, for example, was a period so tragic that it is no wonder that many critics have regarded him as the author of not a few of the more plaintive psalms; and we cannot but feel our emotions deeply stirred in reading many chapters of the simplest prose in the book that bears his name. What an amount of pathos, again, is concentrated in the story, so briefly told in the book of Kings, of the destruction of Jerusalem and the burning of the Temple! (2 Kings xxv. 8-10). What a wailing note sounds in the simple unadorned phrases in which the historian passes under review the mournful scenes that crowded upon one another as the Jewish State fell to ruins! The book of Lamentations is in itself a proof at once how capable the poetical writers of that time were of expressing the most tender emotion in the fittest verse, and how deeply the national heart was stirred by the national calamity. Both from a literary and a religious point of view, the dirges of which each chapter of that book is composed are so finished and mature that we must allow the exercise of the poetic art on such subjects during a long antecedent period. They may not be the work of Jeremiah himself, to whom they are traditionally ascribed; but they are undoubtedly the voice of the sufferers who lived through the dreadful period of the nation's ruin, expressing feelings which were still fresh, and delineating scenes that were actually before the poet's eyes. It has already been pointed out[1] that the *Qîna* or elegy is one of the oldest and most commonly used forms of Hebrew song. And it would seem as if the national muse had been nursing itself for centuries on this plaintive melody, in order that it might find relief to its agony under the heart-breaking misfortune of national ruin. It will, at all events, be hard to believe that singers who had prepared the way for such a touching series of dirges, never rose to the level of composing a few plaintive psalms.

(*c*) Another consideration, which cannot be too much insisted upon, is the fact already pointed out, that metaphor and imagery are woven into the very texture of the language of the Psalms. The image or metaphor is not, so to speak, a photographic reproduction of an isolated event or situation, but is part of the working material and literary apparatus of the poet, by the aid of which he strives to give utterance to his inner feelings and mental movements. The poets had learned to express their

[1] Chap. vii. p. 155.

emotions in terms derived from external phenomena, so that instead of some outward occurrence giving the suggestion for a psalm, it is more likely that an inner experience was the prior impulse, and clothed itself in the only dress available for the purpose. The heaping of metaphor upon metaphor, in the attempt to attain adequate expression, is proof that this was the case. Were we, in fact, to take the metaphors literally, as descriptive of scenes actually present to the eye of the poet, or to seek in mere poetic figures for references to actual occurrences, we should run the risk, in the first place, of turning the loftiest poetry into the deepest bathos, and, in the second place, of allowing ourselves to go astray in search of historical occasions for the compositions. As an instance of the exercise of this unpoetic criticism, may be mentioned Hitzig's reference of Ps. xl. to Jeremiah, because the poet speaks of a "horrible pit" and the "miry clay," and it is well known that Jeremiah was on a memorable occasion shut up in a dungeon. Nor is it much better when some physical phenomenon mentioned in a psalm — as, *e.g.*, waterspouts, waves, and billows — is seized upon as an indication of the spot on which the psalm was composed. It is surely much more consistent with all the operations of the poetic faculty to suppose that the observant poetic eye had long since taken in the varying phases of a diversified landscape, that a poetic fancy had rocked itself into harmony with the pulsations of the warm life that beat in an exuberant nature, and that the figures of speech thus suggested were so many materials ready to hand which, in the mood, the poet seized upon, as any writer of prose seizes the fittest word to convey his meaning. Is it to be supposed that the sight of a panting hart suggested to a poet a pretty figure with which to begin a poem? Is it not more likely that his own inward thirst and longing for divine refreshing was the moving cause, the idea to be expressed, and that this idea found utterance by the aid of an image which was part of the stock of the poetic language, an image which all could understand? Precisely in the same way when an Arabic poet, love-sick, declares that a bird of prey is gnawing at his vitals, we are not to suppose that some vulture seated on its prey before the poet's bodily eyes suggested the figure; but that the torturing pain within him led him to seize upon a figure drawn from a sight familiar to his hearers, the storehouses of phantasy being ransacked for the fittest image.

This metaphorical element becomes more marked the more the poet is moved by violent or conflicting feelings, or is at a loss to give vent to rapidly changing and delicate emotions; as, *e.g.*, when, in the same breath, he represents himself as sick, surrounded by enemies, persecuted, and drawing near to death. Taking his language literally, we should be at a loss to discover whether he means to describe external foes, or bodily ailments, or both together; whereas, allowance being made for the poetic character of the phraseology, he seems rather to be expressing his own inner spiritual straits. Just when he seems to be labouring to lay bare his whole case, the sudden change and crowding agglomeration of metaphors are so striking that we are positively unable to form to ourselves a picture, complete and consistent, of the psalmist's situation; and this feature is continually recurring in all kinds of psalms. To take an easy example, how futile would be the attempt to throw upon one canvas, so to speak, the three short clauses of one verse: "Thou art a shield for me, my glory, and the lifter up of mine head." Translated into abstract terms, the verse is terse, striking, suggestive; but it gives no indication of the poet's outward circumstances. And if we look at such psalms as vi., xxii., xxxviii., we shall find that the complaint turns now upon subjective, now upon objective hindrances and difficulties. At one moment the psalmist is sick, wasted away, ready to die, and then suddenly we hear of enemies, oppressors, mockers, or even ravening lions, dogs, strong bulls of Bashan. It is not one picture, however elaborate, that is before us; it is a rapid succession of pictures thrown upon the field of vision, and fading away the one into the other. "Hebrew diction," says Smend, "exhibits a striking want of precision, which is to be explained not merely by the incapacity of the language" [I should prefer to say, not merely by the *exuberance* of the language] "but rather by the psychological situation of the Hebrew. With the vivacity of his feelings there goes everywhere hand in hand a certain indefiniteness of conception."[1] All which should be carefully borne in mind by the interpreter of the psalmist's *thoughts*, for it is these that present the difficulty more than his historical situation.

(*d*) Closely connected with this is to be taken into account the whole character and nature of the Psalms as literary compositions. However varied are the themes, the poems have one common character; they are not primarily descriptive, but essentially subjective and reflective. The Psalms are usually designated lyric poems, and so they are: songs primarily intended to be sung to the accompaniment of the lyre. "A psalm—a song," we find frequently in the heading, the two words being employed to denote the music and the singing respectively. And though the Psalms may not be so finished in form as the lyrics of Greece, they do not fall behind them, but greatly surpass them in one common feature of the lyric, their

[1] ZATW, 1888, p. 67.

inner subjective element. Milton's three marks of all good poetry are here: it is "simple, sensuous, passionate." And Goethe points to the inner feeling as the soul of all good poetry when he says:—

> "I sing, as sings the little bird
> Upon the tree-top swinging;
> The song that from the throat is poured
> Is rich reward for singing."

The singer seems to sing to himself, or to fondle his lyre and address to it the outpouring of his feelings. Hence it is that we have the abrupt transitions and sudden breaks in the connection, the play of alternating moods, the song at times dying away at the end when the passion is exhausted, like a stream that loses itself in the sand, or gathering itself up into one final *fortissimo*, in which the whole is expressed. Not only is it a difficult thing to follow the singer, his thoughts seem even to outstrip himself; the associations of ideas are subtle beyond detection, or he has thoughts which he cannot express, and he thinks them while the lyre soothes his mind to rest. The key to his meaning is locked up in his own breast, and vainly we look for it in some external situation or historical event. No doubt his song is occasioned by some experience he has had in his life; in many cases it is evidently suggested by the events of his nation, and the situations of his time. But it may be suggested by a thought of a time remote. Moreover, we can never be sure that he keeps to the particular theme with which he started. For it is not an objective scene that he depicts; it is the universal and eternal element in the occurrence, or the experience as a thing moving his own soul, that comes forth in his song. The more he confines himself to that universal element, the more intense is the feeling to which he gives expression. The more his poetry is divested of the temporary and particular, the more numerous are the hearts that are touched by it, and the more lasting his song becomes. Delitzsch, in speaking of what he calls *typico-prophetical* psalms, says: "The mystery of these psalms is at bottom the mystery of all poetry. The genuine lyric poet does not give a mere copy of the impressions of his empirical Ego; an ideal Ego, as Vinet says somewhere, overhears, as it were, this empirical Ego; it is this second soul that makes the poet. The poet does not form a mere cast of his impressions, but idealises them—that is, seizes them by the root of their idea, and stripping off and abstracting all that is adventitious and unimportant, lifts them up into the region of the ideal." [1] The more closely, in fact, we can come to the singer himself, the more we shall appreciate his music; we may deprive ourselves not only of the pleasure but of the meaning of his song by importing into every strain a reference to something

[1] Commentary on the Psalms, Introduction, x.

external to him; and in any case, even if external things are before his mind, we should strive to see them in the light in which they appear to him.

It is this element, no doubt, that explains the absence of detailed description and of precise historical reference which is so striking in the Psalms. This poetry is not of the nature of the epic which evolves some connected story or celebrates the exploits of heroes. Nor is it dramatic, except occasionally and on a small scale, when its own vivacity leads it into sudden transitions, with rapid representation of different thoughts and alternate words of different speakers. It is the singer himself that is embodied in the song. "Though *we* may not know the precise circumstances under which the poet composed his song, yet he himself knew them. But he composes, in the first instance, under an inner necessity. He does not need, for his own information, to expound or detail his own situation, and he has no cause to entertain his hearers, for whose edification he sings, with a statement as to whether the feelings he expresses were experienced by him while sitting or lying, at home or abroad, at work or at leisure." [1] And this, which is true of all lyric poetry, is very characteristic of Semitic poems. The famous *Mu'allaqât* all start with the simple *occasion*—which, however, is an assumed one—of the poet's coming upon the traces

[1] Beer, Individual- und Gemeinde-Psalmen, p. xci.

of the deserted camp of the people of his beloved one, at sight of which he goes off in freest fancy over the fields of memory, the original starting-point being soon forgotten, while the poet's actual situation is never revealed. And so, frequently in the Arabic literature relating to the times of the caliphs, some striking occurrence takes place, or some clever remark is made, and the caliph asks the court poet who is present to take the lute and recite it in verse. Whereupon the poet sings, but his chief care seems to be to eliminate the personal and primary details; and it is only the context of the narrative that enables us to find in his song a reference to the occasion that called it forth. And so the song remains, a little gem in itself, when the manufacture of the setting has been long forgotten. We may perceive the same thing also in the Hebrew prophets, who in spirit and in tone are at one with the poets. "For the real thing," it has been well said,[1] "in the prophets is their faith, not the particular events predicted or projected, in which they give their faith embodiment. These events are always the events occurring immediately around them in their day, which they fill out and animate with the meaning of their own universal conceptions." Therefore it may quite well be that many of our psalms had a far humbler occasion and a far more limited starting-point than

[1] A. B. Davidson in 'Expository Times,' August 1894, p. 492a.

learned critics ascribe to them. It is the inner impulse moving the genius of the singer that not only gives them their charm, but is indeed the thing to be studied and explained. Anything that *inspired* the writer for the time would suggest his song. The clothing of his thoughts might be most variegated, for he had a rich stock of poetic imagery to draw from; and he played with his idea and set it in various lights according to his varying mood. So does the lark start from the sod and begin its carol; but who would seek to explain the lark's song by a reference to the clod of earth from which it sprang upward?

No doubt it may seem at first sight disappointing that we cannot fix positively the actual occasion of each psalm, and it may be thought we lose so much the more in our endeavour to understand it. We may, however, console ourselves with the reflection that the lack of objective precision is more than compensated for by the intensity of subjective effectiveness. If we see the *thing* indistinctly, it is because the life-breath of the *man* is so closely about us. The very fact that the psalmists have given us so little help in this direction should teach us that the outward occasion was not the principal thing to the writer himself; and so the principal and important thing to be reached by us is not the day or hour at which a psalm was composed, or the spot on which the psalmist's feet rested at the moment, but the kind of inner experience which made such composition possible;—to know, not how accurately he has depicted passing events, so much as how true an interpreter he is of all events. In short, it is of the utmost importance to understand the spirit of the psalms and the views of the psalmists, and these we can learn from their own words, in most cases, if we consent to read them in their own light, and refrain from forcing into them far-fetched references. The occasion of a psalm is one thing, and it may be very accidental; the situation of a psalm is another, it is given in the psalm itself, and is essential. The sighing of the wind in the waving trees, the murmuring of the gurgling brook, are more to the poet than an accurate delineation of the landscape; and if we can catch these sounds in his verse we gain more than if we had a photograph of the scene which lay before his dreaming eyes. And many of the psalms, if I mistake not, only yield their secret and their sweetness when we cease to look for the occasion and resign ourselves to the situation. Take such a psalm as the cxxvii.:—

"Except the Lord build the house,
They labour in vain that build it;
Except the Lord keep the city,
The watchman waketh but in vain.
It is vain for you that ye rise up early and so late take rest,
And eat the bread of toil;
For so He giveth His beloved sleep," &c.

I call it the Hebrew "Cotter's Saturday Night."[1] If read as a simple lyric of domestic peace and pious contentment, it moves from beginning to end with the delicate grace of artless life. If interpreted as a "Church" psalm of the building of the Temple and the re-peopling of Jerusalem, it has the stiffness of some creaking piece of dead mechanism. Or take the 8th Psalm :—

> "O Lord our Lord,
> How excellent is Thy name in all the earth!
> Who hast set Thy glory upon the heavens.
> Out of the mouth of babes and sucklings hast Thou established strength," &c.

If we suppose a poet, with perhaps a little child in his arms, contemplating the starry heavens from a flat house-top, we obtain sufficient occasion and suitable situation for such a perfect lyric.

This idealising tendency is particularly manifest in the psalms which treat of the national history, the hope of the house of David, and the glory of the city and temple of Jerusalem. Here there were certain familiar themes which might be suggested to the poet at any moment and by any occasion, themes on which poet and prophet delighted to enlarge; and however they may have been suggested, the immediate occasion would be presently forgotten, and the fancy would take its full freedom of treatment. And just as in personal psalms there

[1] See Expositor, June 1898, p. 414.

is an alternation of hope and joy with sadness and grief, so in these national songs entreaty is mingled with thanksgiving, prayer with praise, and it is not very clear which feeling is uppermost in the poet's mind. Some of them give no indication that there was any exciting cause in the public history of the time to call them forth. They may have been indited in times of peace, by a writer who in calm reflection turned his mind back upon past history, as was common with both prophet and poet. Such a psalm might be one of the longest of them, Ps. lxxviii. :—

> " Give ear, O my people, to my teaching:
> Incline your ear to the words of my mouth.
> I will open my mouth in a parable;
> I will utter dark sayings of old:
> Which we have heard and known,
> And our fathers have told us.
> We will not hide them from their children,
> Telling to the generation to come the praises of the Lord."

Here the psalmist apparently sits down on purpose to recount the great things of the past for the benefit of the younger generation; and only the keen eyes of criticism undertake, from incidental hints or from turns of expressions, to discover the date at which such a song was composed. Thus, *e.g.*, some [1] would have it that, because the psalm ends with David and makes no mention of

---

[1] Hengstenberg, and similarly Delitzsch. See also M. de Harlez, in 'Proceedings of the Society of Biblical Archæology,' ix. 372.

Solomon, it must have been composed in David's time. Others, from Calvin downwards, maintain that the terms in which David is referred to imply a period long subsequent to his reign. Prof. Cheyne,[1] seeing that its "view of the Davidic kingdom resembles that of the Chronicler," says it must be classed with Pss. cv. - cvii., as expressing "the Pan-Israelitish sentiment of the Persian period." Hitzig would bring it still farther down, to the Grecian period. Hupfeld says the salient point in the psalm is the choice of Jerusalem and Zion, and by implication the rejection of Shiloh, which lay in the northern Ephraim (vers. 67-70); but that the didactic treatment of the history indicates a late reflective tendency. The references to the tribe of Ephraim are taken by one set of expositors[2] to point to the revolt of the ten tribes from Rehoboam; by another[3] to the final schism that took place between the Jews and the Samaritans in the post-exilian period. This is but a specimen of the diversity of opinion that prevails as to the historical allusions in the Psalms, and only one example of the manner in which the same facts may be made to support the most different conclusions. From all which it is safe to infer that the conclusions come to by critics reflect their own estimates of the literary and religious capa-

---

[1] Origin of the Psalter, p. 147.
[2] Rosenmüller, De Wette, &c.   [3] Ewald.

bilities of various periods; but that the original writer of the psalm did not keep himself so exclusively and intentionally to any historical occurrence as to enable us to say with confidence what was the first moving cause of the psalm.

In the kingly psalms the idealising tendency of the psalmists attains freest scope. These are no secular odes, celebrating the prowess of heroes or the magnificence of courts. It is in the books of Kings that we find mention of the wars which the kings waged, the might which they showed, the palaces they built, the splendour in which they lived. Even there the writers content themselves with allusions to such things, and refer the reader for fuller information to records which have long since perished. And much less do the psalmists dwell on these things. No court poets are they to flatter their patrons with high-sounding compliments. As far as East is from the West are the kingly psalms removed from the poems in which the great monarchs of Assyria and Egypt are celebrated by their minstrels. And yet they are still more exalted in strain than even such songs. The qualities which the psalmists ascribe to their king are indeed so high, the anticipations they express for him and his dominion are so far-reaching, that we must either give them credit for idealising in the fullest extent, or (if we restrict their words to some actual king, and to definite historical events) we must treat their words as exaggeration to the highest degree. The psalms of this class that stand out most strikingly are ii., xlv., lxxii., cx.; and it is impossible to read these and think that their meaning is exhausted by reference to a mere individual occupant of David's throne, much less to a monarch of any other line. The tone of the psalms as a whole forbids such a supposition, for there is nothing more exalted in the loftiest utterances of prophecy.

Professor Cheyne, however, stoutly maintains[1] that against such a conclusion as this the young sciences of language and religion enter a protest. "The poetic glorifications," he says, "of Egyptian and Babylonian kings, which have been disinterred from the dust of ages, glisten to us of this generation with a strange and pathetic beauty. The high hopes attached to Rameses, to Nebuchadnezzar, to the early Ptolemies, may have been bathed in illusion, but were 'too fair to turn out' wholly 'false.'" And then he proceeds to refer the most exalted of the kingly psalms — not to any king of the line of David, or even to an idealised son of David, but to Ptolemy Philadelphus of Egypt. But to this large liberality it is to be objected that the "young sciences" referred to were not so much as dreamed of in the days when these psalms were composed, and it is not the tolerant wide-

[1] Origin of the Psalter, p. 141 ff.

ness of critical views we have to consider, but the standpoint and outlook of the psalm-writers. It may be very fine to recognise a pathetic beauty in the poetic glorifications of Egyptian and Babylonian kings by the singers of their own nation; but surely it would be no undue stretch of generosity to allow Hebrew poets also to glorify their kings, especially when we consider the very different foundations on which the thrones were established.

One of the most beautiful of the kingly psalms is the seventy-second; and if anything could show the absurdity of the attempt to explain every phrase by a historical reference, it is Hitzig's interpretation of this psalm, in which he finds a consecutive series of allusions to events in the reign of Ptolemy Philadelphus. Prof. Cheyne, while not agreeing with the German critic in details, assigns the psalm to the same period. Nor can his own explanation of the 45th Psalm, which he refers also [1] to Ptolemy, be characterised as fortunate. He admits that the character of this king was not such as a Hebrew writer could admire, and also that the Hebrew poet in his good wishes for the king far surpasses the tone of Theocritus, who wrote odes in honour of Ptolemy; yet he thinks it possible and credible that a high priest at Jerusalem sent this congratulatory poem to the young king on the occasion of his mar-

[1] Origin of the Psalter, p. 166 ff.

riage, believing in all good faith that the new king was in reality what his father was, for the first time in history called, a Saviour. "He wrote it, of course, in Jerusalem, in surroundings happily very different from those in which Theocritus in Alexandria was inditing idylls, to a Jew necessarily so profane."[1] No doubt they "did not know everything down in Judee"; but probably they knew even at that date what their national religion and their national hope were. The book of Chronicles shows the growing regard for and higher idealising of the house of David as time went on; and it would be difficult to prove either that the Jews of Jerusalem were so blissfully ignorant of the state of matters at Alexandria as is here assumed, or that their writers allowed themselves to apply to any Gentile monarch, however exalted and beneficent, the language which the psalmists apply to the personage celebrated in these psalms.

For, even if they were composed with such a reference, a serious difficulty remains, which Prof. Cheyne labours hard to remove.[2] How did such psalms gain admission into the Hebrew Canon? They were written, it is said, at the commencement of Ptolemy's reign, say about B.C. 287, "too soon for the faults of the young prince to have cast a shadow upon his name,"[3] and even before the

[1] Origin of the Psalter, p. 171.
[2] Ibid., p. 172 f.   [3] Ibid., p. 143.

LXX. translation of the Law was thought of.[1] It was therefore long before the translation of the Psalter into Greek, for even the Hebrew Psalter was still in process of formation. Everybody knew in whose honour they were composed. Prof. Cheyne thinks that Psalm xlv. at least was sent direct as a complimentary ode to Ptolemy, and that "there can have been no difficulty in getting it rendered into Greek, for some of the psalms may already have been translated in some shape for private use among the Egyptian Jews."[1] But what became of the Hebrew originals? For the psalms are in the Palestinian collection, from which, and not from the autographs, they were translated into the Septuagint. It must have become apparent before long that the expectations in regard to Ptolemy had been mistaken. Certainly before the Maccabæan rising a "Church" psalm in the form of a panegyric on a heathen king would have been the last thing to be thought of; and Prof. Cheyne says distinctly that "an eulogy on Ptolemy as such would not have been adopted into the permanent Psalter by Simon the Maccabee."[1] Why, then, was it not suppressed or excluded from the still unformed Psalter as soon as the mistake was discovered? Prof. Cheyne's own argument against the ascription of Psalm lxxii. to Solomon applies here with greater force: "Even supposing that a

[1] Origin of the Psalter, p. 172 f.

temple hymn-book existed in Solomon's days, how can one suppose that a psalm which would read like bitter irony would find or at least keep a place within it?"[1] For we have already been told[2] that Simon "as high priest had power to deal as he thought best with the provisionally closed temple hymn-book," even to the extent of inserting in it a highly idealised description of himself in Psalm cx.[3] Instead, however, of likewise appropriating the two psalms in question, or even accepting them with a Messianic reference, it is far more probable, we are told, that both were "explained by Simon (uncritically no doubt) of Solomon."[4] This, however, only increases the difficulty, although supported by the gratuitous assertion that "doubtless in his time the original occasion of the psalm had been forgotten." For a long time had elapsed between the composition of the psalms and the editorial work of Simon, during which they were preserved and used just like the rest of the Hebrew psalms. If the original occasion was forgotten by Simon's time, one would like to know what occasion *was* assigned and what meaning was attached to the psalms by those who in the meantime said or sang them. Is it not clear that, if it was so easy a matter to refer these psalms to Solomon, the general feeling of Palestinian Judaism was already prepared, long before Simon's day,

---

[1] Origin of the Psalter, p. 142.   [2] See above, chap. v. p. 111.
[3] See above, chap. viii. p. 199.   [4] Origin of the Psalter, p. 173.

to recognise a reference to the Davidic King as a matter of course? And does not the careful preservation of such psalms point in the same direction? In fact there is no proof that the consciousness of the nation ever took this strange and temporary aberration of exalting a heathen king to the pinnacle of national hope. The cases of Nebuchadnezzar and Cyrus are quite different. It is one thing to be nursing-fathers to Israel, the Lord's "servants" to bring about the fulfilment of His purposes to His own people; but it is a different thing for a heathen king to be identified with the fortunes of Israel, and celebrated almost as divine. What we do know is that the highest hopes attached to the house of David immediately before these psalms are said to have been composed, that these hopes sustained a succeeding generation in the most arduous struggle in which they ever engaged, and that they blazed up into a bright flame at the Advent in the song of Zechariah :—

> " Blessed be the Lord God of Israel;
> For He hath visited and redeemed His people,
> And hath raised up an horn of salvation for us
> In the house of His servant David;
> As he spake by the mouth of His holy prophets
> Which have been since the world began."
> —Luke i. 68-70.

The probability therefore is that these hopes had never died out.

The important thing to be observed is that, in

any reference of these psalms, a process of idealising on the part of the poet has to be assumed. If that is so, then it is surely most natural to think that the idealising would be done with the legitimate reference (and what other *could* be legitimate to a pious Palestinian Jew?) to the line of David. Such psalms manifestly celebrate some king, actual or ideal, and, even if actual, idealised, who stood in no equivocal relation to the very finest sentiments and highest aspirations of the national consciousness; and if, as the vividness of the description indicates, they were composed when some individual representative of the line was on the throne, they must belong to the time of the monarchy. Seeing that the only choice is between the ideal of one sitting on David's throne, an ideal dating from David's time and never fading from view till the era of the New Testament, and some idealised pagan king, whose character was unknown to the poet or glossed over in his flattering verse, it is not very probable that ordinary common-sense, or sane criticism of Hebrew national literature, will hesitate long as to the alternative. And no one will grudge it to Prof. Cheyne that, by thus exhibiting the insuperable difficulties of his own position, he has demonstrated that the loftiest psalms in the Psalter must be placed in the pre-exilian age.

Finally, the psalms which refer to the worship of the Temple, and the cognate "guest-psalms," exhibit the same idealising tone, and lose their force when explained of the mere ceremonial of the Temple worship, or referred to the dwelling under God's special protection in the sacred territory of Palestine. No doubt the psalmists took pride in the palaces and bulwarks of the capital; they would have been poor patriots had they not. No doubt the moving throng and the swelling chorus of praise thrilled them with emotion; and no one who has felt such influence in the great congregation will find fault with them for being so moved. But that the writers of these psalms were strangers to true heart-devotion, no one who fairly weighs their language will for a moment doubt. Though in the crowded courts, their hearts were lifted up to God's presence, the earthly tabernacle was but an image of a heavenly abode; the same psalm that declares Salem to be Jehovah's dwelling-place a few verses farther on says, "Thou didst cause sentence to be heard from heaven: the earth feared and was still" (Ps. lxxvi. 2, 8). We cannot, in fact, tie down the psalmists' words to external circumstances without restraining their poetic flight and emptying their words of their significance. Whether through the Temple ritual or not, the psalmists had attained to the idea of true spiritual worship, and the external forms were only aids to devotion, and found to be the fittest medium for expressing it.

In conclusion, the Psalms, though a most distinctive element in the national literature, should not be treated primarily as historical *documents*, or even as "disguised history." Instead of beginning with historical criticism, we should approach them with a sympathetic interest, endeavouring to follow the poet in his progress, without interrupting him at every turn to ask what induced him to say this or that. By following him to the end, and allowing his words to tell their own tale, we shall, at all events, come to occupy his situation; and through that, if by any means at all, shall we succeed in understanding the circumstances by which he was surrounded.

CHAPTER X.

RELIGIOUS ELEMENT IN THE PSALTER.

THERE is one fundamental and pre-eminent characteristic common to all the Psalms, of which all the others that have yet been considered may be said to be only varying phases. They are religious songs, else they would not have found a place in the Canon; but they are religious in a higher sense than other songs which are also found incorporated in the canonical historical books. Whereas the latter hold a somewhat secondary place, subsidiary to the history, which as a whole is regarded as sacred, these are not incidental but primarily inspired by the religious instinct or emotion. In looking at the purely poetic characteristics of the Psalms we cannot have failed to perceive that this is no poetry composed for mere æsthetic purposes, or on ordinary literary themes: the deeper feelings of religion stir the mind of the poet, and find expression in the best forms that the poet's art can provide. So, though pre-eminently national, we have seen how the national interest is mainly the religious one: the king is celebrated because he is the Lord's anointed; Jerusalem is glorious because it is the city of the great King, to whom the tribes go up to pay homage; the history is dwelt upon because it is the record of God's wonderful works towards Israel; and the individual comes into significance chiefly and primarily because he is a member of the theocratic nation. When, however, we look more closely at the Psalms, we find a still more distinctively religious element running through them. For, whereas in all of them, even when the immediate occasion can be plainly traced, the theme is treated from a religious point of view, in many of them the theme is so exclusively religious that we cannot trace the occasion at all. For all that the psalm tells us, the singer may be oblivious of the world around him and its affairs, unconscious of all but the feelings of his own heart and the presence of his God.

No writer in the Old Testament, indeed, for any length of time, treats any subject he may have in hand apart from its religious aspect. If it is the history of the chosen people, it is their relation to God that constitutes history; if it is the movements of nations, these are controlled by the Supreme Ruler for His wise purposes. And so in all the other Scriptures: God is everywhere, and everything is viewed in its relation to Him. And yet there is little or nothing of theology; no reasoning about God, no argument for His being, no proof of His attributes. The Old Testament writers start with the assumption that God is there; and any one that denies or doubts His existence is a fool, any one that is indifferent to His providence or blind to His glory is brutish. "The fundamental thought of all Semitic religions," says Kuenen, "is the recognition of the Lord and Ruler of Nature and all her phenomena; the keynote of Semitic piety is submission to the divine power, bowing itself in awe to the very dust. In the one no less than the other lies the germ of a protest against the multiplicity of gods, which is necessarily accompanied by a limitation of the dominion of each, and which divides and therefore weakens the dread they inspire."[1]

Now this being the religious attitude of the Old Testament writers generally, we most naturally expect to find it assumed and maintained by the writers of the Psalms. And in fact we may sum up the religious contents of these compositions under two great heads, corresponding in the main to Hupfeld's broad classification,[2] though subject

[1] National Religions and Universal Religions, p. 24. Cf. Tholuck, Importance of the Study of the Old Testament, in Biblical Cabinet, vol. ii. p. 214 ff.
[2] See chap. viii. p. 175.

to the qualification that the two continually meet and interpenetrate each other : (1) What they say or imply as to God Himself, in His character, His working, His attitude towards His creatures ; and (2) what view they give of nature and the world as related to God, especially the relation in which men stand to Him, whether friendly or hostile, implying, of course, the relation in which they stand to one another in the light of their attitude to God. It will be convenient to consider the religion of the Psalms under these aspects.

The psalm-writers never tell us how or whence they have derived their knowledge of God. They take for evident and for granted not only His being but the character He bears. We cannot even trace an advance in their knowledge in one part of the Psalter compared with another. He may be represented in different attitudes, now favourable and near, at other times standing afar off, hiding His face, or shutting up His compassions ; but He is the same God still in all his essential character. As a recent writer [1] has well said :—

The modern philosophy of the Unconscious, and the fundamental scepticism of the agnostic, would alike have been unintelligible to the Psalmist, who furnishes in popular language arguments which are philosophically impregnable, and which anticipate the doctrines of despair that have gained such strange currency in the nineteenth century.

---

[1] W. T. Davison, The Praises of Israel, p. 107.

In the 94th Psalm they are destroyed before they are born. Teleological arguments, cosmological, anthropological, historical—all lie wrapped up in these cogent questionings, as the oak in the acorn.

> " And they say, The Lord shall not see,
> Neither shall the God of Jacob consider.
> Consider, ye brutish among the people :
> And ye fools, when will ye be wise ?
> He that planted the ear, shall He not hear ?
> He that formed the eye, shall He not see ?
> He that chastiseth the nations, shall not He correct,
> Even He that teacheth man knowledge ?
> The Lord knoweth the thoughts of man,
> That they are vanity."
> —Ps. xciv. 7-11.

Josephus, writing at a late time in his nation's history, interprets correctly the spirit of the old Hebrew writings when he gives as the reason of the superiority of the Mosaic system over all other legislations that Moses regarded all the virtues as subordinate parts of religion, and not religion as a mere subdivision of virtue : in his legislation he recognises all our actions as having ἀναφορὰν πρὸς Θεόν, a relation towards God.[1] Diodorus Siculus calls the true historian " the minister of Providence"; and Plato says " the Deity metes out all things " ('Ο Θεὸς πάντα γεωμέτρει). But nowhere do we see these principles so consistently acted upon and carried out in the treatment of history as in the Hebrew records. They do not lose sight of the Creator in the creature, nor

---

[1] Contra Apion, ii. 16.

forget that the God who metes out all things is in and above the world. He is Possessor of heaven and earth, but reveals Himself to His chosen ones, and exercises a paternal care over the steps of the individual.

This mode of viewing God is apparently deep rooted in the Hebrew mind; and, though attempts have been made to exhibit a growth in the knowledge or conception of the Deity, it has to be confessed that it is not easy to distinguish early and late in the views of the different writers, or to limit the recognition of the various divine attributes to certain times or to successive individuals. If we go back to the representation of the Divine Being which is found in the earliest Hebrew writings, we find the fundamental conception to be that of a Person endowed with qualities to which the human faculties are allied. We speak of the strongly marked anthropomorphism of the Hebrew writers, and some have taken this mode of expression to be an evidence of the low grade from which the Hebrews slowly rose to a more ethical conception. But we find that here in the Psalms, when religious experience and conception have reached the highest point attained by Israel, this anthropomorphism is as strongly marked as in any writings which can be supposed to represent a primitive view. The same faculties are attributed to the Deity, the same human mode of representation is employed as anywhere else — nay, the varying moods and tempers which might be predicated of a human being are ascribed to the Divine. And yet there is no proof that this mode of speech was attended with any degrading or derogatory conceptions of God; nor, we may add, has any better phraseology ever been devised to express the worthiest and most exalted feelings that the most spiritually minded in any age have entertained. Says Prof. Cheyne:[1] "The freedom with which the psalmists use anthropomorphic expressions is a consequence of the sense of religious security which animates them. They have no expectation of being taken literally." And he quotes as true of Scripture generally what the Talmud says of the Torah, "They spoke the tongue of the children of men." And, to quote again from Prof. Davison:—

Personal religion depends upon belief in a personal God. It is common, in these days, to raise metaphysical difficulties over the question of divine personality, whether a characteristic which implies limitation can be asserted of the Supreme Being, and the like; but in the Psalms such questions are never raised. The Psalmist cannot conceive of a God without consciousness, intelligence, and will. His is a God who thinks, knows, feels, and loves, who wills and acts—a God who speaks to men and to whom men can speak, who reveals Himself to mankind as the eternal "I Am," and with whom men may humbly but truly hold communion, echoing an eternal "Thou Art." This feature must not too readily be

---

[1] Original of the Psalter, p. 286.

taken as a matter of course; for, strange though it may seem, in the history of religions, man has been unable, apart from the Scriptures, to preserve in its purity belief in a personal God, and to hold the balance between Polytheism and the errors of earlier times on the one hand, and Materialism and Pantheism, with the errors of later times, on the other. The Bible—and pre-eminent among the books of the old Testament, the Psalter—is the stronghold of those who believe in a personal God.[1]

This so-called anthropomorphism is in fact nothing but man's ascribing to the Supreme Being the qualities which his own better consciousness declares to be the best and most fitting in one who is the Best and Highest. So that, from what the psalmists say of God, we may infer their opinions of what was best and worthiest in man; as we may, conversely, conclude how thoroughly the Hebrews ascribed an ethical character to God from the high ethical standard of duty which they recognised as binding upon man. No vice could be sanctioned under the example of deities such as the Greeks worshipped; nor could there be uncertainty as to the *result* and *reward* of action when one God was supreme, such as might tend to occur under a rule of gods many, each one contending with the other. Tholuck calls attention[2] to the idea of *guilt* produced in the Hebrews by the sense of divine holiness. Even Socrates, he says, was rich in his

---

[1] W. T. Davison, The Praises of Israel, p. 113 f.
[2] Biblical Cabinet, vol. ii. p. 214 ff.

poverty, but was proud of his humility. "And if David had been a tenfold greater sinner than he was, his sins had all been obliterated by that, his simple-hearted humility and penitence, which was, and is, and will continue to be, a folly to all the heathen: 'In my prosperity I said, I shall not be moved: Thou didst hide Thy face, and I was troubled.' 'Before I was afflicted, I went astray, but now have I kept Thy word.'"

The God whom the Hebrew writers know, therefore, and speak of, although the absolute Lord of all, is not conceived of as withdrawn from all relation to His works. On the contrary, it is only in this relation that He is thought of continually. We find very little here of the tendency observable in later Hebrew literature (such as in some parts of the Jewish Prayer-Book[1]) to enlarge on the uniqueness and incomprehensibility of the Divine character. The uniqueness of Jehovah to the Old Testament writers was His incomparable glory manifested in His great works done for His

---

[1] Thus, for example, in the so-called יגדל in the Morning Prayer:—
"1. Magnified and praised be the living God; He is, and there is no limit in time to His being.
 2. He is one, and there is no unity like unto His unity; inconceivable is He, and unending is His unity.
 3. He hath neither bodily form nor substance; we can compare nought unto Him in His holiness.
 4. He was before anything that hath been created—even the first; but His existence had no beginning," &c., &c.— Singer's Authorised Daily Prayer-Book, p. 2 f.

people. And if at times for a space they reflect upon His surpassing character, and the mysteries of His essence, it is only for a brief space, and they return to His "glory," which is the manifestation of His power and majesty in nature and in history. Even His holiness, which separates Him from all that is imperfect or evil, is represented as related to the world and to mankind; and, in a word, the Hebrew writers do not trouble themselves with metaphysical speculation as to the Divine Being, but think ever of Him as One having the closest relation to the world, and exercising on it a constant and righteous rule. From heaven God looks down. He delights in His works. His throne is in heaven; but His eyes behold, His eyelids try the children of men; and whether to rebuke the proud, or to plead the cause of the oppressed, or to heal the broken in heart, He is ever at hand to control, direct, and guide.

Accordingly, there is in the Psalter little or nothing of that element which we habitually regard as of the very essence of poetry: the "love of nature," as we usually express it, is hardly traceable. Sympathy with nature is more apparent—just because nature and man are both regarded as creatures of God's hands, and both suffer His wrath or receive refreshing from His presence. He visits the earth and waters it: He provides them corn when he has so prepared the earth; He maketh it soft with showers, and blesseth the springing thereof (Ps. lxv.) On the other hand, He looketh on the earth, and it trembleth; He toucheth the mountains, and they smoke. And so of animate creation: He opens His hand, they are satisfied with good; He hides His face, and they are troubled (Ps. civ.) But there is nothing of that revelling in nature, and delight in nature for itself, which is so common in other lyric poetry. There is not, for example, to be found a poetical description of sunrise or sunset; but the sun knoweth his going down, and then all the beasts of the forest creep forth; the young lions roar after their prey, and seek their meat from God (Ps. civ.) The Hebrew did not, in fact, know of that personification of nature which is so familiar to us. He could not think of the visible universe and the phenomena of the world apart from the direct guidance of the divine hand; he saw no beauty that was not the manifestation of the divine glory. He knew no Nature with a capital letter. The heavens are the work of God's fingers; the earth is full of His riches. Hence, though there is no *love* of nature, there is the keenest appreciation of its beauty, there is the ready eye to trace all that is fair, orderly, beneficent—for all those things God's hands have made,—and there is the true instinct of poetry to interpret these in the most sympathetic spirit; for man, crowned with glory and honour, is made to have dominion over the work of His hands. Not less ready is the poet to see in the more awful phenomena of nature the working of the Deity whose chariot-wheels roll in the thunder, and whose darts are the lightning. This is strikingly illustrated in that short but expressive psalm (xxix.), which makes us almost hear the crash of the storm and the rush of the tempest :—

> "The voice of the Lord is upon the waters:
> The God of glory thundereth,"

rising to the climax :—

> "The voice of the Lord strippeth the forests bare:
> And in His temple every thing saith, Glory!"

And then the poet having found a resting-place for his soul, the storm dies away into a calm :—

> "The Lord will give strength unto His people;
> The Lord will bless His people with peace."

The psalm from which we have just quoted reminds us, however, of the one aspect of God which ever recurs to the psalmist's thoughts—His attitude towards man and man's world. And the remark that was made a little while ago finds here its illustration, that the noblest qualities of which man is conscious in himself are ascribed by the psalmists to God. Whether in His dealings with the righteous or the wicked, the Lord is righteous in all His ways and holy in all His works. However much the psalmist may lament God's distance from him in distress, however heavily the chastening hand may lie upon him, he never suggests that imperfection, or want of power, or unrighteousness on God's part may be the cause of his sufferings. "The theory," says Prof. Cheyne,[1] "which underlies the prayers of the Psalter is that men should pour out their whole complaint to Jehovah (Ps. cxlii. 3; comp. lxii. 8), but should not rest content till they have emerged from the 'straits' of anguish into the 'wealthy place' of full trust in God (Ps. cxviii. 5). Then they can look out (Ps. v. 3) in the full assurance of faith, and the Divine Spirit conveys to them an answer of peace (Ps. lxxxv. 8)." On the other hand, it is not in caprice or in arbitrary cruelty that God manifests His anger against the wicked. No doubt He is a sovereign God, and man may not question His doing — He fashioneth their hearts alike—yet to the upright He shows Himself upright, and only to the perverse, because they are perverse, He shows Himself froward (Ps. xviii. 26).

In connection with this thought of God's relation to man and the world, we should not overlook those psalms which describe the glorious theophanies, whether these are placed in the remote past or looked forward to in the distant future. Closely regarded, we shall see in them more than a mere poetic representation of God's control of physical phenomena. The theophany is, no doubt, dressed up

[1] Origin of the Psalter, p. 287.

in language borrowed from nature's operations, but it will be perceived that the *purpose* of the theophany is God's revelation of Himself for the advancement of His gracious designs toward His people. So the theophanies of the past time have particular and close reference to the Exodus and the journey through the desert; and all down through the literature these glorious displays are dwelt upon. But not less so is it in the future reference. The burden of the expectation is, "Oh that Thou wouldest bend down the heavens and come down." It is the earnest expectation of the creation for the manifestation of the sons of God. As God was first, so He would be last: deliverance began with Him, from Him alone could come its final achievement. The apocalyptic passages in some of the prophets, such as Zechariah and Joel, exhibit this same expectation in only a varied form, and the fact should not be overlooked in any attempt to set forth the views of the Hebrew writers. Whatever may be the significance, from an eschatological point of view, of the ideal servant of the Lord who is to bring deliverance, this other aspect of the matter must ever be kept in view, that deliverance can only come from God Himself. The combination of the two is worthy of notice, as an adumbration of God and man meeting together in the grand consummation to which the Hebrew seers looked forward.

ABSENCE OF PARTICULARISM. 249

It is remarkable that we find in these religious songs of Israel so little of that so-called particularism, or exclusiveness of spirit, which limited God's favour to one chosen people. There are, no doubt, as we have seen, specifically national psalms which recount God's great deeds for His people, or recall His judgments inflicted on their enemies, to show that He hath not dealt so with any nation. In some also, no doubt, the national feeling becomes intensified to the degree of bitterness, as in the so-called imprecatory psalms. Moreover, many expositors now explain even the psalms which speak in a general way of the righteous and the wicked, as having also a national reference. But what I desire to point out in the meantime is, that even if this is the case, God's dealings with men are not represented as arbitrary, but as regulated by the moral character of those with whom He deals.

And we shall see this more clearly if we turn now to the other side, and consider how the psalmists represent man as related to God, and, by implication, how different classes of men are related to one another in the light of God's righteous character.

Men are broadly divided by the psalmists into two great classes, variously designated, but capable of description as either the good or the bad. The respective names by which the two classes are known are significant either of the relation in which they stand in God's view, or of the qualities which they manifest towards God and to one another. But various as the names are, they do not seem to indicate different subclasses or subdivisions, but simply various aspects of their standing and character. And just as the qualities of God's character are expressed in various ways according to the moral attitude of these two classes, so the dispositions of men towards each other are expressed according to their moral and religious relations to one another in God's sight.

Thus on the one hand the good are represented as righteous, upright, perfect, holy—and this too not only in comparison with other men, but in their standing towards God. It is, however, evident that the psalmists, in using such expressions of themselves or of their fellow-saints, do not employ them as exclusive of imperfection or sin; for in the very connections in which the words stand the writers confess their sins and ask for mercy.[1] When a psalmist says he has walked in his integrity, we are bound to take his words as he employs them and in consistency with what he says in the same breath; just as we interpret St Paul's words, "I have lived in all good conscience to this day," in the light of what he elsewhere says of his own sinfulness. The psalmists, in speaking as they do, claim for

[1] See on this subject Delitzsch, Comm. on the Psalms, Introd., x.

themselves an honesty of purpose and a sincerity of devotion to God and to His cause. They are on the side of the righteous Lord who loveth righteousness. And so, taking the other aspect of their position, they are God's beloved ones, His godly ones, His flock, His faithful ones. They are even described, especially in Asaphic psalms, in more endearing terms, as His turtle-dove (Ps. lxxiv. 19; cf. lxviii. 13), the generation of His children, the man of His right hand (Ps. lxxx. 17).

But there is still another side to the character of the godly. In sharp and sudden contrast at times to these high claims to uprightness, and the touching pleading with God of the favour which He bears to His own, we find the inner moral qualities of the suppliants depicted in another set of expressive metaphors. They are poor and needy; they are meek, weak, broken in heart; they go mourning, for inward grief consumes them; they sigh, wake in the night season, and take no rest. Or they pine away with wasting sickness, or decay under loathsome incurable disease, and draw near to the very gates of death. It is not always clear whether the troubles expressed in such terms arise from external enemies or from inward weakness; but undoubtedly in many cases there is no reference to the persecutions of enemies, and such expressions as the poor, the needy, and the weak are used to denote the thirst of the soul for God, and the humiliation of the spirit before Him. For there is the confession of guilt, guilt sometimes long borne because long unconfessed; and the terms in which confession is uttered leave no room for doubt that it was sin against God, and not merely injury done to fellow-men.

If we turn now to the other class of men we shall find the opposite characters ascribed to them. They are the wicked, sinners, foolish, proud, and that not merely towards their fellow-men, for they set their mouth even against heaven. They are stiff-necked, scornful, boasters; and, in contrast to the poor and needy, they are the rich, who are not in trouble as other men nor plagued like the rest of mortals.

And seeing that the psalmists are not cool ethical philosophers, surveying the moral world and describing it, but lyrical poets expressing their own feelings, they do not calmly contemplate the presence of these ungodly ones in the world. " Do not I hate them that hate Thee?" is the sentiment of the singer as he describes the proud boasters and their doings. God's enemies are his enemies, and indeed, being God's enemies, they actually show their enmity to God's people. From this point of view a light is cast upon the imprecatory psalms, which jar so harshly on the feelings of those who have been taught in the Gospel to bless and curse not. We must not here lose sight of the fact that the Old Testament morality is on a lower standard than that of the New; at the same time, we should not fail to note that the persons whom the psalmists execrate, apparently for personal wrongs, are described as the enemies of God and good, and so we can recognise, even in these denunciations of evildoers, an underlying love of righteousness.

These two classes of men thrown together in the world produce naturally that conflict, jarring, and enmity, the description of which bulks so largely in the Psalms. The wicked plot against the just, they slander them with their tongues—nay, their tongues are as sharp swords, their words like arrows; and the righteous are made continually their reproach, for apparently their poverty is cast in their teeth, their confidence in God, especially in times when God seems far off, is made the bitterest taunt they have to endure. Not only in words, however, but in cruel deeds the righteous are made to suffer. For the proud ones are oppressors, who plunder the innocent, pervert justice to the injury of the undefended, sit in the high places, neither fearing God nor regarding man. In such circumstances the weak man who has no helper, unable to cope with his foe, invokes an unseen Helper, an all-powerful Avenger. God's benison on himself, God's wrath and fury on his enemies, are in turn implored; but whether by the one means or the other, it is the justification and deliverance of the righteous that is asked and expected.

This, then, is the moral world in which the psalmists move. They are on the side of God, they have cast in their lot with God's saints, who are also God's poor; and over against this world of right is the league of evil men, seeking their own gain and advancement, but all united in one common antipathy to God's cause, one common aversion to God's people. There are thus two camps, or opposite parties, into which, according to the psalmists, the world of man is divided. They are opposite, even when not antagonistic—*i.e.*, even when no conflict between them is in question; they are characterised by different dispositions, are known by different external conditions or situations, and in the view of God stand on different grounds. But, as a rule, they are in conflict; and the psalmist himself speaks as if he were a party, or indeed often the only party, on the one side of the strife. And the strife is a never-ending one. If it does not always come to open hostilities, the enemy is ever on the watch; the psalmist may lie down in peace under God's protecting care, but on the morrow he has to stand to his arms, or at least to be on the watch. And it must be confessed that sometimes the battle is described in so highly figurative a manner that it is almost or altogether impossible to form a har-

monious or connected picture of the scene. In one
and the same psalm the psalmist may describe himself as assailed by wild beasts, attacked by fierce
enemies, and wasted by long-continued sickness
and ready to perish. Nay, he contemplates the
near approach of death, and sometimes laments
that he is going down to Sheol, where he can no
longer praise God; while at other times, with a
miracle of faith, he refuses to admit that even
Sheol will separate him from his God, and comforts himself with a thought of the beatific vision
beyond.

When he attains such lofty utterances, it is plain
that the psalmist is again idealising; and just because
he is now in the region of the most delicate and spiritual experiences, and endeavouring to depict the
most intense feelings of the soul, his metaphors are
the more bold, more complicated in their collocation, more rapid in their transition.

This heaping together of metaphors to express
spiritual feelings is an evidence of an acquired
habit of religious language. Each figure is not a
photograph of an isolated incident or a line in
a stated delineation of a historical experience;[1]
for the pieces do not so harmonise as to enable
us to grasp the whole in one picture. And such
a habit could only supervene on a long discipline of
personal experience and education in the spiritual

[1] See chap. ix. p. 213 f.

life. How far such an experience was attained or attainable in the pre-exilian period we shall have to consider in the sequel. In the meantime, it may be pointed out that, in its main features, the view that is given in the Psalms of man's relation to God, and of the moral distinctions of human society, is one that would occur to reflective minds in a very simple and even primitive condition of things. Given a conception of the Deity as essentially righteous in all His ways and holy in all His works, the moral sense would of natural consequence infer the rest. And the spectacle presented in the Psalms, of the wicked plotting against the just, of the rich oppressing the poor, of the proud lording it over those who have no support, is the spectacle exhibited in the social condition of the East apparently from of old—a condition in which the feelings of individual freedom and individual responsibility have not been cultivated, where the rulers and wealthy have it in their power, if they choose, to abuse their influence, and the oppressed have no redress. The hardships of life must have impressed themselves upon the minds of even ordinary men from an early time and in many Eastern lands, though the feeling has not found voice in literature. It is not to be supposed that the millions who toiled and fought to build up the great empires that rose and fell in the East never gave a thought to the arbitrary doings of their masters, nor felt the pain of oppression. Their cry and their groaning went up to heaven, though only the boastful words of their lords and kings have survived on the monuments reared by their pride to commemorate their victories. But it would not be wonderful if in Israel, where, as all allow, a higher ethical conception was earlier attained than elsewhere, and where there was at least, as it cannot be denied, some general consciousness of a righteous law, and a common conviction of the existence of a righteous Ruler, the lyre of a musical people was early tuned to the strains of pious reflection and humble complaint, and the spirits of the singers were quieted, and their troubles eased as they poured out their simple prayers and cast their burden upon the Lord.

CHAPTER XI.

THE SPEAKER IN THE PSALMS.

THE specifically religious element in the Psalms, of which we have been speaking, is by far the most important feature of these sacred songs. The psalms in which it comes most prominently into expression are consecrated by usage in the Christian Church as vehicles of the deepest feelings of the heart. The devout Christian in these last days finds no words more suitable than the words of the old psalms to express his penitence, his submission to God's will, his utter helplessness apart from divine aid. The Saviour Himself poured out His last breath with their words on His lips. And none of His followers, who in the centuries have borne their crosses after Him, whether on the road to martyrdom or on the *via dolorosa* of a painful life, have ever found themselves in a situation in which some word from a psalm failed to describe their case or to give relief under their burden. Unquestionably in the Psalms we reach the high-water mark of Old Testament practical piety, the best that the Old Testament can exhibit of heart-religion. If they are early, so much the more will our estimate of the pre-exilian religion of Israel, at least in certain circles of the people, be enhanced. If they are late, then we shall give full acknowledgment to the final and pure development of religious experience which they represent, as we feel bound in a common brotherhood to the pious singers who composed them. For, whether early or late, it is this personal and experimental aspect of religion which has always been specially recognised in the Psalms, and gained for them a place not only in the public praise of the Church but in the private devotions of its members. It has wonderfully helped many a penitent, to discover that sinners as great as himself have found mercy. And many a perplexed heart, doubting even the reality of its own experiences, has received a new access of faith by finding that all who have sought God have been led to Him in the same way, and that the whole course of divine guidance has followed one consistent method, leading plainly forward to full redemption in the Gospel.

We have, however, already seen incidentally that another voice than that of an individual is now by many heard in the Psalms. Accordingly we are confronted with the question, Who is the speaker in the Psalms, whether an individual or the Church collectively? And to this question the present chapter must be devoted.

There are about eighty psalms, or more than one-half of the whole Psalter, in which the Psalmist speaks in the singular number, and the experiences, hopes, fears, difficulties expressed seem at the first sight to be those of an individual. Now it is contended by many modern critics that in the great majority of these, or indeed in all of them,[1] it is not an individual that speaks for himself, but that the speaker is the personified Jewish Church, whose vicissitudes are described; and that it is only on this supposition that the Psalms yield a consistent and reasonable meaning, being explicable by the historical situation of the times in which they were composed. Closely connected with this view of the speaker, and in fact implied in it, is the supposition that the "wicked," the "enemy," and so on, who is spoken of, is no individual nor a number of separate individuals, but a corporate or collective adversary, either a heathen foe or a hostile party within the nation. On this view, in short, the struggle is not between the

[1] A full exposition and defence of the view is given by Smend, in an article "Ueber das Ich der Psalmen," in ZATW, 1888, pp. 49-147, in which all the "I-Psalms," with three or four exceptions, are explained as uttered by the Church. Afterwards, in a review of Nowack's edition of Hupfeld's 'Psalmen,' in the 'Theologische Literaturzeitung,' Nov. 2, 1889, he explained even these exceptions in the same sense.

Psalmist individually and his personal or social adversary, the arena of the strife is not the soul itself or the sphere of personal experience; but the struggle is between two embodied parties, and the arena is the open field of national history or political life.

Now it is to be conceded at the outset that personification is largely made use of in the Old Testament. Not only Israel, but other nations, either speak or are addressed in the singular. "Perhaps thou dwellest in the midst of me," says Israel to the Gibeonites (Josh. ix. 7, Heb.); "Thou shalt not pass through me," says Edom to Israel (Num. xx. 18: comp. vers. 14-21, xxi. 22; Deut. ii. 27-29; Judges xi. 19); "I will flee before Israel," says the Egyptian (Exod. xiv. 25, Heb.). So the house of Joseph speaks to Joshua (Josh. xvii. 14 ff.), the tribe of Judah to Simeon (Judges i. 3), the city of Ekron (1 Sam. v. 10, Heb.), the Jews of Bethel (Zech. vii. 3), and the heathen of the same city (Zech. viii. 21). These and innumerable other examples, to say nothing of the way in which Israel is addressed as "Thou" both in the Law and the Prophets, show that the figure of personification was common from the earliest times. It is therefore neither new nor strange that Israel is often represented collectively in the Psalms, and that in some of them we have undoubtedly a personification and a corporate reference. There is, for example, the alternate use of "I" and "we" in many psalms, showing that even if there is one speaker, he speaks along with or in the name of others. We could not have a better instance of personification than in Ps. cxxix. :—

> "Many a time have they afflicted me from my youth up,
> Let Israel now say;
> Many a time have they afflicted me from my youth up:
> Yet they have not prevailed against me.
> The plowers plowed upon my back;
> They made long their furrows.
> The Lord is righteous:
> He hath cut asunder the cords of the wicked.
> Let them be ashamed and turned backward,
> All they that hate Zion," &c.

In the same manner in Ps. cxxiv. :—

> "If it had not been the Lord who was on our side,
> Let Israel now say;
> If it had not been the Lord who was on our side,
> When men rose up against us:
> Then they had swallowed us up alive,
> When their wrath was kindled against us," &c.

In this latter psalm Israel is represented as the speaker, though the pronoun throughout is in the plural; and in the former, though the "I" is employed, there is no doubt of the sense in which it is used. The psalmist has indeed taken the trouble to tell us that he is uttering what might be the language of Israel as a whole; and, be it observed, the personification is so well maintained that the most superficial reader is not misled by it. It is different, however, with other psalms, in which it is only by the most laboured exegesis that it can be made to appear possible that the speaker is Israel or the Israelite Church.

This theory of personification in the Psalms has been so warmly taken up by the most recent writers, and is so fully carried out by some, that we must understand clearly what it amounts to.

It is not merely meant that a psalm, written in words that express the inner experiences of an individual, may be said or sung by a whole congregation. We are familiar with that in our modern hymns; and most people believe that the same is the case with many of our most cherished psalms. These are supposed to have been first the outpouring of one pious soul, and because they came from one true heart they are appropriated by the many, the whole congregation singing as one, while each individual appropriates the sentiments to himself. So far from objecting to such a general reference in the Psalms, we have already argued [1] that this is a characteristic of a genuine lyric that it passes lightly over what is temporary or special, and seizes upon the abiding and universal, so as to enlist the sympathies and interest of a greater number of hearers.

Nor is it merely asserted that a psalm originally composed with a reference to some definite situation

---

[1] See above, chap. ix.

in the life of an individual may be taken as applicable to a corporate body—to the Church, in fact, either of the Old Testament or of the New. In this way the ancient Rabbis explained many of the psalms as descriptive of the fortunes of "Israel" as a body, though they regarded them as having been first composed by David at critical periods in his history. And so Christian commentators have explained many of the psalms as referring to the Church, making the speaker sometimes the Church itself, sometimes Christ the head of the Church. This mode of "applying" the Psalms—whatever may be said of it as a mode of interpretation—is not what is meant when it is said that the "I" of the Psalms is the Church personified.[1]

What, in fact, these critics claim as demonstrable and proved is, that psalms in which "I" alone is found, and which could be read from beginning to end and give a fairly coherent sense if taken as the utterance of an individual, were yet from the first

[1] It is somewhat unusual to find modern writers appealing for support of critical views to the Rabbis and Church Fathers. Yet Smend (*loc. cit.*, p. 56 f.) buttresses his corporate reference of the Psalms by the exposition of these venerable authorities. No doubt the Rabbis were always looking for Israel, and the early Church Fathers for the Church, in the Bible, and so they naturally found the Psalms capable of application in their favourite sense. But was it not just because they were *uncritical* that they so proceeded; in other words, because with a theory of prophetic inspiration in their minds, they took no account of the primary historical situation of the psalm-writers?

composed, so to speak, in the name of the people or the Church of Israel, and intended to express the situation not of one person but of the people as a whole.

It is evident that the difference of view which thus arises implies a very wide divergence in the estimate of the history and the value of Old Testament religion generally. For example, it will make all the difference in the world if we ascribe the confident expectation of immortality in Ps. xvi. 8 ff. to an individual or merely see a reference to the perpetuity of the nation; and the confession of sin in Ps. xxxii. will have a very different significance when regarded as merely the acknowledgment of national backsliding, and when taken as the utterance of a heart broken by remorse. The greater the extension, the less the intensity.

In order to observe how the theory is carried out, and with what results, let us select such a familiar psalm as the twenty-third, and observe its treatment by Smend, a leading advocate of the theory of personification.[1] There is no doubt that an ordinary reader takes this psalm as the expression of individual experience; and, though a whole congregation sings it together, each singer appropriates it as his own. But let us hear

[1] It is but right to mention that Prof. Cheyne (Origin of the Psalter, p. 319) admits this and other psalms to have an individual reference, although he adopts largely the theory of personification.

how Smend, carrying out Olshausen's hint, expounds it:—

"The Lord is my Shepherd." But the shepherd, says the critic, does not tend a single sheep but a flock, and Jehovah is always called Israel's shepherd. It is true, no doubt, that Jacob is represented as saying that Jehovah had tended him all his life long (Gen. xlviii. 15), but then Jacob was not an individual; he stands for the people as a whole— he is the people in germ. Moreover, Jehovah is to lead the speaker in paths of righteousness for *His name's sake*. But Jehovah's honour attached to the people as a whole; it was in the fortunes of Israel that His sole divinity was manifested, and not in the daily walk of individuals. So also the expressions—" Thou preparest a table before me," " Surely goodness and mercy shall follow me "—can only be rightly understood if the Church is the speaker. The Church knows itself to be Jehovah's guest, client, and house-inmate, so long as it dwells in His land and has access to the Temple. Herein not only has it the pledge of divine grace, but all the grace of Jehovah is seen to be herein included. The dwelling in the holy land and in the vicinity of the Temple signifies for the Church salvation in the fullest extent,—to be driven out from which amounts to the rejection and destruction of the Church. Once did it so happen, but never shall it occur again. The Temple was indeed, as for the

Church so for the individual, of the highest significance (Ps. cxxii.), but scarcely could the individual so regard himself as Jehovah's guest and house-associate. This confidence belonged only to the people as a whole. Further, the individual might live far from the Temple, and his nearness to it did not shield him from distress. But the driving of the Church from the holy ground would have made an end of the religion.

This summary of Smend's treatment of the 23rd Psalm has been given, not for the purpose of entering into a detailed criticism of this particular application of the theory, but in order to exhibit the ground-principles on which he proceeds, and which to a greater or less extent are adopted by others who, like him, carry out this theory of personification with rigour. It will be observed that it is not for constraining reasons in the language of the Psalms themselves that Smend gives them this corporate reference. He has to take pains to make apparent to us how this reference inheres in the words, and at most he barely succeeds in showing how it may be read into them. The constraining reasons lie behind, in certain postulates, expressed or implied in his whole mode of argumentation.

One of these assumptions, deemed of such importance that it is declared to be the starting-point of the whole subject of psalm-criticism, is that the Psalter was the praise-book of the Second Temple.

This assertion proves nothing, as has already been pointed out,[1] as to the date and first occasion of individual psalms, nor does it warrant the inference that all the psalms are " Church psalms." Even if it could be shown by an examination of their contents that the Psalms were composed for common or public worship, that would not prove their *post-exilian* origin, for the corporate feeling was as strong in early as in late times; and it is quite possible that psalms may be of pre-exilian date and yet have been composed for the use either of the Temple worshippers or for assemblies larger or smaller of a more private kind.

No doubt, if Smend's contention were established —*i.e.*, if it were certain that the Psalms were originally composed primarily and directly for *Temple* use—it would go so far to prepare for the acceptance of the other position, that they were composed in the name of the Church. For the poet, writing what was to be recited and engaged in by the assembled congregation, would naturally adapt his words for the destined use. But it is by no means to be admitted without question that the Psalms were thus composed. On the contrary, a close examination of them shows such a diversity of situation, such a variety of conception and expression, that it is only by the most violent straining, or by obstinate adherence to a theory, that they can be

---

[1] See chap. iii. p. 57 ff.

viewed as having this primary reference. There is, for example, a very marked contrast between psalms found toward the end of the Psalter, in which public praise is the avowed theme, and many of the compositions in earlier books, where the themes are most diverse, and the appropriateness to common worship is far from evident.

Having the courage of his convictions, however, Smend carries out his principle with a rigour that gives a most constrained and unnatural tone to many of the simplest and sweetest of the Psalms, as we have just seen in his treatment of the 23rd. The 1st Psalm also, he says, is generally misunderstood. For here it is not the pious and the godless individual that are opposed, but in both cases it is collective bodies that are spoken of. The godless are to come to nought in Messianic times because they want the inner quality of continuance. But since the closing verses speak of the godless, we must understand the earlier verses to speak similarly of the godly collectively. The "man" who in verse 1 is pronounced "blessed" is just the Church. So, he maintains, in the passage Jer. xvii. 5 ff, which is so strikingly parallel to the 1st Psalm, it is the totality of the people that is spoken of.

A few other passages on which he greatly relies may be quoted, to familiarise the reader with what at first sounds strange. *E.g.*—

"But as for me, I am like a green olive-tree in the house of God:
I trust in the mercy of God for ever and ever.
I will give Thee thanks for ever, because Thou hast done it:
And I will wait on Thy name, for it is good, in the presence of Thy saints."
—Ps. lii. 8, 9.

"The righteous shall flourish like the palm-tree:
He shall grow like a cedar in Lebanon.
They that are planted in the house of the Lord
Shall flourish in the courts of our God.
They shall still bring forth fruit in old age;
They shall be full of sap and green."
—Ps. xcii. 12, 13.

"Blessed is the man that maketh the Lord his trust,
And respecteth not the proud, nor such as turn aside to lies."
—Ps. xl. 4.

"Blessed is the man whom Thou chastenest, O Lord,
And teachest out of Thy law."
—Ps. xciv. 12.

And even Ps. cxxviii. :—

"Blessed is every one that feareth the Lord,
That walketh in His ways.
For thou shalt eat the labour of thine hands:
Happy shalt thou be, and it shall be well with thee.
Thy wife shall be as a fruitful vine, in the innermost parts of thine house:
Thy children like olive plants, round about thy table.
Behold, that thus shall the man be blessed
That feareth the Lord.
The Lord shall bless thee out of Zion:
And thou shalt see the good of Jerusalem all the days of thy life.
Yea, thou shalt see thy children's children.
Peace be upon Israel."

He admits that this psalm is "somewhat different" from Ps. i., referring as it does to the present, while

Ps. i. refers to the future; but he maintains that since the first verse pronounces happy *all* pious Jews, and the last verse mentions Israel, the whole psalm must refer to the collective Church personified.

Even if we admitted that such psalms as these were made for the public service of the Temple, it would be difficult to imagine the mental attitude of the poet, if poet he might be called, who composed such a psalm as the one last quoted in the name of the Church, or even with reference to the Church as a whole. And if we reject the idea that the Psalms were all composed primarily for public worship, the corporate reference seems quite out of place. Now, as has been said, there is absolutely no proof that the Psalms were thus composed for public use. To assume it is to beg the whole question as to the origin of psalmody. The only *proof* worthy of the name must be drawn from the Psalms themselves; and any one can see from Smend's own examples how weak the proof is. On the other hand, it would be easy to produce expressions from the psalms in question in which it would be altogether inappropriate to regard the Church as the speaker,[1] *e.g.*—

" I am become a stranger to my brethren, and an

---

[1] Schuurmans Stekhoven has done this in reply to Smend in ZATW, 1889, p. 131 f. Cf. also Sellin, Disputatio de Origine Carminum, &c., p. 36 f. The few passages quoted, which might be indefinitely increased, may be allowed to speak for themselves.

alien to my mother's children" (Ps. lxix. 8). "Then I restored what I took not away" (lxix. 4). Indeed this whole psalm is personal.

"Unrighteous witnesses rise up; they ask me of things that I know not" (Ps. xxxv. 11), which Smend says may be a proverbial expression.

"Cast me not off in the time of old age; forsake me not when my strength faileth" (Ps. lxxi. 9); which he explains: "May God show Himself in the later history as He has done in the past."

"Oh, turn unto me, and have mercy upon me: give Thy strength unto Thy servant, and save the son of thine handmaid" (Ps. lxxxvi. 16); the latter expression is never used of Israel, and is quite inappropriate.

"When my father and my mother forsake me, then the Lord will take me up" (Ps. xxvii. 10).

"Behold, Thou hast made my days as an handbreadth; and mine age is as nothing before Thee" (Ps. xxxix. 5).

"The Lord will support him on the couch of languishing: Thou makest all his bed in his sickness" (Ps. xli. 3).

"Behold, I was shapen in iniquity; and in sin did my mother conceive me" (Ps. li. 5).

"For it was not an enemy that reproached me; . . . but it was thou, a man mine equal, and my familiar friend," &c. (Ps. lv. 12-14).

"Thou tellest my wanderings: put Thou my tears

into Thy bottle; are they not in Thy book," &c. (Ps. lvi. 8).

"At midnight I will arise to give Thee thanks" (Ps. cxix. 62).

It seems almost superfluous to argue seriously against such a rigorous pushing of the theory of personification as would give a corporate reference to words like these. It is necessary, however, to point out some of the stronger objections to the theory as a whole, in order that the basis on which it is rested may be made the more evident.

In the *first* place, it is difficult to see what is gained by it. All the objections that have any force against an individual reference of the psalms in question are just as valid against the corporate reference. There is the same heaping of metaphor upon metaphor and sudden transition from one figure to another, leading to a vagueness of presentation on either supposition, as Smend himself is forced to admit.[1] And then the brave assertion that all the Psalms are Temple songs, which was to solve all difficulties, breaks down in the actual exposition; for the "I" which ought consistently to be always the assembled congregation, is explained sometimes as the whole ideal Israel, sometimes as the Palestinian Jewish Church as distinct from the Jews of the Dispersion, and sometimes even as the Church of the

---

[1] ZATW, *loc. cit.*, p. 66 f., 79. Cf. Sellin, p. 27 f.

Exile. And so, when enemies are referred to, Smend is uncertain at times whether it is hostile nations or renegade, apostate, and time-serving Jews, parties, in fact, within the nation, that are in question.[1] Equally insufficient is the theory to explain a feature which is very common in the psalms referred to—viz., that the speaker draws a distinction between himself and God's saints or the congregation. Thus :—

> "I will declare Thy name unto my brethren :
> In the midst of the congregation will I praise Thee."
>
> "Of Thee cometh my praise in the great congregation :
> I will pay my vows before them that fear Him."
> —Ps. xxii. 22, 25.
>
> "I will wait on Thy name, for it is good, in the presence of Thy saints." —Ps. lii. 9.[2]

All that Smend can do by way of explaining such language is to keep repeating that Israel may be distinguished from the Israelites (Hos. i., ii.) and Rachel from her children (Jer. xxxi. 15 ff.), and so the Church of Jerusalem may in its own name speak of the whole Church of the Dispersion. The 22nd Psalm, he says, is evidently post-exilian; and though, in the time of the Dispersion, distress primarily fell on the Church in Judæa, it affected also the Judaism of the whole world, which, in

---

[1] See, *e.g.*, his remarks on Ps. viii., *loc. cit.*, p. 90 f.
[2] Such passages are numerous. See, *e.g.*, Pss. iv. 4-6, xxxv. 18, lxii. 8, cxvi. 14. Comp. Sellin, p. 37.

this connection, would be the "congregation."[1] But he does not tell us, for example, what *Church vows* were, nor does he make clearer the idea of the Church celebrating God's praise in the midst of the Church. Even could we maintain in our minds these nice distinctions between the Church and its parts, what, we ask in the name of common-sense, are we to understand by the father and the mother of the Church, or the wife of the Church in the innermost parts of the house, and similar incongruities? Such exposition only tends to make the Psalms unintelligible; and I take it that the psalmists were too good poets, and too sober and earnest thinkers, to give way to such conceits. And this suggests

A *second* objection, of a more positive kind—viz., that this carrying out of the personification theory does violence to the lyric character of these psalms, which, on this view, cease to be the spontaneous outflow of the poet's reflective spirit, and become highly artistic, or rather highly artificial compositions. For the poet is not giving vent to his own thoughts and feelings, but is continually thinking for some one else, putting himself in the place of some imaginary David or some idealised Church or community, and systematically proceeding upon intricate distinctions and elaborate personifications, which are in the highest degree forced and un-

[1] ZATW, 1888, p. 80; also Theol. Literaturzeitung, *loc. cit.*

natural in lyric poems. Thus, instead of coming warm from a glowing heart and expressing the rapidly changing feeling of the poet, the psalms are turned into descriptive sketches of the fluctuating fortunes of the Church as a whole, as the speaker is now execrating foreign enemies or censuring lukewarm kinsmen and apostate Israelites, or again appealing for divine favour on the plea of a worship faithfully performed at the Temple, and a tie indissolubly connecting Jehovah with the Holy Land. In short, to empty the Psalms of all personal reference is, as has been said,[1] to make these lyrics a species of poetry entirely unparalleled in the world. Whereas, in contending for an individual and personal significance, we do not exclude a wider collective reference, just because it is the property of a good lyric to express what is deepest in the poet's own feelings, and what appeals to the hearts of the largest number of readers. Hence, on this view, the rapid interchange of the "I" and the "we," which to the personifying theorists is so difficult of explanation, is really the best mark of the genuine lyric.

In the *third* place, the theory, in the unsparing way in which it is carried out, not only fails to do justice to the literary character of the Psalms, but does violence to their religious spirit; for it implies a movement of a retrograde kind, and is inconsistent

[1] Beer, Individual- und Gemeinde-Psalmen, p. xciv.

with the very position from which the critics themselves start. One of the reasons most strenuously insisted upon for the post-exilian origin of the Psalter is that the tone of religion in the Psalms is far too high for pre-exilian times. It needed, we are told, a long time for the teaching of the prophets to sink down into the general consciousness and come forth purified in the spiritual songs of the post-exilian Church. Yet, though the critics are continually repeating that the tone of the Psalms is too high for pre-exilian times, when they apply this theory of personification, they are ever attributing to the psalmists the very same circumscribed views and narrow local considerations which they are in the habit of describing as the pre-exilian or even pre-prophetic religion. What could be balder than Smend's explaining [1] those passages of the Psalms which speak of delight in nearness to God and dwelling in His house as the expression of the Church's confidence of safety because the Temple was standing, and of its belief that the celebration of worship was the pledge and assurance of His presence? Or what shall we say of his estimate of the post-prophetic religion and of the "Church"-consciousness of post-exilian times, when he writes: [2] "The prayers [of the Jewish Church] referred to concrete ends, the support of the Church against the ungodly and the heathen, their deliverance from immediate

[1] ZATW, 1888, p. 115.   [2] Ibid., p. 55.

danger; and they importunately demanded an answer by visible facts, for on such an answer the truth of the religion and the existence of God depended." Was it then for this that the teaching of the prophets required so long a time to sink into the general consciousness—to come forth again in corporate national religion? Why, these were the very things for which all the prophets, early and late, reproved their formalist contemporaries. And one would rather expect Smend's elaborate toning down of the spiritual meaning and his careful elimination of the individual reference of the Psalms, in order to make them the suitable expression of the religion of a *Church-nation*, to lead up to the conclusion that compositions of so narrow a spirit must be taken as products of the pre-prophetic religion.

In fact, the expressions "Church," and "Church-religion," as used in these discussions on the Psalms, are misleading. For the Church that is indicated is not an invisible body of believing souls, but a visible community, constituted, no doubt, on a basis of common religious belief and worship, but existing for "concrete ends," and exercised to a great extent with the very secular and material measures necessary for self-defence and self-government. The Church of Jerusalem, in whose mouth Smend puts some of the loftiest Psalms, was, after all, but the municipality—at best, all that survived, or all that could be revived, of the old national order. If it deserves the name of a Church, it is a very broad one, for all were members of it as a matter of course; and however passive or indifferent they might be, so long as they formed no party hostile to the general good, they were of the "saints" or "godly ones" who made up the collective "I" that speaks in the Psalms. Of necessity, therefore, if the Psalms are to be explained as the utterance of a body like this, their language must be restricted in its application to relations that could be predicated of such a body. And it is here that the incongruity appears; for the language itself, being derived from inward spiritual experience, is so strikingly expressive of spiritual relations, that we feel it to be no advance, but a retrogression, to give it a lower application. When, for example, a psalmist (and he may have been David himself) sets divine gladness in the heart above the increase of corn and wine (Ps. iv. 7), and can sleep in quietness though surrounded by myriads armed against him (Ps. iii. 5, 6), it is doing violence to his words to assert that his faith and his religion depended upon such "concrete ends" as plentiful harvests and signal victories.

Let us, however, look into the matter a little more closely, in order to discover if possible—what is the essential point to be settled—not how the

Psalms might be sung or applied, but how they came first from the hand of the composers. From a merely literary point of view it must be confessed that there is a certain want of lucidity in the view we have been considering; and it is worth while to examine the question from this point of view, in order to try to represent to ourselves what the position and literary situation of the first authors of the psalms in question must have been.

First of all, it is undeniable that, not only in the so-called "I" psalms, but in every psalm, the primary speaker was one person. It was no company that sat down, each to contribute a line, or all together to concoct a poem; but the person from whose pen or whose mouth the song first came, whatever were his thoughts, thought them himself as an individual. Be it picture or experience, he saw the picture before him; he imagined, conceived, or felt the experience. It came first of all from his mind. If he recounts facts that are known to all, yet it is he that supplies the words and provides the poetical setting. If he says "we," thereby associating himself with others, he has something in common with others, yet he speaks primarily and directly of and for himself. And if, speaking for all, he uses the simple "I," he *may* be using a personification; but, if it is a matter of experience he is relating, one would expect him not to say "I" unless he had made experience of what all feel.

Let us now suppose that a poet sets himself deliberately to employ personification. It is an art, and it will have to be artistically worked out. A certain collective body, whether all Israel, or the true Israel, the nation or the Church, is to be represented as a person,—clothed upon, so to speak, with the dress of an individual. A nation or Church has not, *e.g.*, a face, hands, feet, bones, soul, spirit, and so forth. All these are attributes of the individual, and they are to be predicated of a Church or community. Our artist must get his materials somewhere before he can effect the personification; and if he has the true artistic taste, he must choose the suitable materials for the case. Just as the panting hart, the rushing torrents, the rapid lightning, the thirsty ground, and the hundred other figures by which mental states and attitudes are described, had been seen by the poet's eye and taken possession of by his fancy, forming the poetic stuff with which he worked,—so every touch that he is to give in his process of personification must have been suggested by his observation or his experience; and his observation must have been accurate, his experience wide, if he is to portray the Church in a personification that shall answer to the life.

Now if we look closely at what we may

call the material with which the poet produced the alleged personification, we shall see that a very great part of it is drawn, and could only be drawn, from personal experience. The very idea of personification implies the attributing to the collective what is properly the quality of the individual; and even when the psalmist employs such objective figures as holding by the hand, entertaining as a guest, and so forth, he must first of all have formed an image of the individual in his mind. But when he goes farther and speaks of purely moral and spiritual relations, he must have formed a conception of these relations in an individual sense, before he could apply them artistically to the whole body or to the people. How could he employ such expressions as a broken spirit, a contrite heart, a clean heart, delight in God (or in His law), communing with one's heart, unless he had first experienced what the expressions imply? Smend himself admits[1] that in such a psalm as the lxxiii., in which the poet describes his victory over doubt, the subjective experience of the individual may be of special interest for the whole, if each saint has had to pass through it. But if this be so, then such a psalm would be intelligible as a *Church* - psalm only on the supposition that individuals had made experience of what the psalm describes—in other

---

[1] *Loc. cit.*, p. 51. Comp. p. 124 f., also p. 70 f.

words, on the presupposition of a pretty general experience of religion on the part of individuals. So Prof. Cheyne says:[1] "Granting that David, like other poets, might idealise himself, how could he work into his poetry thoughts and experiences which had no root in his inner and outer life?" But this is only the statement in regard to particular cases, of a truth of general application, that personal experience is anterior to, and the foundation of, religious personification.

Both Smend and Cheyne appeal[2] for confirmation of the personification theory to the choruses in the Greek plays, in which the collective chorus speaks as one person. Be it so. Yet it is the writer of the play who is the first concipient of the idea that is expressed, and the Greek tragedians, in fact, especially Euripides, are fond of putting into the mouth of the chorus their own conceptions as a kind of commentary or reflection on the course of the play. So that the poet himself speaks, as it were, from under the mask of the chorus, and, in any case, the thoughts are first of all those of an individual.

It would not be difficult, I think, to prove that even the prophets learned in this way by private experience the great truths they were called on to impress upon the people in their corporate

[1] Origin of the Psalter, p. 260 f.
[2] ZATW for 1888, p. 60, Anm. 2 ; Origin of the Psalter, p. 262.

capacity. The comparison of Israel to an unfaithful wife is one of the most striking figures of prophetic diction. But we cannot forget that Hosea, who employs this figure with most touching effect, is believed to have been taught the fulness of its meaning in his own bitter personal experience. We see also how Isaiah, whose duty it was to impress upon the Israel of his day the holiness and greatness of Jehovah, was set apart for his ministry by that vision in the Temple, when a live coal from the altar was taken and put upon his lips in token that—unclean as he felt himself to be—his iniquity was taken away. It was the same with the prophets Jeremiah and Ezekiel, as they expressly tell us: they had first to be taught themselves before they were sent to teach others.

If the prophets were thus taught by experience the spiritual truths they were to declare, much more must the psalmists, who, as it is alleged, ascribe to the Church the feelings and experiences of the individual, have made trial of these in their own souls before they could apply them to the body as a whole, so aptly and unerringly that the most deeply experienced and spiritually minded even under the Christian dispensation acknowledge their fitness and force.

The conclusion, I think, is inevitable, that if we have personification in these psalms, then we must postulate the existence, at an earlier stage, of a heart-religion, an experimental religion as the possession of the Israelite poets. It is surely an extraordinary position to maintain, that it was only after and through the use of a personification so very appropriate and striking that susceptible souls came to know what personal experimental religion was. For when Smend asks incredulously,[1] "How came it that the Jewish consciousness drew so enormously from religious individualism?" I would simply ask, What else could it draw from in the nature of the case? And what he declares to be "quite natural and self-evident"[2] I think is quite unnatural and absurd—viz., "that individual piety would borrow from the common consciousness and not the reverse,"—for religious experience, in any proper sense, must first be an experience of one, and the common consciousness in such a matter could only be the aggregate consciousness of separate individuals. Smend himself in his more recent work[3] expresses himself with more moderation: "The religion was primarily represented by the totality of the pious, but the party of the pious rested ever on the personality of its leaders, who furnished with their trust in God a support to the totality of the pious." Prof. Cheyne more adequately represents the true position,

---

[1] ZATW, *loc. cit.*, p. 53. [2] Ibid., p. 143.
[3] Lehrbuch der Alttest. Relig., p. 475.

though in somewhat hazy language, when, contending that the speaker in Ps. xxii. is the Church, he says [1] the writers "spoke for the community, having absorbed that passionate love of God and country which glowed in each of its members." With more lucidity in another connection, when speaking of certain "mystical" psalms, he says: [2] "I know that, according to some critics, the speaker in these passages is only the nation personified. For my own part I do not think so; but even if they be right, such expressions could not have been assigned to the nation if they had not first been uttered by individuals."

Instead of admitting, therefore, that these psalms were merely the expression of the national vicissitudes or social movements of the post-exilian community, the very use of the language which they embody could not have failed to keep before the minds of the pious singers who composed them the personal feelings which they so aptly express. Since the metaphors and images employed are such as could only be drawn from personal experience, there must have been in the minds at least of the poets themselves, and probably these were not few, such a stage of spiritual experience as made that phraseology natural to them and adequate in the circumstances. So much for the poets who first composed the Psalms.

[1] Origin of the Psalter, p. 264 f.   [2] Ibid., p. 385.

But we must go further. When these Psalms came to be sung by the congregations of Israel, what, we ask, was the consciousness of each individual worshipper who joined in the words? I think any reader at the present day, trained though he be in abstract thinking, requires to make an effort to keep up the feeling of personification which is said to be expressed in the Psalms; and I take it that the Jewish worshipper, who came the nearest to occupy the alleged standpoint of the poet, would retain this consciousness also only by a constant effort. If he was one who also was in sympathy with the poet's religious experience (which I maintain must have furnished this clothing for the personification), then he was construing continually his own inner feelings into an image of the Church. And as for the ordinary Jewish worshipper, it will be hard to believe that he did not, as we know an ordinary worshipper at the present day who is not trained in abstract reasoning and nice distinctions does spontaneously, take personal language in a personal sense. So that, in fine, the worshipper who already had the personal experience would have it fostered and cherished, and the man who had little of it would be educated into it. The conceptions of the Psalms are coined in a personal mint, in the chamber of the individual soul; and whatever they did to foster national or corporate religion, they would also infallibly foster personal religion.

It seems to me, therefore, beyond question that, just as each individual psalm must have been individually composed, after being individually conceived in one poet's mind, before they could be collectively used as a Church liturgy, so the experience of sin, penitence, pardon, peace, was made in the individual heart before the expression of it could be put into the mouth of a personified Church. And that, after all, is the point we wish to reach—viz., the ultimate source of psalm-religion. It came from the one heart and appealed to the hearts of many. It did not first express itself as the attribute of people in the mass, who then discovered that this was a fit expression for private religion.

The feeling of the Christian consciousness, and of the religious heart generally, should count for something here. For what is internal, subjective criticism but the bringing of the matter to the test of our best faculties of discriminating? And the religious sense can be trusted as a good judge of what is religiously conceived. The readiness with which the individual consciousness has in all ages appropriated the Hebrew psalms as the expression of its best moods and feelings is a proof of this at least, that in these songs the Hebrew poets have come the nearest to the deepest instincts and the most sacred experiences of religious man. The Christian Church —having Christ for its head—furnishes a far higher and more perfect subject of personification than the Jewish Church was fitted to be. And Christian expositors have, just as Jewish expositors in their field, applied these psalms, or many of them, to the Christian Church. Yet beyond that, and in a more special sense, have the Psalms been felt to be Christian hymns, expressing the feelings, attitudes, and relations of soul which are cardinal to Christianity. Whatever may be said of the religious basis of the Jewish consciousness in matters of religion, there can be no doubt that in Christianity religion begins in the individual heart, the essential soul-relations are those of the individual, each believer being a "lively stone" in the great living temple of the Church. And it would seem strange, therefore, that the Psalms — the closest approximation to Christian truth — should furnish as their highest type of religion a mere national attitude of Israel to Israel's God, surrounded by enemies, not even of a spiritual kind, but merely of a political or at most a social description.

We cannot take these highly metaphorical descriptions as war-bulletins, detailing the progress of campaigns; we cannot form out of them a connected picture of national and social situations. Whether the psalmist is speaking of himself alone as beset by enemies, or is describing the situation of his nation at any given time, we cannot construe a hard historical counterpart of fact out of every

T

detail, every figure, every metaphor of the psalms in question. We shall have to admit here again, as in regard to the kingly psalms, for example, that the singer takes an upward flight into " an ampler ether, a diviner air." Instead of forcing into or out of every detail a reproduction merely of an event or an experience in the outward life of the individual or the nation, we should simply confess that the poet is thus, by the aid of his poetical symbolism, doing what a modern thinker would do by the aid of his abstract terms; that he is moving in a spiritual and supersensible world, and describing—as one who has been engaged in it— the eternal struggle between the opposing forces of good and evil. Thus and thus only, it would appear, can we obtain a clue to the meaning of those deeper, mysterious psalms, which seem to be written under the very shadow of the cross of Christ, and in which the psalmist seems to catch a glimpse of the evangelical truth that through death lies the path to eternal life.

CHAPTER XII.

PERSONAL RELIGION IN PRE-EXILIAN TIME.

AT every successive step in this inquiry it becomes more and more apparent that a broader and deeper question is involved than the mere dates of the composition of the Psalms. Expressly or by implication there is the underlying question as to the character of the religion of Israel in pre-exilian times; and it becomes more and more evident that upon the varying conclusions reached, or the presuppositions held, on that subject depend mainly the conclusions or attitudes of different inquirers into the subject of the Psalms. When, for example, one critic [1] says of a certain psalm (Ps. viii.) that he cannot understand how the "eminently spiritual tone" of its words can be attributed to Israelite antiquity, and even to the time of David; and when another [2] is continually dropping such remarks

---

[1] Smend, ZATW, 1888, p. 55.
[2] Cheyne, Origin of the Psalter, pp. 99, 231, 237.

as that "such highly spiritual hymns" (as Psalms lxi. and lxiii., for example) obviously cannot be pre-Jeremian, and that "such ripe fruits of spiritual religion" (as Ps. xxii.) could not have been produced before the period which preceded Nehemiah's first journey to Jerusalem; and, again, that "such sweet expressions of resting faith" as are found in Ps. xxiii. and others cannot be pre-exilic; it is obvious that the writers employing such language have an anterior controlling view of the history of Israelite religion which excludes the psalms in question from pre-exilian time, and that the subsequent work of the critic is merely the detail of determining *how* late the compositions are to be placed.

We are, accordingly, now brought face to face with this fundamental question, Whether there was room in pre-exilian time for such a religion as is expressed in the Psalms? For greater clearness, however, we must consider a little more closely what those critical writers mean when they assert for the Psalms a tone so spiritually high that it is inconceivable before the Exile. In the preceding chapter the opinion has been expressed that the critics here take a retrograde view of the religion, and that their exposition is neither consistent with their own theory of development nor adequate to account for the language of the Psalms. And it behoves us to inquire what they understand by *post*-exilian spiritual religion in order to perceive what they expect *pre*-exilian religion to be.

It is plain enough that on the personification theory, which resolves the speaker in the Psalms in all or most cases into the collective Church, the religion which is described as so eminently spiritual and high-toned is not regarded, primarily at least, as the experience and sentiment of individuals—is not, in short, personal piety and "heart-religion" as we usually understand that expression, and in the sense in which we nowadays read and appropriate the Psalms. Critics like Smend tell us that in no single instance does the "I" of the Psalms stand for an individual; and others who would not go so far, even while they admit a sporadic and occasional personal reference, yet find the experiences and situations of the post-exilian Church in the great majority of places where the words appear to read as the experiences of an individual psalmist. It is plain, therefore, that the "spirituality" and "high tone" are to be understood on this interpretation. So Smend has told us that the 8th Psalm refers without doubt to "the discomfiture of Jehovah's enemies by common prayer," whereas in early pre-exilian times "Jehovah manifested His power in quite a different way." Prof. Cheyne also speaks [1] of the individual consciousness being all but lost in the corporate, and gives it as his opinion that

[1] Origin of the Psalter, pp. 265, 277.

"in most cases the supposition that the original psalmist sometimes speaks as any pious Israelite, who shares the joys and sorrows of his nation, would speak, is sufficient." "Rarely," he says, "do the Hebrew psalmists disclose their personality. They had indeed their private joys and sorrows, but they did not make them the theme of song. The individual consciousness was not sufficiently developed for this, and so an unselfish religion was easier for them than it is for us." Smend, while confessing that the disappearance of the individual in the mass, which is characteristic of ancient Israel, is to our psychological understanding incomprehensible, says that it comes in fine to be a question whether the religious individualism, which people are wont to get out of the Psalms, existed at all in pre-Christian Judaism.[1] And Prof. Cheyne indicates what he means by high spiritual tone when he says of Ps. xvi. : "Certainly no one who thinks that, upon the whole, history is marked by progress rather than degeneration, can, without inconsistency, affirm this psalm to be Davidic. It cannot even be preexilic at all, but is the fruit of that long weaning from the world, begun in Babylonia, and perfected under another foreign yoke in Israel's recovered home. It is, in fact, one of the finest Church-songs. The "excellent" and the "holy ones" can be no

---

[1] Review of Nowack's edition of Hupfeld's Psalms, Theol. Literaturzeitung, 2nd November 1889.

other than the priests, who, as represented by the "high (literally, great) priest," were more and more found to be Israel's firmest support against heathen aggression."[1]

We gather, then, from statements like these, that the eminently spiritual religion of post-exilian Judaism, which finds its brightest expression in the Psalter, was a *corporate* religion, in which the wants and feelings of the individuals as such were subordinated to or swallowed up in the necessities and situations of the Church as a whole. It is the heathen world-Powers who in turn held God's people in subjection that are especially His enemies, and this because their rule over the Holy Land and the chosen people was sacrilege; and those words in the Psalter denoting enmity to God—such as *the wicked, the impious,* or even *man* generally— are so many designations of these heathen Powers.[2] Sometimes, however, these heathen Powers assumed a friendly or actively favourable attitude to Israel, as in the times of Ezra and Nehemiah and the Ptolemies, and in such times psalms like the seventy-second and the forty-fifth could be indited in their praise. On the other hand, not only outside the chosen nation, but within its bosom, there might be and actually were enemies of God, a hostile party, opposed to His law,—not, indeed,

[1] Origin of the Psalter, p. 197 f. Compare p. 163 and related note.
[2] Smend, Lehrbuch der Alttest. Relig., p. 379 ff.

openly taking part with the nation's enemies, but yet treading down and oppressing their poorer brethren,—a condition of things which finds expression in the sighing of the poor and the cry of the needy which are heard so often in the Psalms.[1]

Meantime, till God's power shall be revealed in the discomfiture of His enemies, it is the duty and privilege of the Jewish Church to celebrate His glory and testify to His greatness. He sits enthroned on the praises of Israel (Ps. xxii. 3); the Jewish Diaspora in its widest extent makes His name known to the ends of the earth (xlviii. 10, lxv. 5, 8), and the Jews were even prepared for the idea that the homage of the heathen would also be ultimately offered to their God (Mal. i. 11, 14). But meanwhile the existence of the religion depended on them alone. The nation must not disappear, else God's praise would cease from the earth (Ps. vi. 5, xxx. 9, lxxxviii. 10 ff., cxv. 13 ff., cxviii. 17).[2] It is, in fact, on the language of many of the psalms in this connection that Smend bases one of his strongest arguments for the theory of personification. The speaker, he says, applies to himself terms, and claims for himself an importance altogether unbecoming in an individual Israelite, and therefore these psalms must be understood

---

[1] Smend, Lehrbuch der Alttest. Relig., p. 387 ff.
[2] Ibid., p. 386 f.

of the Church as a whole. He speaks, for example, as if God's cause depended on the issue of his own private case, so that the deliverance of the psalmist would amount to the justification of God, and his desertion or downfall would be an occasion for reproach to God's enemies, for it would be tantamount to the annihilation of pure religion.

The Church, says Smend,[1] stood in quite a different attitude towards God and the world from the individual. It had greater sins and sufferings, greater responsibilities and hopes. In relation to God it felt itself under wrath, because the enormous collective guilt of the past rested upon it. Its sufferings also were the greatest conceivable contradiction between the ideal and the reality; the whole of mankind must have been viewed by it as its embittered enemy. . . . The religious consciousness of the individual, on the other hand, rested always in Judaism on the general consciousness, the individual in the last resort must always fall back on his relation to the whole, when he wished to conceive of his belonging to Jehovah.

To many readers all this will appear to fall very far short of the spiritual religion which they have been accustomed to find in the Psalms, and to be but a little advance, if an advance at all, upon the religion of pre-exilian Israel. And the statement of it will prepare us for the conception of pre-

[1] ZATW, 1888, p. 54 f. Cf. pp. 79, 90, 96.

exilian religion as it is represented by writers of this school. These writers are in the habit of repeating that after the Exile Israel was no longer a nation but a Church. Old Israel was destroyed, as the prophets had threatened, and prophetic men like the authors of the Deutero-Isaiah had laid the foundation of the post-exilian Church in a truer sense than Ezekiel and the authors of the Priestly Code. The latter merely drew a practical inference from the situation of things, but the former made the personal faith of the prophets the faith of the whole Church. Their ideas, however, got modified by altered circumstances as time went on, as is always the case with the ideas of pioneers. The Church, in fact, became more and more legalistic, and its relations to the world, which these great theologians had regarded as temporary, proved in the end to be abiding. Israel found itself to be no longer one nation among many, but one nation against all the world; the honour of Israel's God was enlarged into the honour of the Lord of the whole earth. And this is the situation depicted in the Psalms.

Now, even admitting this to be in the main a true statement of the position in the world of the post-exilian Judaism, it might be argued that it does not differ essentially from the situation in pre-exilian times; and also that it is inadequate to account for the remarkably spiritual tone of the

Psalms. It could be shown that the absence of national independence in the post-exilian time was always regarded as accidental and temporary, and that the expectation of a restored monarchy was never absent, blending with and fading into the more spiritualised Messianic hope. And, on the other hand, it might be shown that in the pre-exilian period the God of Israel was distinctly recognised as the Lord of the whole earth, and that Israel's cause was sacred just because it was His cause. But the point chiefly insisted on now is that what is described as the highest spiritual religion of the Old Testament is still regarded as merely a refined national feeling, and that what, on the simplest construction of the language, is a spiritual warfare, is ever being explained as contests waged with carnal weapons. One would certainly have expected to find more than this as the efflorescence of Old Testament religion. And if this is the highest that is to be found after all the teaching of the prophets and the discipline of experience, we need not be surprised at the poor account that is given of pre-exilian and of pre-prophetic religion.

We must, therefore, consider whether there is not proof that the individual counted for more, and personal piety was not a more general experience, than this view implies. It is a question not merely of comparative date, but of comparative standard, a question not of lateness but of lowness—the question, namely, as to whether, early or late, we are not justified in reading these Psalms as the expression primarily of the thoughts and feelings of the individual soul.

We must, however, here recognise a distinction between the old and the new dispensations. When Smend says it is a question whether individualism, as we understand it in the Psalms, existed at all in pre-Christian Judaism, we must concede his contention to this extent, that a conception of personal religion in the absolute sense of there being no difference between Jew and Gentile was entirely foreign to Judaism. The history of the Christian Church in the New Testament age shows plainly that even the apostles of Jesus had not surmounted the position of national religion so far as to apprehend that in God's sight, and in the new order of things, there was no difference. The question put by the disciples (Acts i. 6), "Wilt Thou at this time restore again the kingdom to Israel?" shows the standpoint occupied by them after the Ascension; and the reluctance of St Peter to hold intercourse with the Roman Cornelius (Acts x.) was only overcome by a special vision making known to him the truth that "God is no respecter of persons; but in every nation he that feareth Him and worketh righteousness is acceptable to Him" (Acts x. 34, 35). It was not without an effort that the Church of apostolic days allowed Gentiles to enter its precincts without passing through the porch of the Law; and St Paul speaks of the mystery which, in other generations, was not made known unto the sons of men, that the Gentiles are fellow-heirs and fellow-members of the body, and fellow-partakers of the promise (Eph. iii. 4-6).

Individualism of this kind is not to be looked for in the Old Testament, in which even the most glowing passages of the prophets anticipate an expansion of Judaism and a glorification of their nation, not a breaking down of the high privilege which had been bestowed in ancient promise. Yet the corporate religion of the Old Testament leaves room for an individual and personal religion, just as the individualism of the New Testament is in nowise inconsistent with a Church-religion. Not only within the pale of the post-exilian Jewish Church but in the sphere of pre-exilian Israel there are so many proofs that the thing was understood as a matter of course, and was an active influence in life, that it seems strange that it should be denied. When Smend goes the length of saying[1] that even in the book of Jeremiah the "I" who speaks is sometimes Israel, sometimes the prophet, who in his person represents the true Israel, and that no later individual found himself in Jeremiah's situation, and so on, one feels that there is here a case of pushing a theory in the face of all obstacles; and, in general,

[1] Theol. Literaturzeitung, 2nd November 1889.

the account which he gives of the pre-exilian religion proceeds upon an exegesis of the historical and prophetical writings which is open to the same objection.

It is to the pre-exilian writings that we must turn for proofs on this subject; and the inquiries we have to make are such as these: Did individuals in early Israel, apart from or within the corporate relationship in which they stood to the nation, feel that they stood in direct religious relationship to God, in such a way that they were responsible for their individual actions, and acknowledged the divine control of their daily lives? Were these relations of such a kind as to imply a moral and spiritual consciousness, which would lead individuals to express such feelings and to look to God for such blessings as we find in the language of the Psalms? Was there, in short, within the bosom of collective Israel, the recognition of the individual as an ethical quantity, standing in immediate spiritual relationship to God, and of the requirements of the religion which all professed as binding upon individuals as well as on the nation?

(1) Now, in the first place, it may be argued that the very existence of *law* in ancient Israel implies the recognition of individual responsibility, and was calculated to educate the individual moral sense. This argument is not based upon any assumption of the Mosaic antiquity of the legal code or codes as

such; indeed it will gain in strength on the modern critical hypothesis of the origin of these codes. The coming of the individual Israelite to the priest for *torah* or instruction, whether that was embodied in formal enactment or merely given orally as occasion demanded, implied the need of individual guidance, the confession by the worshipper of some defilement or trespass, or the acknowledgment of some personal or family blessing. Every basket of fruit that was brought to the sanctuary, every firstling of the flock that was redeemed, impressed upon the individual the fact that the requirement of the general law reached to his particular case; and that Law being regarded as of divine origin, the individual as subject to it was brought into direct relation to the divine will. "Thou shalt do no murder," or any of the most fundamental moral obligations, though addressed to the nation as a whole, could be kept or broken only by particular personal act; and as often as a case of judging between man and man, between stroke and stroke, had to be decided, so often was there a case of moral and individual discipline, a step in the education of the conscience, and a recognition of individual responsibility before God.

(2) In the second place, the books of the writing prophets, with their reproof of sins and commendation of virtues, draw a clear distinction between good and bad individuals in the nation, and proceed

upon the recognition of personal responsibility and upon the existence of a personal judging moral faculty. The very function of the prophet as a reprover implied this. We may turn to almost any page of the very earliest of these witnesses and we meet with catalogues of virtues and vices which could only be exemplified in individual acts. When Amos denounces as transgressions of Israel the land-grabbing and oppression of the poor by the rich (Amos iii. 10, iv. 1, v. 11, 12), are not these individual sins, and does he not imply a discerning conscience in his hearers? We hear the very plaint of the poor and needy that is directed to God in many of the psalms, though it is uttered in the sterner tones of the prophet as addressed to the oppressors themselves. So the prophet Hosea depicts a *social* and not merely a national condition of things when he says: "The Lord hath a controversy with the inhabitants of the land, because there is no truth, nor mercy, nor knowledge of God in the land. There is nought but swearing and breaking faith, and killing, and stealing, and committing adultery; they break out, and blood toucheth blood" (Hos. iv. 1, 2). And what these earliest prophets say is repeated by Isaiah in the bloom-period of prophecy, and echoed on to Jeremiah at the close of the national history. "Run ye to and fro through the streets of Jerusalem, and see now, and know, and seek in the broad places thereof, if ye can find a man, if there be any that doeth justly, that seeketh truth" (Jer. v. 1). "As a cage is full of birds, so are their houses full of deceit: therefore they are become great, and waxen rich. They are waxen fat, they shine: yea, they overpass in deeds of wickedness: they plead not the cause, the cause of the fatherless, that they should prosper; and the right of the needy do they not judge" (Jer. v. 27 f.) Here and elsewhere we have the very words and phrases that occur so often in the Psalms, and there can be no doubt of their individual personal reference. Moreover, it is particularly to be observed that, though the offences specified are mainly injuries done by man to man, yet the Lord proclaims Himself the avenger of all such; it is He that "hath a controversy with the inhabitants of the land." In other words, the whole prophetic work was directed to the quickening of that feeling of individual responsibility which finds expression in the Psalms: "Against Thee, Thee only have I sinned."

It would be easy from almost any of the prophets to bring forward passages which, if translated from prophetic language into that of the Psalms, would exactly depict the condition of things set forth in many of these plaintive prayers. That is to say, if instead of the prophet addressing his words of rebuke to the rich, the proud, the unjust, and so forth, we represent the poor, the meek, the oppressed directing their complaint to God, we have only another aspect of the same situation. The poor they had always with them; and though it has been objected that there is more frequent mention of the "wicked" under various epithets in the Psalms than in the prophetical books, this can easily be explained by the fact that the prophets speak directly *to* the wicked, and do not require to name them (every prophetic rebuke implies their presence), while the psalmists speak *of* the wicked in their plaintive appeals to the righteous Judge of all.[1]

But, indeed, we can hardly suppose any condition of society existing in ancient Israel in which such a distinction did not prevail as is implied in language like this. On however low a plane we may suppose their ideas to have moved, they were a people with the ordinary institutions of an organised society, possessing property, living under laws written or consuetudinary, subject to the variations of fortune incident to such a life, and, like other ancient Eastern peoples, having no defined middle class between rich and poor. No doubt many countries in the East at the present day present a fair parallel to the social condition of Palestine during long periods of the monarchy. The social inequalities are just such as are reflected in the Psalms. The evils under which the individual in modern times complains are not mainly or not

[1] Sellin, Disputatio, &c., p. 51.

primarily of a political kind, as, *e.g.*, that the rulers are of foreign blood or different faith, but that the ruling class as a whole is unjust. And the injustice, which is sometimes most severe when the superior is nearest in social station or kindred to the oppressed, poisons the whole social life, producing want of truth and fidelity between man and man, the circumventing and slandering of the poor man by another who is but little above him in the scale, and, in general, the oppression of the man who has no "back," as the phrase goes. In such a state of society, where justice — in the sense of legal decisions — can be bought and sold, the oppressed man is very literally and truly the "poor" man, having nothing wherewith to buy; and the case of the orphan, the widow, and the stranger—the man who has no kindred to intercede for him or to sustain his cause—is as pitiful as it is anywhere depicted in the pages of the Prophets or the plaints of the Psalms. It is to be added, that such a condition of things induces, as might be expected, a religious tone very similar to that of the psalmists—a spirit of prostration and helplessness, reacting now into passionate appeals to heaven for deliverance, again into lurid imprecations upon the oppressor; or, in stronger and more pious souls, expressing itself in dumb unquestioning submission or struggling hope. It may, indeed, be partly owing to the imperfections of the social order in such countries, the weakness of human law and the uncertainties of moral issues between man and man, that Oriental peoples have acquired the *religious habit*, as we may describe it, of referring things more directly to God than people do who can count upon the even working of the principles of justice. Accordingly, a type of faith which is pre-eminently *submissive* comes readily as a relief and support, and the religious attitude towards unavoidable trouble or distress is summed up in such a formula as that so often on the lips, "There is no strength nor power but in God." We are accustomed to regard this as a product of Mohammedanism; but it is, in fact, deeper than any formulated creed, and no doubt it has made the reception of Mohammedanism easier in those countries where that religion chiefly prevails. There is more truth than we usually think in Mohammed's claim that Islam (which simply means resignation) is as old at least as Abraham.

(3) In the third place, the very oldest of the historical writings show that the individual was reckoned as the moral unit, and that personal piety as well as individual transgression were well understood. If we turn to those parts of the book of Genesis which modern critics declare to be among the earliest attempts at written history, we find that that history is indeed mainly a record of indi-

vidual lives and characters, and that, like all the Old Testament history, it is set in a religious light. When the writers proceed to set down the origin of the nation and the source of their religious beliefs, they trace all from the individual, through the family, to the nation. In the period up to the Deluge we find a righteous Abel, a translated Enoch, who had walked with God, a just Noah, upright in his generation,—all sharply distinguished from their godless neighbours, and even from members of their own families. And it is the same in the patriarchal history. Where shall we find a better picture of the pious individual than that of Abraham, who believed in God, and it was counted to him for righteousness? And with him as an individual was the covenant made. It had reference to a nation, no doubt—nay, it was to be world-wide in its range of consequence—but it was with Abraham, the friend of God, that it was in the first instance concluded. And there is no need to go in detail into the subsequent patriarchal history, which is all conceived on the same plan of selecting one and rejecting another, and the gradual enlargement of the family into the nation. National religion, in a word, at whatever rate it may be appraised in ancient Israel, is based on, and grows out of, individual religion.

No doubt critics interpret these patriarchal stories as legends, and Smend, as we have already seen,[1]

---

[1] See above, p. 266.

explains away Jacob's words that Jehovah had tended him as a shepherd all his life long by saying that Jacob is personified Israel. But the writers of these patriarchal stories did not write as modern critics; to them each patriarch was most evidently a distinct individual. In other words, the popular conception, at the time at which these narratives were told, was that individuals stood in direct religious relationship to God, and that the distinction of good and bad individuals was universally recognised. The whole story of Abraham's intercession for Sodom (Gen. xviii. 23-33) turns upon this: "Wilt Thou consume the righteous with the wicked?" "That be far from Thee to do after this manner, to slay the righteous with the wicked, that so the righteous should be as the wicked: that be far from Thee: shall not the Judge of all the earth do right?" (ver. 25). And the narrative makes it plain enough what the wickedness of the men of Sodom was. It was not because they were heathens, or because they oppressed Lot and others like-minded, but because of wickedness in their lives, that divine judgment was executed upon them. And it is particularly to be noted, in view of what Smend is continually saying of the undue importance of the individual, how in the end it came to this, that if even ten righteous persons could have been found in Sodom, the whole place would have been spared for their sake. Indeed, Smend cannot but perceive that this whole narrative is dead in the teeth of his theory. And he makes no attempt to reconcile it with his view, but simply says [1] that the whole passage, vers. 22 *b*-33 *a*, is an insertion by a later hand. But the thing is too deeply engrained in the whole mode of thought of these early historians to be excised in this way. The Hebrew writers show beyond question that it was the common belief that the knowledge of good was communicated first to individuals: "Enoch walked with God," "God spake to Abraham"; and the distinction between a pious man and a wicked man was clearly enough apprehended apart from any relation in which they stood to the nation.

When we come down to the period when the nation had taken more corporate shape—the time in which this "national religion," as it is regarded, was in full exercise—we find that the individual is *not* lost in the mass, as Smend would make us believe. For instance, we have the account of the man who gathered sticks on the Sabbath-day when Israel was in the wilderness (Num. xv. 32-36); and the narrative told in minutest detail of the sin of Achan in taking of the spoil of Jericho (Josh. vii. 10-26). We have also the record of the rebellion of Korah and his company (Num. xvi.); and it is to be observed that, though sins committed by individuals entailed suffering upon the community, yet the

---

[1] Alttest. Relig., p. 474.

individuals are singled out for punishment. And we could not have a clearer proof of the fact that there was a recognised individual consciousness in the matter of sin than in the simple words put into the mouth of the poor woman of Sarepta with whom the prophet Elijah went to live during the famine: "Art thou come unto me," she says, "to bring my sin to remembrance?" (1 Kings xvii. 18).

The same sense of individual responsibility and direct relationship to God is exemplified in all the instances—and they are numerous—in which we find individuals offering up prayers for themselves or for others. Thus Abraham, as we have seen, prays for Sodom (Gen. xviii. 23-33), and entreats God on behalf of Abimelech (Gen. xx. 17). His servant Eliezer, recognising God's guidance in his journey to Padan-aram, prays at the well for a token of assurance (Gen. xxiv. 12-14). We read frequently of Moses interceding for the people, and praying for himself. The people also entreat Samuel to pray for them, and he declares that it was his constant work to do so (1 Sam. xii. 23). David's prayers are frequently mentioned, as on the occasion of the promise given to him of a sure house (2 Sam. vii. 27); and in that sorrowful night when his child was stricken with sickness (2 Sam. xii. 16).

There cannot be either a virtuous or a vicious nation without virtuous or vicious individuals; and as personal relationships are the nearest to men, the virtues or vices of individuals in a mixed community impress themselves upon the most unobservant attention. Nor should it be forgotten that ancient Israel was differently constituted from some of the great Eastern monarchies, in which the people as a mass were subjects of one despotic ruler. The blood-kindred that united the tribes, the tribal and family divisions and autonomies, and the limited power of the king, were all of a character to educate the feeling of individuality both in social and religious matters.

Many prominent critical writers on the religion of the Old Testament, from the time of Vatke, have a short and sharp method of dealing with the subject of individual religion : they simply deny its existence. "Not the individual Israelite," says Stade,[1] "but the whole people of Israel, was a religious quantity. It was the national misfortunes that first raised the question, of which even the prophets had never once thought, how the fate of the individual stood related to his own actions on the one hand and to the fate of the people on the other." "The popular religion," says Marti,[2] "as well as the pre-exilian prophets, knew nothing of individual retribution; the individual was involved in the fate of the people,

---

[1] Geschichte, i. pp. 507, 513, ii. p. 24.

[2] August Kayser's Theologie des Alten Testaments, 2te Auflage, von Marti, p. 185.

and had to endure with the people its punishment as he participated in its blessings." And other writers repeat the same thing in similar terms,[1] overlooking or ignoring the fact that, though undoubtedly the ancient view was that the nation was the religious universe, so to speak, beyond which was a world lying in wickedness, yet within that pale there was free play for individual action, and a clear enough conception of individual responsibility. Smend has, in his recent History of the Old Testament religion, relaxed the rigidity of former writers, and admits that there is such a thing as individual religion in the Old Testament. But he maintains[2] that the relationship of the individual to God was altogether arbitrary, and not governed by ethical considerations. Some were favourites of heaven, others without assignable reason were not; sons might be favoured for their fathers' sakes, and yet even from His own favourites God might without reason withdraw His kindness. The most that one could do was to submit patiently, taking what Heaven sent, or perhaps get into the good graces of those who were observed to be prosperous and so share in their good luck. At best the individual could *hope* in God, but could not have confidence in Him. The examples, however, which he adduces fall short of establishing such a sweeping conclusion. No doubt they exhibit a some-

[1] See Sellin, Beiträge, i. p. 140 f. [2] Alttest. Relig., § 7, p. 99 ff.

what primitive conception of the divine operation—and ancient Israel could hardly be expected to have attained a firm persuasion of the unerring working to minutest detail of moral principles. As Smend himself says, God was regarded as a living person, not an impersonal Law; and we can observe the tendency in Israel, as among Orientals generally, to magnify the divine sovereignty almost into fatalism. Yet Smend's own examples prove that the God of Israel concerned Himself with the smallest affairs of the individual, and though He gave no reason for His actions, He never relaxed His control. Moreover, He was the unquestioned Judge of the widows and the fatherless, the avenger of right and wrong; and even if the sufferer could not trace the connection between sin and punishment, he firmly believed there was a connection, and was willing to own his personal guilt even though his conscience was not quick enough to bring it home to him. As Sellin has pointed out,[1] the belief in a personal retribution underlies all the forms of oaths and imprecations, which play an important part in the early religious life; and we find the principle formulated in the most general terms: "Whosoever sins against Me, him will I blot out of My book" (Exod. xxxii. 33); "Them that honour Me I will honour, and they that despise Me shall be lightly esteemed" (1 Sam. ii. 30); "The Lord shall render

[1] Beiträge, Heft i., p. 149.

to every man his righteousness and his faithfulness" (1 Sam. xxvi. 23).

There does not, therefore, appear sufficient reason for drawing so broad a distinction as is made between national religion before the Exile and Church-religion after it. In both periods the mass bulks largely, but not so largely as to exclude the free play of individual responsible action. In the earlier period as in the later the individual had his desires, his hopes, his sins, his sufferings; in the later, no doubt, all these were accentuated, and, as the wall of nationality was more and more broken down, the individual felt himself more intimately face to face with a moral law and a spiritual requirement that were broad as the world. Nevertheless, in the earlier period also the individual was accounted a "moral quantity" in the sight of God; and it seems to me that the refusal to admit this fact not only leaves the later and more spiritual religion without adequate explanation, but tends to lower the level of that religion itself, till there is found scarcely anything worthy of the name of individual religion in the Old Testament at all.

In contending, however, that we have in the Psalms what may have been the expression of individual piety in times before the Exile, we do not necessarily imply that the persons who composed these songs occupied, say, the same level of spiritual apprehension and experience as persons in these days who use the Psalms as vehicles of devotion. The remarkable thing is—and surely it is very remarkable—that we may put into the language of the Psalms as much spiritual meaning as we please with a full sense of their fitness to our own experience, and this itself is a strong presumption that their primary meaning and reference was of an individual kind. Robertson Smith, in speaking [1] of individual and collective psalms, says that the poets in many of these compositions give expression to their own religious experiences, but they purposely do so in such a general manner that any other pious man may straightway appropriate those feelings to himself. And Tholuck finely remarks [2] that it partakes to a certain degree of morbid religiousness when the pious poet cannot break away from his own individual relations, whereas it is a sign of power when he can sing his own feelings in such a way as to touch the universal feelings of humanity. The more a Christian advances in piety, he says, the more does he find, even in special necessities, an appropriate expression of his wants in the simple and familiar Lord's Prayer. We may compare the religious phraseology of the Psalms to the picture thrown upon a screen before the exact focus of the lens has been found. The image is there, though dim in outline and vague in expres-

---

[1] Old Testament in the Jewish Church, second edition, p. 189.
[2] Uebersetzung und Auslegung der Psalmen (1843), p. xxvi.

sion. It is the same picture that grows in clearness as the light is concentrated into true focus. The experience is true from the beginning, though it may be weak and vague; and the phraseology has been so well chosen and controlled that it is capable of ever new applications, and will never become inadequate nor antiquated while human nature lasts.

CHAPTER XIII.

DAVID THE PSALMIST.

IN the preceding chapter, though we have proved little directly as to the authorship of the Psalms, yet the discussion of the inevitable previous question as to the possibility of psalm-religion in pre-exilian times has given us good reason for maintaining that personal piety was a thing not unknown but actively in exercise and generally presupposed.

We can now advance farther and consider whether we know of individuals in that period whose piety was of the type expressed in the Psalms, and whether their circumstances and situations were similar to those of the psalmists.

1. And, first of all, let us look at the individual prophets. In them, if anywhere, and in them without question, we have instances of good men. The very calling of each prophet implies an individual relationship to God, and implies also an antithesis between him and others. No doubt we are here

still within the sphere of the nation; it was the God of Israel that called the prophet, and the prophet was sent with a message to the people. Early or late in the history of Israel, we cannot get away from this national reference. Yet the singling out of one from his contemporaries, the sending of one on a mission to the many, the assurances of help for his work, the distinction of the true prophet from the false, the universal belief that a prophet must be specially called and sent,—all these are so many different aspects of the individual standing of the man. Look at Amos, as depicted in his book. He stands sharply and clearly alone,—taken from his herds and his sycomores, hurried away from his native town and country, confronted with the power and opposition of the northern kingdom, avowing no connection with prophetic guild or class. "The Lord took me," he says; and we could not conceive a better example of a direct relationship to God. And before him we have Elijah, towering in solitary grandeur over king, people, and powerful prophetic opposition—not indeed so solitary as he supposed, but yet testifying all the more by his conviction of loneliness that one man might be the mouthpiece of God, and receive in his own soul all the strength and comfort needed for the religious life. And before him we have Samuel, the great Scripture pattern of youthful piety, communing often with

God, and mediating in intercessory prayer for the people. Moses himself, to whom the Old Testament writers trace back prophecy, is delineated so plainly as a type of personal religion that nothing but the existence of such a piety could have made the delineation so exact. Any one of all these is a fit character to be assumed as the speaking subject of a psalm, understanding by such a composition the outpouring of the soul's fulness to God. And in every one of the cases mentioned we have the very situation implied in so many of the most spiritual of these songs. We have the one faithful individual against a multitude of gainsaying, perverse, unbelieving people,—a "godless people," in the sense that they refused God's ways. The cause of each one of them becomes at the crisis the cause of God against the world, the world being then, before political events had broken down national barriers, the commonwealth of Israel. And, finally, we are allowed to penetrate so deeply into the consciousness of these men, that we can detect the pain and anguish caused by this isolation, the helplessness of the man apart from divine aid, with the struggling faith in the divine righteousness and goodness, or the submissive resignation to the mystery of the divine will, exactly as these are seen fluctuating in the Psalms.[1]

---

[1] See, *e.g.*, Exod. xxxii. 11, xxxiii. 12, Num. xi. 11-15; and compare 1 Sam. xx. 3, xxvii. 1, 2 Sam. iii. 39.

It is no wonder that critics like Hitzig have attributed so many psalms to Jeremiah. This prophet more than others gives us full details of his outer and inner experience; he is by nature peculiarly sensitive and prone to give full expression to his sensitiveness. Whether or not we have in the Psalter productions of his pen, there are certainly not a few psalms which, in respect of experience, language, and situation are entirely and eminently in keeping with his life and character, so that no fair-minded critic, on a comparison of them with Jeremiah's known work and place, would say that they were above or beyond his range. Now, though no doubt Jeremiah stands well down in the prophetic roll, and the events through which he lived were of a nature to sadden even a bolder spirit, yet from the nature of the case there is to a great extent an essential similarity in the personal experience of all the line of prophets, just because the duty laid upon all was essentially the same, and the situation involved in the national environment was essentially unchanged.

These considerations, of course, are so general that they do not entitle us to say of any particular psalm that it was written by any particular prophet; yet they are of such force that we may affirm that any one of the prophets was quite capable of composing *some* psalm. We have already[1] put the

---
[1] Above, chap. xii. p. 305.

matter in this way, that many of the Psalms, if turned into prophetic style, might read as passages from the prophets. And we may now say conversely that there are many passages in the prophets that embody all the essential elements of the Psalms; and, what is more, there are not a few passages which, even in the unessential features of style and form, might be taken from the context and read as psalms. The book of Isaiah contains several such pieces; the greater part of the seventh chapter of Micah is quite psalmic in thought and expression; Jeremiah is particularly prone to lyric meditation in the style of the Psalms; and the books of Nahum and Habakkuk have each a chapter entirely psalmodic in construction (Nah. i.; Hab. iii.) There is also the psalm, already spoken of, in the book of Jonah (chap. ii.) And then we find in some of the historical books specimens of psalms ascribed to prophets or to persons under immediate prophetic influence, as the song of Hannah (1 Sam. ii. 1-10) and the prayer of Hezekiah (Isa. xxxviii. 9-20), to say nothing of pieces ascribed to David, whether or not included in the Psalter (2 Sam. xxii., xxiii. 1-7). In point of fact, as Prof. Cheyne reminds us, prophetic and poetic inspiration were closely connected in primitive times, both Miriam and Deborah being called prophetesses.[1]

This being the case, it is far from admissible simply

[1] Origin of the Psalter, p. 15 and note.

to set aside all these lyrical pieces found outside the Psalter as insertions in the historical and prophetical books belonging to a later age when psalm-composition had become prevalent. It is true, no doubt, that the critics who would reject these pieces support their decision on the ground that there are no such precise references in the pieces as would warrant their being assigned to the occasions to which they are referred by the Biblical writers. But this is just because the critics insist on finding in a lyric what is in reality a drawback to its excellence; for, as we have already argued, the less particular and precise such a song is, the more it appeals to the common heart, and gains in universal application and esteem.[1]

To the question, Why we do not find a greater number of sacred lyrics outside the Psalter, and to the other question, Why the pieces existing outside the Psalter have not been embodied in the collection, we may not be able to return satisfactory answers. It would be equally difficult, I suppose, to answer the question, Why so few pieces have been preserved from the Book of Jashar or the Book of the Wars of Jehovah, both of which seem to have been collections of valuable national songs. It is possible that from a comparatively early period a collection or collections of this special kind of composition were

---

[1] So Beer argues in regard to the songs in question (Individual- und Gemeinde-Psalmen, p. lxxxii. ff.)

formed, so that, finally, all religious lyrics, not already embedded in other books, were brought together into one Psalter. We need not expect to find more than one Psalter. But the existence of psalms in the historical and prophetical books proves, at the very least, that the authors or editors of those books believed that psalm-composition was not restricted to a particular class of psalm-composers. And there is this to be said in favour of the early inclusion of these pieces in the books where they are now found, that the later we come down, there is the more probability of the separate existence of a specific collection of sacred songs in which they could have readily found a place, without being thrust, as the critics say they are, into books whose connection they disturb. So that, on the whole, it seems there is sufficient presumption that the composition of psalms or lyrics of a religious character was not a late achievement, as certainly there is sufficient proof that there were men adequate to this class of composition.

2. Hitherto we have spoken mainly of single prophets or prophetic men, and their fitness to become psalm-writers. It is now, however, to be observed that each prophet did not stand isolated and alone in his generation. We have positive proof in the case of Jeremiah that he had a certain number, at all events, of faithful adherents like-minded with himself. Isaiah also makes mention

of his disciples. Indeed to represent, as is too often done, each prophet as standing utterly and absolutely alone, giving expression to some truth that no one had ever before heard and no one but the speaker accepted, is a supposition scarcely conceivable, and probably entirely opposed to all that we know of the history of reformers and the growth of religious ideas. If in Elijah's dark days there were seven thousand, *unknown* to him, who had not bowed the knee to Baal, we get a glimpse also of a faithful Obadiah, whom the prophet did know (1 Kings xviii. 3-13); and we may—nay, we must —assume all along the existence of a certain number of faithful ones, who followed the preaching of the prophets and who trembled at their words, and were thus the representatives and continuators of the better faith of the nation. Let us for a moment consider the prophetic work of such a man as Isaiah or Jeremiah. Is it conceivable that, having delivered some discourse in the court of the Temple or in some place of public concourse, the prophet was silent till his next public appearance, and his hearers departed, one to his farm and another to his merchandise, giving no more thought to his words? We learn from Jeremiah himself, what we might safely infer from what we know of his temperament, that, having publicly warned and rebuked the people of his day, he was in the habit of interceding for them in prayer (Jer. vii. 16, xi. 14). And what a later prophet has mentioned as customary in his time (Mal. iii. 16), would most naturally occur at other times: "They that feared the Lord spake one with another." The prophets' addresses would form the themes of meditation in lonely chambers or in small circles of the pious—translated, so to speak, into prayer and attuned to song on the lyre. The very secrecy and isolation of these little bands would furnish the plaintive key in which their meditations were composed, and so the poor and the meek never failed from the land.

In this connection we may refer again to those psalms found outside the Psalter — the song of Hannah, the prayer of Hezekiah, and the prayer of Jonah, along with which may be taken the Apocryphal prayer of Manasseh, and that of Ben Sirach (Ecclesiasticus li. 1 ff.) Whether these, critically examined, are considered to suit the occasions to which they are referred or not, is another question; but in the meantime it is plain that they are by the writers assigned to the individuals named, which in itself is a proof that in the writers' estimation psalms expressing the experiences of an individual were possible — in other words, that individual religion was well recognised. Smend's contention,[1] that these personages are types of the true Israel, needs no refutation.

3. The preceding argument goes to prove that

[1] ZATW, 1888, p. 145.

there is nothing in the essential character of the Psalms that places them above and beyond the reach of prophetic circles in pre-exilian times. No doubt some are loftier in tone than others, deeper in insight, wider and firmer in faith and hope. But similar variations are seen in the Prophets, and these variations are not dependent on chronology. After all has been said, the difference between prophetic and hymnic religion is a difference in form of expression, a difference at most of audience and of speaker, not of substance. The prophet declares the truth to others, the poet repeats the same truth in other words to himself or tells it in prayer to God. And who knows how often the prophet may have been nerved for his public ministrations by such private exercises of prayer and meditation ministered either by himself or by others? For we need not look always for a prophet or a king or a prominent official of State as the composer of a psalm. "Bring me a minstrel" (2 Kings iii. 15) may have been a common formula in the gatherings of the pious; and the gift of song, like the gift of prophecy, was no doubt given in richer measure to some than to others, and to individuals who were by nature more receptive. Persons who could freely and readily express their own and others' feelings in song may have been little fitted for taking up the utterance of the Lord in a great and gainsaying concourse.

This line of argument converges with another which has been already pursued,[1] to the effect that the practice of lyric poetry was common in ancient time—that, in fact, poetry was engrained in the Hebrew temperament. And it meets the objection that occurs at this point, that the specimens of lyrics found outside the Psalter are all of a secular character, and therefore that psalmody was a later and special acquirement. We have already said that we cannot expect to find *two* psalters; and the objection in hand can only be maintained by excising from the prophetic and historical books any specimens of sacred lyrics that occur. But if it has been shown that psalm-religion could exist, and did exist, in prophetic times, and also that lyric composition was practised from the earliest times, there seems nothing to hinder us from believing that psalms, whether many or few, now found in the collected Psalter, may be the work of pre-exilian authors.

And thus we are brought again to the question of Davidic psalmody by a new route. The question at the present day is, Have we sufficient reason for ascribing to David *any* of the psalms included in our existing Psalter? for to this question the advanced critics give a decidedly negative reply. Admitting that David was both a musician and a poet, they say that the music

[1] See chap. vii. p. 153.

was much too rude for use in divine worship or altogether worldly, and that his poetry was secular. Moreover, the Psalms, it is alleged, are of such a spiritual tone as to be inconsistent with the character of the historical David. His lament over Saul and Jonathan (2 Sam. i. 19-27), and his lament for Abner (2 Sam. iii. 33, 34), it is maintained, though creditable to him as a poet and a man of tender feelings, do not warrant us in regarding him as a man of such religious experience as would find utterance in the Psalms. So we are told that "if we wish to know David as he really was, we must put the contents of all these songs completely on one side, and rely exclusively upon the narratives of the books of Samuel and Kings";[1] and the account of his life and character contained in the books of Samuel, *when critically sifted*, reveals to us, it is maintained, quite a different man from the David of tradition.

There are here two things, the estimate of David's poetry and the estimate of his character. As to his poetry, Prof. Cheyne himself expresses[2] astonishment that although dancing with song—joyous music, in fact—was so characteristic of ancient times,—and David appears himself in this attitude, —yet the specimens of poetry ascribed to him in the

---

[1] Bible for Young People, vol. iii. p. 83.
[2] Origin of the Psalter, p. 192.

historical books are of an elegiac or mournful character. The astonishing thing here, however, is that Prof. Cheyne, with his broad literary sympathies, takes such a narrow view of the poetical faculty. When the same poet, Cowper, has left us the poem of "John Gilpin" and the eminently spiritual hymn "God moves in a mysterious way," to take but one instance out of an indefinite number that will occur to the reader, we should make some allowance for the versatility of the ancient muse, and admit the possibility of David, who could pen these elegies which are exquisite in their pathos and delicacy of sentiment, being able also to indite a poem expressing faith in God.

So also we may hesitate before accepting the estimate of David's character presented by many critical writers. Here, for example, is the estimate given by one very outspoken writer,[1] already quoted: "It is easy to understand how David came to be regarded as the chief psalmist of Israel. In the third century before Christ, when the book of Chronicles was written, the time of David was looked upon as the golden age of Israel, and David himself as a model king. Hence the writer of this book gives him as much as possible of the honour of having built the Temple. Now, since the ancient tradition represented David as a great singer and player on the harp, and the Jews of this later period

[1] Bible for Young People, vol. iii. p. 81.

could not conceive of a model king composing any but religious music, they imagined David to have been the father of psalmody." The only thing that is "easy" here is the entire ignoring of the difficulty. Where did these traditions come from, and why was it that, at the late period referred to, the age of David was looked upon as the golden age of Israel? This habit of explaining the early as the backward projection of the late is always liable to the objection that it leaves the late itself without explanation. Moreover, this habit of refusing to admit complexity in the capacities of Biblical characters is exceedingly hazardous and unsafe, when history is so full of instances of the combination in one person of qualities the most diverse. We have not only poets who can harp upon more than one string, but we have religious leaders who have united the most fervent piety with the exercise of poorly developed virtue, or the practice of very questionable policy.[1] A critic, if he has not a single measure of large enough capacity for a historical character, should not think himself at liberty to measure him out in two half-bushels, making one man of each.

Reuss too, in his Introduction to the Psalter,[2]

[1] Macduff, in his 'Tales of the Warrior King' (p. 345), compares David with Constantine the Great, "who was by turns the docile believer and the cruel despot, devotee and murderer, patron saint and avenging demon."

[2] Das Alte Testament, vol. v. p. 47 ff.

makes a great deal of the disparity between the historical David, as described in 1 Sam. xvi., 2 Kings ii., and the sweet singer of Israel as he has been idealised out of the Psalms. It is not, however, the case, as he asserts, that people in modern times have formed their conception of David's character by overlooking the historical picture. Rightly or wrongly, the popular idea of David has been formed by persons who have their eyes quite open to David's personal moral faults; and perhaps it is because the ordinary conscience is aware of the possibility of coexisting contradictory elements of good and evil in one heart, that it is not staggered at the disparity. However creditable it may be to the Christian consciousness of the critics to deny this possibility, it is to be feared that such a *sancta simplicitas* is far from common. Unfortunately history has found room for moral contradictions as great as any that can possibly be found in David. We have our own Robert Burns, whose irrepressible poetic energy impelled him to disclose himself in both aspects of his moral character. We have also the secret communings of men with themselves in their private diaries and meditations,[1] which come to light after they are gone; and in many more instances the secrets of the heart go down to the grave with men who have been tempted, and good men who have fallen.

[1] For example, Samuel Johnson's Prayers and Meditations.

> "Then at the balance let's be mute,
> We never can adjust it;
> What's done we partly may compute,
> But know not what's resisted." [1]

The "tradition" of David is not to be so summarily set aside as some critical writers would have it. That is but saying in other words that the son of Jesse must have combined in one person such qualities and such a variety of qualities as to seize strongly the national consciousness of Israel and to mould materially the subsequent history. It is not sufficient to say that at a late period his reign was looked back upon as a golden age, and that he was invested with this and that quality. People do not at late periods first begin to look about for some name to which to attach their national associations and convictions. And we must remember that, on the lowest estimate of David's character, he *did* consolidate his nation and raise it to eminence as no one before him had done, and that his successors, so far as they were successful, followed in the lines he had laid down. It must have been a character of no ordinary breadth and force that could thus make its influence felt down through the centuries of the monarchy; and since the most exacting of critics cannot deny to him the two attributes of patriotism and poetry, it will be hard to exclude

[1] Burns, Address to the Unco Guid.

the other strand that makes up the threefold cord of permanent national influence — religion. "The spirit of Poetry is akin to that of Religion";[1] and as poetry was inborn in the Hebrew race, so it was in the name and by the power of religion that the nation achieved all the greatness which has made their history imperishable. In the wonderful Providence that guided that nation, the man was raised up at the fit time with all the strength — and with all the weaknesses—of a national poet, a man after God's own heart in the place which he gave to the national religion in his "policy." The personal qualities which drew to him the best of the nation in the days when he was an outlaw were just those that a people like Israel would regard as strength of character; and if we may judge by the devotion of these adherents to his person, we may say that his character was as highly "idealised" in his lifetime as it could possibly have been in any subsequent age. It may have been flattering Oriental rhetoric that prompted the words of Abigail (1 Sam. xxv. 28-31) and the wise woman of Tekoah (2 Sam. xiv. 17-19): "The Lord will certainly make my lord a sure house, because my lord fighteth the battles of the Lord, and evil shall not be found in thee all thy days"; "As

---

[1] William Scott Douglas, in introductory note to the "Cotter's Saturday Night" in his edition of Burns.

an angel of God so is my lord the king to discern good and bad, and the Lord thy God be with thee." But brave men would not put their lives in danger to humour a passing longing, as did the heroes who broke through to the well at Bethlehem (2 Sam. xxiii. 13-17), nor would the best of all classes of the nation have thrown in their lot with a persecuted man and adhered to his cause when it was at the lowest ebb, unless he had captivated their hearts by more than appeals to their own selfishness. Struggles like those that issue in the birth of national independence and greatness are not to be explained on the worst but on the best aspect of the qualities of human nature. The "tradition," in a word, is just the continued throb in the national pulse of the life that was quickened to intensity under a unique leader, and the age of David was looked back to as a golden age, because every recurring crisis that stirred that life freshened the memories that were never forgotten.

Prof. Cheyne, if I understand him rightly, feels the force of the tradition attaching to the name of David; but it is not easy to follow him in his attempt to explain the persistency of the tradition. He feels bound, he says,[1] to assume the existence of a "David" (using the name in a symbolic sense) subsequently to the poet-king, to

[1] Origin of the Psalter, p. 194.

account for the literary character of the book of Amos. "He cannot indeed have been alone; he must have had able followers, by whose help he influenced his age, and left a deeper impress than the historical David, not only upon Amos, but after Amos upon the authors of the earliest extant psalms (Deut. xxxii.; Ps. xviii. ?)." For, he says in the same connection,[1] "as critics, we cannot consistently suppose that the religious songs of David (if there were any) were as much above the spiritual capacities of the people as the psalms which, I will not say the later Jews, but which Ewald or Hitzig or Delitzsch would assign to him."

The uncritical reader may be disposed to dismiss all this with the scoff that it merely amounts to saying that the Psalms were not written by David but by another man of the same name. But we must make the best attempt we can to discover what is precisely the position assumed, and it seems to be this. The historical David, "the hero of the transition from rudeness to culture,"[2] "the versatile *condottiere*, chieftain, and king,"[3] whose "posthumous fame rested chiefly upon his secular poetry,"[4] may indeed have composed songs of a religious character, but of these none remain. Yet the literary character of the book of Amos is such that the space between him and the historical

[1] Origin of the Psalter, p. 192 f. [2] Ibid., p. 194.
[3] Ibid., p. 211. [4] Ibid., p. 192.

David must be filled up not merely by one poet, greater in spiritual and lyrical gifts than the poet-king, but by a succession of such men—whose works in like manner have all been lost, but whose influence we must postulate to account for the earliest extant psalms, belonging at the earliest (Ps. xviii.) to the age of Josiah.

It is certainly a large assumption that is here made; and if it is necessary in the interests of a general hypothesis in regard to the Psalter, one is disposed to say, So much the worse for the hypothesis. It will occur to the reader as remarkable that not a word should have been preserved of the sacred songs of David, while so great care has been observed in preserving his secular compositions. Equally remarkable is it that all the glory of these imaginary Davids has been transferred to the one of them who least of all deserved it. Confining ourselves, however, to facts, it is undoubted that the Biblical writers tell us nothing about such symbolic Davids, and know only one poet of that name. There is no concealment of the fact that David had contemporaries and successors in the lyric art; an Asaph, a Heman, and sons of Korah, whoever these were, have their names preserved in this connection. And whatever Prof. Cheyne may say of the "elder orthodoxy" making the great mistake of confounding the two Davids, that mistake is as old as Amos at least.

That is to say, in Amos' day, two centuries after David, the "tradition" of David is put so strongly in words that, had it occurred in the books of Chronicles, it would have been contemptuously rejected as the dream of a later age. In plain terms, the impress made by David, the poet-king, —for Amos recognises his pre-eminence in both capacities (see Amos vi. 5, ix. 11),—was so deep and lasting that it required no late imagination to magnify it. It is most arbitrary and unwarranted to explain the former of these references of Amos to David as implying that his poetry was entirely secular and his music sensuous; and it is equally unwarrantable to reject the latter reference merely on the ground of its giving too high an estimate of the Davidic house. An unbiassed criticism will see in the former an indication that the sin of the nobles whom the prophet rebuked consisted in their employing upon their own selfish pleasures the best of everything they could lay hands on or contrive, even to making instruments like David's for their luxurious feasts; and in the latter reference the promise given through Nathan of the divine choice and perpetuity of the Davidic house is clearly implied. So that in Amos' time David was looked back upon as the great poet-king, as he is described in the historical books and as all subsequent tradition regarded him.

That "the man of whom we are speaking was

no isolated student poet," [1] may be freely conceded. The Biblical writers who mention the prophetic companies of Samuel's time, and record the names of distinguished men who aided David in the musical accomplishments with which his name is associated, leave us free to infer as much. And to the question, "Why may not successors of David have been his equals in natural and his superiors in spiritual capacities?" [2] we can only answer, Why not? If by a succession of Davids is merely meant a series beginning with him who carried on the exercise of psalmody, this is but the contention of the preceding pages. But no proof is forthcoming to support the assertion that poets between David and Amos first introduced a religious element into poetry or surpassed the historical David in spiritual expression. And equally unfounded is the assertion [3] that "the reorganisation of the people in Ezra's time was too complete to allow any considerable influence to archaic liturgical formulæ," so that "it is not possible to hold that there is any large admixture of old and new in the Hebrew Psalter." On the contrary, I hold that it is perfectly within the bounds of possibility that a considerable part of the earlier portion of the Psalter, which presumably was the first collection, may come from the time of David. This

---

[1] Cheyne, Origin of the Psalter, p. 190.
[2] Ibid., p. 191.   [3] Ibid., p. 194.

can only be denied by a manipulation of the historical books in a manner to produce a "critically" revised account of his character, and at the same time by insisting on reading into the Psalms a "Church" reference which detracts from the obvious simplicity of these lyrics. When one has excised from the historical books all details that represent the higher religious side of David's character, and rejected the sacred songs that are in these books attributed to him, it is no great feat to say that such a David as is left cannot have composed any of the psalms in the Psalter. And again, when the Psalter is declared at the outset to have been composed for use in the post-exilian Temple, and its language is rigidly construed of the situations and experiences of the post-exilian Judaism, it is plain that David could have had no share in their composition. But when the psalms are read, especially those in the earlier part of the Psalter, in the obvious sense of the language, and when the sentiments and situations are compared with the unvarnished accounts of David contained in the books of Samuel, it may be maintained that many of them are quite appropriate in his mouth, and indeed eminently suited to his circumstances.

It may be indeed that the collectors, or those who added the superscriptions to the Psalms, have not in all cases put down the precise situation to which the several psalms called Davidic refer;

but this much may be confidently asserted, that in the accounts that have been given of David's life in the historical books we have the delineation of a character quite in keeping with such psalms, of an experience wide enough and checkered enough to explain their varied references, and of a poetic sensibility very strongly marked even when poetical composition is not in question. What would the critics have? Do they demand formal statements in the historical books that David at such and such times wrote such and such psalms? Why, when such statements are produced they reject them as incredible, and relegate the psalms in question to some later time. Or do they expect each psalm to bear a categorical declaration of its authorship? Such declarations as are contained in the headings being discarded, the authorship must be determined or conjectured from the Psalms themselves; and the whole history of psalm-exposition, with the extraordinary diversity of view among expositors, shows how difficult a matter this is. The most that the expositor can generally do is to point to situations in which a psalm may have been composed; and but for the preconceptions as to the character of David and the "Church" character of the Psalms, my contention is that adequate situations can be pointed to in the life of David; or, what is better, that his whole character, literary and religious, is adequate to account for many psalms in the collection.

The events in the eventful life of David are set down in the books of Samuel with a fulness that enables us to form a very vivid conception of his character, and with a candour and simplicity—faults and failings being placed side by side with merits and virtues—that give every guarantee of veracity. And when all is done in the separation of "late" and "early" elements in these narratives, it comes to this, that if we cannot believe the late, we have no better guarantee of the truth of the early. A king's courtiers and contemporaries are, one would think, more liable to exaggerate a monarch's virtues and slur over his vices than a later writer. If critics insist on believing all the bad things that are said of David and rejecting all the good, they have the more difficult task of explaining how later accounts have grown out of the earlier, and, to speak generally, the task of showing how the attenuated character whom their criticism leaves was able to fill the position he occupied, achieve the work he performed, and bequeath the name by which he is remembered.

The vicissitudes and situations in David's life presented in these narratives are of such a nature that, though we may not be able to say precisely that such and such a psalm was composed at such and such a time and place, yet we may confidently say, Here is a man who has passed through certain experiences and borne himself in such wise that we are not surprised to hear that, being a poet, he composed this and the other psalm. It is very doubtful whether we should tie down any lyric to a precise set of circumstances, the poet being like a painter, who, having found a fit landscape, sits down to transfer it to canvas. I do not think it likely that David, finding himself in some great perplexity or sorrow, called for writing materials in order to describe the situation and record his feelings. But I do think it probable that the vicissitudes through which he passed made such an impression on his sensitive heart, and became so inwrought into an emotional nature, that when he soothed himself in his retirement with his lyre, they came forth spontaneously in the form of a psalm or song or prayer, according as the recollection was sad or joyful, and as his singing mood moved him.

There is one day in David's life—a long and sorrowful day, not untouched with gleams of brightness—of which the sacred historians have left a minute description as it waxed from early morn till it closed in the rest of night.[1] It was the day on which, at the revolt of Absalom, the aged king set out from Jerusalem, and, attended by faithful friends as well as encountered by ruthless enemies, made his way

---

[1] A description of this day is given in his own inimitable style by Dean Stanley ('Jewish Church,' Lecture xxiv.), who draws attention to the fact that it was reserved for Ewald (Hist., iii. 228-235) to bring out the singular interest of this day.

slowly over the slopes of Olivet, down into the valley beyond, and finally slept on the other side of Jordan. Without presuming to tell each turn of the road at which a psalm was suggested, we may say in a word that, if there is poetry in actual life, if there is pathos in meek endurance, that long and eventful day is a psalter in itself, even had the mouth of David been closed and his voice silent from morning to night. The few words he speaks to his faithful adherents, the submission with which he bows to the divine will, his meekness under rebuke and reviling, his tender regard for the welfare of his friends and his greater solicitude for the honour of his God,—all breathe the very spirit of the Psalter, and reveal a character than which no period of Israelite history, late or early, can produce one more closely in keeping with the tone of many of the psalms. The 3rd Psalm bears in the superscription that it is "a psalm of David, when he fled from Absalom his son." It may or may not be that it was composed, as expositors have been in the habit of explaining, on the morning after that anxious day, when he awoke (see ver. 5) refreshed by sleep and in safety from his enemies. But at all events, no one who is not possessed by a theory can read dispassionately the prose account of that day's events and then say that such a psalm as this is out of keeping with David's character and far beyond his experience. It is true that Hitzig, who reckoned this among the Davidic psalms, placed it not at the crisis of Absalom's rebellion, but at the time after the capture of Ziklag, when "David was greatly distressed, for the people spake of stoning him, but David strengthened himself in Jehovah his God" (1 Sam. xxx. 6). This is proof, at least, that there were various occasions in David's life on which such a psalm as this might have been suggested. By the more modern criticism, which finds the spiritual tone of the psalms too high for any individual, late or early, we are told that this psalm, and others which by the comparative method go along with it, belong to "the period when faithful Israelites were so sorely oppressed both by traitors in their midst and by their Persian tyrants";[1] and the situation of the psalm is one in which "the sources of danger to the spiritual kernel of the nation are, first, an Israelitish faction openly opposed to the *khasidim*, and secondly, the many desponding friends of the cause of truth, who are discontented at the prosperity of the strict Jehovists." I confess that such knowledge is too wonderful for me. The reader may peruse the psalm, first with the traditional title, and then with this revised critical heading, and judge for himself. I would merely hazard the remark that the psalm is at least better poetry if read in the older fashioned way.

[1] Cheyne, Origin of the Psalter, p. 227.

This reference to one eventful day in David's life has been made, however, not for the purpose of finding *occasion* for any particular psalm, but to direct attention to the way in which his character was manifested in a very special set of circumstances. Let us now call to mind the long and checkered life in which that character was developed and matured—the peaceful home-life of the boy, the stirring activities of youth, and chiefly, in that the most receptive time of life, the peculiar influences favourable and adverse that bore upon him during the years of Saul's reign. And then there is the long period of his own reign, as he passed from vigorous manhood to feeble old age, building up a kingdom out of jealous warlike tribes, ruling unruly men by a strange attractiveness, yet himself ruled by men far his inferiors in principle, falling a prey to his own passions, suffering the penalty of over-indulgence to his children. No life's day ever opened brighter, none had so many and so strange variations, few a more sombre even-time. Let the accounts be criticised to the last degree, enough remains to show us a character of extraordinary sensitiveness and susceptibility; and it is passing strange that he should be declared to be susceptible of almost any impression but that of religion, or, at all events, so little influenced by it that, though he is presented to us in almost every conceivable aspect, there was no religious aspect worth presenting, no word from him of a religious character worth preserving. Did he not, in all those years of persecution by Saul, lift up a thought to the God of Israel? or was his religion in truth nothing but a mechanical consulting of the oracle as to the success or reverse of a projected raid? Was it for the mere love of adventure and the passion for fighting that he took his life in his hand all those years? And when some new turn in his fortunes came, and in retired cave or on remote hillside he found breathing-space from his enemy, was his lyre tuned to some secular song to solace his spirits, and did he and his followers regale themselves like those nobles of Samaria in Amos' time who are said to have so closely imitated him? Among all the thoughts that passed through his busy brain, was God not in any of them; and though admiring posterity has preserved his elegy on Abner, has it not been able to preserve a single line of a religious character that he uttered? It is hard to believe all this of one who confessedly had a pre-eminent faculty of song, and was so richly endowed in almost every sensibility that is akin to religion—tenderness of heart, love of country and home, devotion to friends, magnanimity towards enemies. And all because these apparently simple and heartfelt lyrics are the expression of the fortunes of the "Jewish Church," and in David's time the Jewish Church did not exist.

Whatever may be said of "Church-religion," readers of all grades of intelligence for thousands of years have recognised and been touched by "the broad humanity of the book of Psalms";[1] and what is maintained here is, that the character of the historical David, as a fair reading of the historical books enables us to conceive it, exhibits just the kind of humanity in the sufficient degree of intensity that is reflected in many of the Psalms. After all, what is the religion of the Psalms in its broader and firmer features? For an answer to this question we must address ourselves not to the theologian and the scholar, but to men with all the fulness of human nature, even with "passions wild and strong," like our Scottish poet. They will tell us how a psalm has the power to soothe their feverish unrest, or "allay emotions when their strength threatens harm."[2] When friends prove false, when the foundations of the earth seem to be dissolved, when justice and kindness alike seem to have become words without meaning, it is a psalm that gives the assurance that—

"God's in His heaven, all's right with the world."[3]

When the evil part of nature has gained the upper hand, when falls already confessed have anew to be

---

[1] Ker, The Psalms in History and Biography, p. viii.
[2] Currer Bell, in Shirley, chap. xii.
[3] Browning, "The Year's at the Spring." Compare Ps. xi. 4.

deplored, when progress upwards seems impossible, and speech fails to express contrition, the familiar words of a penitential psalm recur to the memory with unexhausted meaning. Nay, when unsolved problems and "questions over-queried" rush in upon the mind in mad confusion, and deep darkness threatens to envelop the soul, the mysterious weird images of the Psalms—bulls of Bashan, lions' mouths — recur to the mind, and suit the mood of the perturbed affrighted spirit. We know not how, we know not why; but a human soul seems to have drawn near and passed by us, and there was warmth and life in the passage. The Psalmist is not a "poet's poet," nor is he a theological versifier. It is because the Psalms touch the broad sympathies of humanity at its tenderest parts that they have been, and will continue to be, the prayer-book of stumbling, erring, hoping, believing mankind. And it would seem that David was raised up, so richly gifted with poetic talent, so severely trained by a unique experience, that he was able to strike the chords of those sympathies, and has had his name indissolubly associated with the Psalms. The note once struck re-echoed in the ages that followed, with more art no doubt, with growing intensity perhaps, but never with truer tone or deeper pathos. It would seem almost incredible that the experiences through which David passed should never have awakened in a soul so sensitive the religious sentiments they seem so purposely adapted to awaken, and that one who could compose the exquisitely tender lament over Jonathan was not sympathetically touched by the countless situations in which his own dramatic life was laid. It seems almost cruel to deny to one who so grievously sinned the relief of a *sacred* song to express his penitence, and to one who was so deeply oppressed by sorrow the consolation of a song of resignation. Silent he was, no doubt, when God's hand lay heavy upon him; but by the power of divine grace he was able again to look up, again to tune his harp, though in a subdued note and minor key; and the world of sinful erring souls who have been cheered by his words will not grudge him his due place as the sweet singer of Israel.

CONCLUSION.

THE aim of the preceding chapters has been to vindicate for the Psalms an earlier place in the history of Israel, and a higher place in the religion of the Old Testament, than a modern school of criticism is willing to concede to them. It has been necessary to lead an argument of a broad and general kind, because, on the one hand, the critical estimate of the pre-exilian religious history would preclude even the possibility of sacred lyrics like the Psalms being composed before the Exile; and because, on the other hand, the interpretation of the Psalms in a "Church" sense, while professing to enhance the spirituality of their meaning, seems to deprive them of their simplicity as expressions of individual heart-religion. The attempt has been made by two main converging lines of proof to reach the twofold conclusion—*first,* that though many of the Psalms belong to a comparatively late period in the history, psalmody has its origin far back in pre-exilian times, having been prepared for in the very earliest religious songs, and brought to the definite psalm-type at the hands of David; and, *secondly*, that beneath the forms of expression, and behind the temporal occasions of the Psalms, we must recognise as the great moving impulse to psalmody the stirring of a true spirit of individual religious experience, which itself, though perhaps somewhat unformed and vague, is also of great antiquity.

No doubt any conclusion at which we finally arrive in regard to the Psalter as a whole must be based primarily on an exegesis of individual psalms; and hence a more minutely detailed examination or classification of these lyrics may be desiderated in an inquiry of this kind. But when we are met by sweeping assertions as to the impossibility of pre-exilian psalmody, it becomes necessary to examine the foundations on which such broad statements rest, in order to have clear ground on which to carry out the examination of the individual pieces. It is lost labour disputing whether such and such a psalm came from David, if one party in the discussion takes the firm position that David could not have composed a psalm. On the other hand, if it can be made probable that David was capable of psalm-composition, it is then a fair subject of inquiry whether psalms ascribed to him are really his. There is, moreover, this advantage gained, if our general position can be made good.

If the pre-exilian time as a whole was a time in which psalmody was practicable and practised, we have a pretty wide field in which to look for the occasions of individual psalms, and are not precluded from assigning them to authors known or unknown during the period. That is to say, the choice is not between David alone and the post-exilian time.

It would, of course, be deeply interesting if we could say definitely of each psalm who was its author and under what circumstances it was composed. Yet even could we call back the original singers of these lyrics and question them, perhaps after all they would tell us little to satisfy our curiosity. The history of the composition of modern lyrics shows how evanescent an occasion has often led to the production of many an everlasting poem, and how, in most cases, it is the *mood* of the singer more than his surrounding that explains the song. So that it may be misdirected labour to search for some historical occasion underlying a psalm, while the mental situation that explains it is written plainly on its face. The very fact that it should be possible to assign a given psalm with varying plausibility to half-a-dozen different periods before or after the Exile, and to explain it either of individual experience or of the vicissitudes of the nation, is sufficient proof that the theme in the psalmist's mind was no accidental and transient event or feeling, but something so deep and universal that it could not but continually recur, and could not be circumscribed by too definite terms. Instead, therefore, of resolving the Psalms into "occasional" pieces, all arising out of the conflict of the post-exilian Jewish Church with the world-Powers or with faithless adherents, a truer view, as I take it, is, that we have in them the conflict between the right and the wrong on the largest scale — a conflict which is as old as the dawn of conscience, and has taken more and more definite shape as conscience became enlightened, and as experience of man and of the world was extended. But they are not poems descriptive of the conflict; they are the sighs or the shouts, the prayers or the praises, of the men actively engaged in the conflict. And so in all succeeding ages they have appealed to the hearts of men who have still the same combat to wage, and they are as fresh to-day as when they were first composed. Epic poetry was, as Dean Stanley [1] finely observes, denied to the Semitic races; but this defect is to a great extent supplied by the ivy-like tenacity with which the growth of the Hebrew lyrics winds itself round and round the more than epic trunk of the Hebrew history. But then, be it remembered, that history gains all its interest and significance from the religion. Take

[1] Jewish Church, Lect. xxv.

away from the history of Israel the religious element and it would shrink into insignificance, even as the states that were contiguous to Israel have sunk into oblivion. And it seems to me that to deny to pre-exilian Israel such a religion as is expressed in the more general of the psalms, is not only to denude the trunk of its clinging ivy, but to take away the life-sap of the trunk itself.

Here, in fact, the whole subject comes to a point, and here lies the justification for this whole discussion. Without the existence of a genuine vital godliness in pre-exilian Israel, it seems to me that the whole history of that people becomes an insoluble riddle, because nothing would be left whereby to explain the persistence of the nation on a religious basis—the tenacity with which, through all misfortune, they clung to the national faith and institutions, the devotion which enabled them to survive political wreck, and to spring up into new life on the ruins of the old order of things. There would, in short, be no living materials to constitute a nation such as Israel was.

The religion of the Psalms is but the counterpart of the religion of the Prophets. Even if it should be affirmed that the teaching of these men had first to work itself into the national consciousness before it could come forth again in the religion of the Psalms, yet the two extremities of this process cannot be separated by centuries. A power must operate where it exists; and the prophetic voice, to be effective on the heart, must not be dissipated into the air. Now, what have we in the Psalms but the process actually going on — the religion taught by the prophets being echoed back in the language of devotion and personal experience? There is no dividing line in history at which we can say the teaching of the prophets ends and the response of the Psalms begins. Accordingly, the estimate we form of the one will control our estimate of the other. If we are convinced that the prophetic religion attained a high tone at an early period, it will not be difficult for us to believe that there are pre-exilian Psalms. On the other hand, to lower the tone and bring down the date of prophetic influence will lead to the depreciation of the Psalms as expressions of vital personal religion, and to the relegating of them to a later and later point of time.

We cannot leave the whole pre-exilian period without religion altogether. It is bad enough to eliminate from it the great names which the national memory has set up as landmarks—to present us with a pre-prophetic period without the patriarchs and without a Moses; to offer us, instead of David, the sweet singer of Israel, a series of hypothetical Davids, whose attempts at sacred song, however, have, like his, all been forgotten;

and, now in these last days also, to reduce the genuine Isaiah to very insignificant bulk. The landscape of pre-exilian history becomes tame enough when the towering trees are so ruthlessly hewn down; but it will become a bleak wilderness if we remove also the soil which was necessary for the growth of even the humble vegetation that is allowed to remain. Did the prophets themselves have no pious mothers to instil into their minds the fear of God and the love of goodness? no godly homes in which the religion they taught was practised? Is it indeed possible to believe that these men stood up, one by one, with nothing behind them, absolutely alone in their conceptions of the truth and their devotion to it? How then were they understood by their contemporaries? How were they not only tolerated but feared, unless their words were known to be but the expression of the better mind of the people? And it is this better mind that finds utterance in the Psalms. Be it that the prophets towered above the mass of their contemporaries, still there were those who heard and followed their words; and the nation has religiously preserved their utterances, even when they sound as the nation's condemnation. So also in the Psalms, the response of a narrower or wider circle of such susceptible hearers, there has been preserved a witness that the religion was not entirely without a heart.

THE ANSWER OF THE CONSCIENCE. 359

And, as time went on and the general conscience became more and more tender, there was an increasing number who could appropriate to themselves the language of these sacred songs, till they became indeed and in the truest sense the voice of the Jewish Church.

It may not be possible for us to identify the psalms which are David's, and to tell precisely whose are the others. If our view of the history is correct, the song was continuous, only ebbing and flowing with the ebb and flow of national life. But old songs, as they were repeated from mouth to mouth, may have been modified or added to; and it may be that, side by side with the most ancient, there are now some of the most recent utterances of the psalmists. The history of psalm-writing and psalm-transmission would be different from the history of all other lyrical collections, whether secular or sacred, if it were not so. The most popular of songs are most freely handled, and, like the commonest coins in circulation, most frequently conceal their image and superscription. Zunz has shown[1] how many of the hymnic pieces now incorporated in the Jewish Prayer-book were first of all the compositions, for private individual or social use, of the leaders of prayer in the synagogue, or of other men in positions of prominence; that these pieces were first repeated by their authors

[1] Gottesdienstliche Vorträge, p. 392 ff.

in the hearing of their pupils, then introduced into the local synagogues, and finally became part of the common prayer-book, whose history and composition can thus be traced step by step. And very probably the Psalter had a similar history. We know almost to a certainty that it arose, as a whole, out of more limited collections; but in all probability the first beginnings were simple enough. As the persistent tradition assigns to David the origin of psalmody, so the earlier psalms in the collection have a more personal tone, and the public liturgical use reveals itself more markedly as the collection grew.

But psalmody once exercised, became the outlet for the expression of the best that Judaism had of vital religion — earnest heart-searching and the seeking of God's face and favour. As the God of Israel was never without a witness during all the vicissitudes of His people's history, so He never left His chosen ones without a consolation, giving them songs in the darkest night of their distress, expressive of the faith which they had in His promises, of the influence which His revelation through Law and Prophecy had upon their hearts, and keeping alive a *practical* religion till the time came for the Hope of Israel to be manifested.

www.ingramcontent.com/pod-product-compliance
Lightning Source LLC
Chambersburg PA
HW061422300426
4CB00014B/1499